DRUKHARI

RAIDERS FROM THE DARK CITY

CONTENTS

PRODUCED BY GAMES WORKSHOP IN NOTTINGHAM

With thanks to the Mournival and the Infinity Circuit for their additional playtesting services

Games Workshop Ltd, Willow Rd, Lenton, Nottingham, NG7 2WS
games-workshop.com

INTRODUCTION

The book you hold is the ultimate guide to the Drukhari, piratical raiders who prey upon the denizens of realspace. Inside these pages you will find everything you need to assemble your collection of Drukhari miniatures into an army of sadistic fiends, ready to carve a gruesome path through the galaxy.

The Drukhari are an ancient and technologically advanced race that feeds on the suffering of others. Their ancestors ruled the stars long before Mankind first ventured outward from Terra, and over long millennia the ennui of their vast lifespans led them to ever greater acts of depravity and violence. Now, from the nightmare city of Commorragh nestled in the black heart of the webway, the Drukhari launch their raids on the worlds of realspace, slaughtering to sustain their withered souls and gathering up slaves to take back to their morbid torture chambers.

Gaming with the Drukhari offers a distinct and challenging experience in which you forgo heavy armour and durability for exceptional manoeuvrability and firepower. Whether you field a force of Kabalite soldiers, airborne warriors of the Wych Cults or hulking, Haemonculus-created monstrosities, *Codex: Drukhari* provides the rules and the resources you require.

The Drukhari offer fantastic opportunities to any collector. Many of the models in their range come with a wide variety of cruel and unusual weaponry to choose from, as well as wonderfully grotesque appendages and implements of torture. You can truly let your imagination run wild when assembling and painting such a collection, or you can build your army to fit the history and battle style of one the many Kabals, Wych Cults or Haemonculus Covens that inhabits the Dark City.

Contained within this book you will find all the information required to collect a Drukhari army and field it upon the tabletop.

EVIL INCARNATE: This section delves into the grisly history of the Drukhari, the Dark City's most infamous organisations and denizens, and how their forces organise for war.

PAGEANTRY OF COMMORRAGH: Here you will find a showcase of gorgeously painted miniatures and example armies to inspire your own collection of Drukhari Citadel Miniatures.

THE DARK AELDARI: In this section you will find datasheets for every unit in the Drukhari range, as well as wargear lists and weapon rules.

COMMORRITE RAIDERS: Finally, this section contains additional rules – including Warlord Traits, Artefacts of Cruelty, Stratagems and matched play points – that will transform your collection of Citadel Miniatures into a terrifying Drukhari raiding party.

To play games with your army, you will need a copy of the Warhammer 40,000 rules. To find out more about Warhammer 40,000 or download the free core rules, visit warhammer40000.com.

Emerging from the webway like a nightmare unbidden, the Drukhari strike swiftly and mercilessly. With each new depravity enacted they feed their withered souls, growing stronger from the pain they inflict upon their enemies – yet the hunger within them can never be completely sated.

EVIL INCARNATE

Fiercely intelligent piratical raiders who feed upon anguish to stave off the slow death of their souls, the Drukhari epitomise everything wanton and cruel about the ancient Aeldari race from which they are descended. Their boundless potential is put to every terrible purpose they can imagine, and because their lives span millennia, they have all the time they need to perfect their stygian arts.

The Drukhari turned their backs upon the material dimension long ago, and now only emerge from their twilight realm to revel in the torments of the lesser races. The warrior Kabals strike swiftly and without warning from portals opened within the webway, only to disappear like ghosts when enemy resistance becomes too severe. They launch their piratical raids from above, whole armies screaming into the midst of the foe, firing from the decks of baroque grav-craft before leaping down to experience the slaughter first-hand. Sprays of arterial blood and spasming corpses mark their passage, the laughter of these merciless warriors the last thing their victims ever hear.

To the sadistic Drukhari, the sweet fruit of horror is as pleasing as the caress of a razored blade across soft flesh. They relish breaking the bodies of their captives, but prize even more highly the process of crushing their spirits, for nothing is more gratifying to the denizens of the Dark City than securing utter dominion over those who have resisted them. They drink in every nuance of woe until their captives gibber and plead for death – a mercy the Drukhari are famously slow to grant.

The warriors of the Drukhari are tall and lithe without exception. Their alabaster skin is almost corpse-like in its pallor, for there is no true sunlight within their shadowy realm. Their athletic physiques are lined with whipcord muscle, honed and enhanced until they are superior even to those of their craftworld cousins – the Asuryani – for the warriors of Commorragh prize martial prowess most highly. They stride through the fires of battle with the surety of those who have lived for millennia, and they rarely sully their tongues with the grunting languages of the inferior races, using translator technology

on those occasions when communication is unavoidable. But their magnificence is only skin deep – viewed with the witch-sight, Drukhari are repugnant monsters, eternally thirsting for the anguish of others in order to fill the aching void at their core.

The Drukhari are masters of fighting with every weapon at their disposal – survival amongst their society demands nothing less. Little distinction is drawn between the sexes, for an individual's skill and cunning is far more important than traits such as height or gender. Their senses are keen to the point of paranoia, their shadowed eyes and tapered ears alert to the slightest disturbance. In the Dark City in which they make their lair, the incautious do not survive for long.

While countless generations of conflict have ensured the Drukhari's bodies are even more suited to physical combat than other elements of the Aeldari race, the innate psychic abilities possessed by their forebears have, by necessity, been allowed to atrophy. To channel the energies of the warp within the Dark City would be to invite disaster, for doing so could draw the gaze of the Chaos God Slaanesh, the one the Aeldari fearfully call 'She Who Thirsts.' As such, the use of psychic powers is one of the few things forbidden in Commorragh.

The weaponry manufactured within the Dark City is just as advanced as that which is psychically grown upon the craftworlds. In matters of war the Drukhari are artisans supreme, their technology refined to such a point that it may as well be magical. Their endless imagination and skill have led them down a sinister path indeed – their favourite tools of war include splinter weapons that can set every nerve aflame with pain, darklight beams, whips that bleed acidic ichor, and eldritch soul-traps. The Drukhari are so confident of their own abilities that their lightweight bodysuits incorporate bladed plates not only for protection, but also to give them yet another weapon to use upon their prey. Collectively, the warriors of Commorragh know all the ways there are to kill the galaxy's myriad creatures, and delight in perfecting as many as they can.

'When I look upon the lesser races I am filled with disgust. Left to their own devices, they lead lives that are pitifully brief and completely devoid of meaning. How many of their generations have passed by in my lifetime? The answer is beneath my attention. Yet with the correct application of my art, each of those wretched beings can be made to endure an eternity of suffering, and it is through their screams that they show me their value.'

- Urien Rakarth,
Master Haemonculus of
the Prophets of Flesh

THE LABYRINTH DIMENSION

For the Imperium of Mankind, travel between distant stars is made possible by passing through the warp – the twisted dimension of the Chaos Gods. To do so is to invite peril, for the predatory servants of the Ruinous Powers are able to scent the emotional trace of interlopers, devouring the souls of those they find. For the Drukhari – as with all members of their race – this danger is even greater, for where the soul of a human is but a dim flicker in the warp, that of an Aeldari is a blazing beacon. To enter the immaterium is to draw the attention of She Who Thirsts, who was created millennia ago by the unfathomable decadence of the Drukhari's ancestors. But there are other ways to traverse the stars – such as through the interstitial nether-realm known as the webway.

Sometimes called the labyrinth dimension, the webway is a construct of shimmering arterial pathways that spans both realspace and the immaterium. It is defined by the fact that it sits between the material realm and the roiling tides of the warp, comparable to the surface of a mirror, or the fabric of a veil cast over something foul. The ancient Aeldari discovered that it was possible to exist within that silvered surface, to move between the threads of that veil. It is here that the Drukhari have made their home, and it is by using the innumerable hidden portals that connect the webway and realspace that the raiding parties of Commorragh are able to terrorise the galaxy. Since the Fall – the great tragedy of the Aeldari race – the webway has been a realm both shattered and dangerous, its splintered reaches infested by strange beings from different realities. Yet this is the perfect breeding ground for the warriors of the Drukhari.

COMMORRAGH

In the depths of the webway lies Commorragh, named by many in fearful whispers as the Dark City. Commorragh is to the greatest megalopolises of realspace as a soaring mountain is to a mound of termites. Its dimensions would be considered impossible if they could be read by conventional means, its population greater than that of whole star systems. Although called a city, Commorragh is more akin to a vast collection of satellite realms linked by myriad portals and hidden pathways, its far-flung nodes spread throughout the arteries of the webway like a malevolent virus. While

Drukhari raids are launched with such speed and voraciousness that many defenders are slain before they even know they are under attack. Without question, those who die ignorant of the fiends that have come for them are the most fortunate.

inside that labyrinth dimension the gap between each sub-realm can be crossed with a single step, Commorragh's clustered concentrations are in reality scattered across the galaxy, in some cases thousands of light-years apart.

Commorragh appears within the webway as a composite entity of impossible scale, a shimmering, contradictory realm that plucks at the sanity of those who approach it. Thousands of ships dock each day within its out-flung spines, for the Drukhari are far more numerous than even their craftworld kin suspect. It is not only the society of the Drukhari that festers within this terrible realm – Commorragh plays host to many of the galaxy's most disreputable and villainous individuals, including alien mercenaries, bounty hunters, corsairs and renegades, all risking their souls in the hope of claiming the riches of the Dark City.

LORD OF DARKNESS

The occupants of the Dark City are sadistic murderers all, abjectly self-serving and incapable of compassion. Violent civil skirmishes are omnipresent, yet descent into complete anarchy is prevented by the ruthless hand of the Supreme Overlord of Commorragh, Asdrubael Vect. A master strategist and tactician, Vect's mind is as sharp as the blades he puts to the throats of his detractors. It is by his cunning that the warring Kabals are kept in balance – unable to devour each other completely, yet still spurred to brutal competition with one another as they vie for the Supreme Overlord's favour. In this way the political statuses of these bitter rivals are in constant flux, the ebbing and flowing of their power driven ever by Vect. Those killers who are able to thrive in this environment whilst remaining in Vect's graces are given permission to put their practised brutality to use during realspace raids.

DARK ORIGINS

Ten thousand years ago, amid the apocalyptic screams of a newborn god, the mighty Aeldari empire fell to ruin. Yet the architects of this catastrophe were spared the worst of its wrath, as they were hidden deep within the bounds of the webway. They lurk there still, a race of unrepentant monsters damned to suffer an eternal thirst for the pain of others.

The ancient empire of the Aeldari was the greatest civilisation since that of the Old Ones, the various cultures that exist in the 41st Millennium mere reflections of its glory. Yet the Aeldari fell from grace in the most profound of ways. The origins of those who now call themselves the Drukhari can be found hidden amidst the atrocity and mayhem of that terrible time.

The ancient Aeldari had perfected their sciences to such an extent that they could travel vast distances in a heartbeat, reforge planets to their liking and quench stars at a whim. With the galaxy prostrate at their feet and arduous labour but a distant memory, the Aeldari were gradually overcome by an arrogant sense of entitlement. Free to indulge their every curiosity, they spent ever more time engaged in esoteric pursuits, desperate to escape the ennui that set in over the course of their centuries-long lives.

The Aeldari psyche is a thing of extremes and intense complexity; it can experience zeniths of bliss and nadirs of horror far more keenly than that of other races. It is just as capable of falling into corruption as it is of transcending to the sublime. With so much power at their beck and call, the core of the Aeldari realm – once a masterpiece of civilisation – became centred around self-gratification and the pursuit of individual fulfilment. Slowly, the proud empire began to rot from within.

Amongst the pleasure-seekers and the interminably curious were those whose pursuit of excess became increasingly extreme. These included a great proportion of the aristocracy of ancient Aeldari society; those with the wealth and the time to truly explore every aspect of decadence. One by one, the leaders of the cults of excess that were growing within Aeldari society became obsessed with their own power. They relocated into the labyrinth dimension known as the webway, taking over hidden ports and setting up strongholds at key nodal points within to continue their debased pursuits. Almost invariably, these realms were linked via portals to the sprawling and exhilaratingly lawless city of Commorragh.

Commorragh was originally the greatest of the webway port-cities, impossibly vast and able to transport a fleet to any of the most vital planets of the Aeldari empire by virtue of its many portals. Because of the access it granted to the far-flung corners of realspace, this mighty metropolis was reckoned to be the most important location in the entire webway. It was too valuable to the Aeldari as a whole to belong to any single aspect of their empire, so it existed outside the jurisdiction of the great Aeldari councils of that time. Precisely because of its autonomy, the city-port quickly became a magnet for those that wished their deeds to remain hidden from prying eyes.

The realm of Commorragh expanded unstoppably as wealth flowed across its borders. It spread outward into the void, consuming other webway port-cities, private estates and sub-realms with each new expansion. Commorragh grew ever larger and more impressive as it fed on their plundered resources. Unseen, the dilettante lords who ruled Commorragh's spires and dens of vice grew in status alongside their adoptive city, initiating more and more of the Aeldari into their shadowy creeds.

The Aeldari are exceptionally psychically gifted as a race, and as they wallowed ever deeper into corruption, echoes of both agony and ecstasy began to ripple through time and space. In the parallel dimension of the warp, the reflections of these intense experiences began to coalesce, for the shifting tides of the empyrean can take form around raw emotions, feeding on them and growing strong, even sentient. The constant stream of indulgence and depravity pouring from the Aeldari empire was as unstoppable as a tide. It nourished and empowered that which crystallised at its centre – a nascent god of excess, content at first simply to wait, and to grow.

THE FALL OF THE AELDARI

As the Aeldari empire began its descent into madness, there were some who foresaw disaster and fled to safety. The first of these were the Exodites, those who perceived their peril clearest of all. They chose to establish a network of colonies far away from the blighted heart of the empire, exiling themselves so that they might survive. Many of them exist

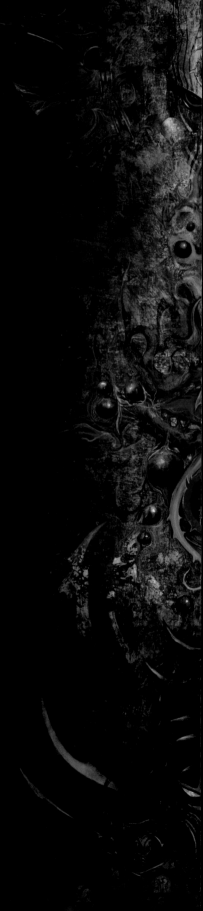

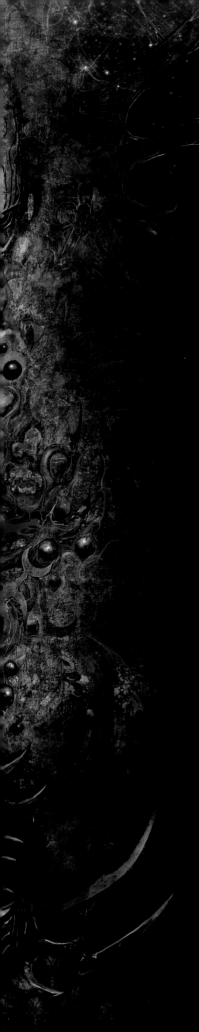

there still, their cultures living in a symbiotic relationship with the world-spirits of their planets.

Those who escaped later were the forefathers of the Asuryani. As their parent society became ever more depraved, they recoiled in horror from what their once-noble kin had become. Realising that they stood upon the brink, they turned their considerable resources to the construction of immense craftworlds: graceful space-cities the size of small moons. The Aeldari of the craftworlds fled into the void, desperate to escape from the punishment that must surely fall upon their race. Some would even succeed. Those left behind jeered at the craven flight and narrow minds of their departed cousins. Yet the more cunning amongst them watched, and wondered, shoring up the defences of their occluded webway strongholds even as they continued their hedonistic pursuits.

As depravity riddled every aspect of Aeldari society, the cults of excess sought ever more violent thrills. Before long the streets of the empire's cities ran with blood. The elegant architecture of their palaces became battlegrounds as the Aeldari preyed upon each other, delighting in the cruellest of crimes. Their insanity and tainted passion poured into the warp until it achieved critical mass. With a thunderous metaphysical roar that tore the heart out of the empire, a new god was born – Slaanesh, the Dark Prince of Excess.

Slaanesh's birth screams destroyed countless souls in a psychic shock wave that rolled across the galaxy. Whole star systems fell amid orgies of cannibalism and violence. In that instant, most of the Aeldari race was destroyed, consumed by a cataclysm of terror and pain. The epicentre of their realspace empire was sucked into the warp, leaving a yawning maelstrom of pure Chaos in its place – a place the Imperium would later call the Eye of Terror. Slaanesh gorged upon the despair of the Aeldari. Unstoppable in its ascendancy, it consumed the deities of the old Aeldari empire, scattering the few survivors to the corners of the warp.

The Aeldari civilisation was reduced to a broken diaspora, their realm destroyed by the aftershock of Slaanesh's inception. Yet those hidden in the webway remained all but untouched. Great swathes of the labyrinth dimension itself were shattered into ruin, but many of those Aeldari who had built personal empires in and around Commorragh survived the birth of Slaanesh. The echoes of the new god's arrival had wrought insidious changes within them – changes whose horrific nature

would not be fully comprehended until later – but the Commorrite Aeldari had escaped destruction. In their supreme arrogance they did not cease their quest for excess, even for a moment. Repentance and atonement were alien concepts to a people who acknowledged no limits to their power.

The Aeldari sealed within the webway had not escaped the Fall, though this horror would only dawn on them slowly. Rather than having their essence consumed in one great draught, their souls were slowly draining away into the warp – consumed over time by Slaanesh, the entity the Aeldari call 'She Who Thirsts'. The Aeldari fear Slaanesh above all, for the god was given life by their actions, and now waits hungrily on the other side of the veil to claim each and every one of them. Where the Aeldari of the craftworlds learned to deny Slaanesh's hold upon them using the mystical spirit stones and infinity circuits, the Commorrite Aeldari became expert at ensuring that lesser beings suffered in their stead.

Provided they steeped themselves in the most extreme and decadent acts, the Aeldari of the webway found that the curse of Slaanesh could be abated. The agony of others nourished their withered souls and kept them vital and strong, filling their frames with unnatural energies. Assuming they could feed regularly enough, the webway dwellers became physically immune to the passage of time. So it was that the Drukhari were born, sadistic parasites who subsist upon the anguish of others in order to prevent the slow death of their immortal souls. Ten thousand years later, in the 41st Millennium, Slaanesh's thirst pulls at them still. There truly is no escape. The Drukhari have unwittingly doomed themselves, exchanging a horrific but mercifully swift end for an eternity of ghoulish starvation.

To this day the Drukhari raid the galaxy from the canker that is Commorragh, sowing misery and destruction wherever they emerge and spiriting away countless captives to their lairs for their own horrible ends. They are masters of torture and degradation, for the longer a Drukhari can drag out the punishment of a captive, the greater the nourishment that can be derived from it. A Drukhari who has recently fed upon the torment of others shines with a cold and startling aura, their physical form restored to perfection even as the spirit within festers. One who is starved of such energies for long enough will become a shadow, desperately hunting for a taste of pain with which to stave off the gnawing pangs in the depths of their soul.

RAIDERS OF REALSPACE

Though the Dark City is a self-contained realm, hidden from the eyes of those outside the webway, the Drukhari have a constant need to send their warrior castes on campaigns of slaughter. Only by launching massed raids across the galaxy can they feed their insatiable hunger for suffering, and secure the slaves and resources that allow Commorragh to thrive.

The webway gates that connect Commorragh to realspace are dotted across planets, moons and empty patches of space from one end of the galaxy to the other. Dating back to when the Drukhari's ancestors ruled the stars, these portals allowed the ancient Aeldari to travel quickly across their empire. Since that time they have remained hidden in the folds of reality, and the Drukhari now use them to terrorise and butcher the inhabitants of realspace, emerging unexpectedly to carry out their slaughter before hastening back to the Dark City with their mutilated captives.

Though some of the entrances to the webway have been discovered by the lesser races, most are known only to the Drukhari and their Aeldari cousins. As such, raiding parties will often prey on the same worlds again and again, appearing as if from nowhere before each massacre. Other times, Commorrite warlords use their spy networks to keep watch through a particular portal, silently observing as a decimated planet rebuilds over decades, centuries or even millennia. When the fruit of their populous is deemed ripe for harvest, another raid will come screaming from the shadows, giving face to the nightmares that have been buried in the collective conscious of the society for generations.

The first sign of a Drukhari raid is usually the appearance of the barb-prowed Raiders. The silhouettes of these grav-craft are feared by many species across the galaxy and are synonymous with doom. From the decks of the Raiders come fusillades of splinter weapon fire that rake the rows of defending infantry, and beams of darklight that rip through armoured vehicles and gun emplacements. Smaller craft carrying Drukhari champions and their elite retinues follow in the wake of this destruction, quickly overtaking the larger Raiders to stab through the rents in the lines of defence.

Such raids are swift and brutal, for the Drukhari avoid attritional warfare unless the potential rewards in suffering are monumentally high. Besides, the defenders are often eradicated before they have had

a chance to fortify their position. This is not to say that the Drukhari mindlessly kill all before them – far from it. Many of their foes are merely neutralised and taken as prisoners, though this is in no way a mercy. Those who are aware of the Drukhari's sadistic proclivities know that to die screaming on the battlefield is a far kinder fate than to survive and be taken to the torture chambers of Commorragh, where the sweet release of death can be denied indefinitely.

The strike forces of the Drukhari, despite consisting of treacherous and scheming murderers, work like well-tuned machines upon the battlefield. Raids are planned in meticulous detail by the Archons, Succubi and Haemonculi that lead them, and hidden routes through the webway are opened to allow passage for their forces before the assault. Only the most capable are recruited for each realspace raid, which is why Drukhari warriors are such determined opponents, and why their bitter rivalries are set aside during battle. Working in concert ensures that not only is the greatest amount of punishment inflicted upon the denizens of realspace, but also that the maximum number of victims can be taken back to Commorragh. Vendettas are revisited only once the captives are divided, for above all the Dark City requires a steady intake of fresh souls.

Enormous militant gangs known as Kabals regularly launch piratical invasions, and there is much to be gained from being

part of such an organisation – the thrill of hunting lesser beings, the chance to capture new slaves, but most importantly, the revitalising feast of unbridled destruction at hunt's end. Upon a Kabal's return to Commorragh, thousands of captives are traded as currency, put to work in the hellish depths of the weapons shops, rendered down in flesh-troughs or tormented unto death, their demise drawn out so that their captors can gain the greatest sustenance from their misery.

Though many raiding forces coalesce around a particular Archon, Succubus or Haemonculus, the Drukhari armies that fall upon realspace are far from uniform in composition. The Wych Cults who entertain Commorrite society with their nightly displays of ultra-violence are powerful military organisations capable of devastating raids. In addition, many Archons will recruit bands of Wyches from the Cult they patronise, for such warrior-acrobats make deadly shock troops. Similarly, the vile Haemonculus Covens that lurk in the bowels of Commorragh have standing armies of their own. These shambling hordes of flesh-twisted nightmares are often purchased to bulk out a raid with frightening and resilient warriors, or else accompany their leering creators as bodyguards and assistants both.

Typical raiding parties have their ranks swelled further by hirelings or opportunists from the many mercenary subcultures that exist within Commorragh. Whooping gangs of Hellions and hurtling Reaver jetbikes perform high-speed fly-by strikes. Jagged supersonic aircraft and flocks of murderous Scourges supply the Kabalites with air cover, while hovering Ravager gunships pick off armoured targets with contemptuous ease. Incubi, Mandrakes, Grotesques and other freakish specialists lend a raiding party strength and versatility, and it is common for a powerful Archon to surround himself with as many of these varied warriors as he can. The process of assembling such multifaceted raiding parties is known in the Dark City as *K'lthrael Aht'Ynris Khlave*, or 'tailoring the toxin to the blade', and is intended to ensure a strike force can swiftly and decisively overcome any opposition, no matter its nature or strengths.

Sometimes a powerful Wych Cult will organise its own raid, marshalling whole fleets of Raiders and Venoms to bear its bands of gladiatrixes into battle. Such raids are often executed with a specific acquisition in mind, be it deadly new beasts for the arenas or esoteric living ingredients to render down into the potent cocktails of combat drugs that the Wych Cults favour. A raiding force of Wyches prefers close assault over all other forms of warfare, and will often be supported by Beastmasters, Reavers and other such warriors of the arenas. Some Wych Cults, most notably the Pain Eternal, are as active in raiding realspace as the most warlike of the Kabals, channelling their fearsome resources into proving their skills in battle against the varied foes of the galaxy at large.

Similarly the Covens of the Haemonculi will sometimes launch raids of their own volition. Though usually content to squat like bloated spiders amid their webs of shadow and pain, the Haemonculi need a steady flow of victims as much as any other part of Commorrite society. Many of the more discerning Haemonculi prefer to orchestrate raids of their own, picking out those they wish captured with a connoisseur's eye, or savouring the act of indulging their own peculiar tastes with the relish of a gourmet. A Coven at war is a terrifying sight – a rampaging tide of warped bone and bulging, veined muscle that glitters with a myriad of blades and needles. Grotesques thunder into the enemy ranks alongside buzzing, clicking Engines of Pain, while the gruesome weapons of the Haemonculi torment, rupture and liquefy the foe in spectacular fashion.

On occasion, a Drukhari raiding party will join forces with other factions of Aeldari when the desires of each lend them a shared purpose. The Masques of the Harlequins, the Reborn warhosts of the Ynnari, even the Asuryani of the craftworlds – all find reason to fight alongside their Commorrite cousins against the younger races and ancient enemies that pervade the galaxy. While some of these distant kin may disapprove of the Drukhari's wanton cruelty on the battlefield, they do not deny its effectiveness. Though they are but the flickering embers of a dying empire, together the disparate Aeldari peoples can bring whole systems to their knees.

A GALAXY IN SHADOW

With the arrival of the *Dathedian* – known in the Imperium as the Cicatrix Maledictum or Great Rift – the outpouring of warp energy shattered many arterial spars of the webway. Whole sections were cut off entirely, reduced to isolated islands that were abandoned by their former inhabitants. Many rune-gates were ruptured completely or subsumed by the hungering Chaos dimension, their passages emptying into howling rents in reality. However, the calamity that befell those outside the webway was even greater, for the Dathedian had cleaved the galaxy in two. Countless human worlds that were once part of the wider Imperium floundered in darkness, unable to communicate or travel as they once had, alone amidst the menacing darkness of a hostile galaxy. The Drukhari have plunged headlong into this shrouded hunting ground, sending their raiding parties to harvest worlds once thought to be impregnable fortresses of Humanity. From these worlds they have taken slaves in greater numbers than ever before. Every day the Imperium sends more forces in a desperate attempt to salvage this section of their realm, and every day more and more captives are taken to die in the arenas of Commorragh. Among them are breeds of warriors previously unseen such as the Primaris Space Marines, who sate the spectators' thirst for variety in bloodshed. Though the Dathedian wrought great ruination upon the webway, those Drukhari who endured its birth spasms are now free to savour the torment it has created across reality.

The Drukhari do not rely on cumbersome armour, slow-moving tanks or static fortifications in battle; they consider a swift and merciless offense to be the best form of defence, and wish to be as directly exposed as possible to their victims' pain and despair.

THE DARK CITY

Commorragh's long descent into depravity stretches back millennia, to a time when the Aeldari civilization was at its zenith. It is a city in which the sadistic rule as tyrants, fuelled by the torments of the helpless, and the technologies created by the Drukhari's ancient ancestors are used to form progressively nightmarish sub-dimensions.

Commorragh is the eternal hub in which the Drukhari plot and implement their atrocities. The reaches of space around the city are stitched with seemingly endless trails of scintillating light as vessels pass to and fro between the Dark City and the portals that surround it. Some of these gateways into realspace are small and dim, but the arterial portals above the largest city-states blaze with ethereal luminescence. Each can accommodate a pirate fleet with ease. To focus on the city that these portals serve is near impossible. Each distant peak of spires and starscrapers is larger than the last, each border below almost fractal in its complexity. A profusion of thorned dock-spars jut from every archipelago and tower, and ornate spacecraft, held fast in crackling beams of electromagnetic force, occupy every berth. The Dark City seethes with a constant flow of corruption, as it draws evil to itself only to breathe it back out into the void.

Commorragh today is an endless nest of architectural contradictions and spatial anomalies. Each of its estates has been overdeveloped to such an extent that their growth has been forced into the vertical plane, the rival regions sprouting upwards like a tangle of needle-plants fighting for a scrap of sunlight. Each of the spires and towers is linked to its fellows by hundreds of curved arches and strands, and crested with complex silver structures that glow with stolen energies. Its towering eyries and palaces reach both upward and downward, spiralling into the depths of captive space. With every passing year, the parasitic city seeks to devour ever more of the hidden dimension that acts as its host.

IMPOSSIBLE REALMS

Commorragh is complex on a dimensional scale, a monolithic and ever-changing tangle of impossibilities that could no more be accurately or comprehensively mapped than could the currents of the warp themselves. Yet it is navigable, for the Dark City has many recognisable districts within its shifting bounds, though their number is almost beyond counting. Some are well-known and well-travelled, densely inhabited regions of tangled spires and bone-paved streets carved into fiercely defended territories by warring Kabals. Others are death to enter unbidden, the personal realms of powerful Archons or cadaverous Haemonculi who do not take kindly to unsolicited intrusions. Yet most dangerous are those regions that have fallen into disuse, due to either structural or dimensional collapse. These may take the form of monster-haunted wastelands of vitreous wreckage and ossified remains, or lakes of seething poisons and screaming shadows. The latter will often have suffered dimensional breaches due to the partial or total collapse of the webway around

Commorragh is less a city and more a conglomeration of nightmares, brought into existence by the most twisted Drukhari minds. Its fang-like spires and plunging abysses house the most depraved devices of agony imaginable, and from its slave pits and torture chambers come the endless screams of countless wretched slaves.

them, and may be bombarded by the light of dying stars, or exist within fields of entropic radiation that wither living creatures to dust in seconds.

DESOLATE OUTSKIRTS

Girdling the titanic central spires of the Dark City, Low Commorragh is a hotchpotch of shattered ruins and scavenged glories. Once-proud fortress complexes and barter-ports spread out in all directions, and the black and angular spires of lesser Kabals riddle their extremities with opportunistic growth. Many areas are haunted by packs of Ur-Ghuls and Khymerae, and are twisted beyond recognition by the tremendous upheavals of the Fall and the Great Rift. Their pitch-dark catacombs are prowled by far larger and uglier things than the Drukhari, for in Low Commorragh the lost and the feral thrive like carrion in a graveyard.

A vast swathe of these war-torn ruins form a region known as the Sprawls. Through their bleak streets wander the Parched – cadaverous Drukhari who have fallen far from grace. These ghouls gather on the periphery of others' fights and misfortunes, vicariously feeding on pain like freezing men flocking to a flame. Another region, known colloquially as Central Corespur, plays host to the torturous bends and falls of the acid-green River Khaïdes. Along this river race Hellions and Reavers, who compete in blisteringly fast aerial duels. The losers are sent spinning to their deaths, their dissolving corpses adding to the potency of the caustic sludge that swills around them.

Further coreward can be found the mercenary district Sec Maegra, more popularly known as Null City – a nation-sized shanty town permanently riven by internecine conflict on a scale akin to civil war among the lesser races. A thick mist of poisonous smoke hangs over its roofs, and with every passing minute fresh screams pierce the silence. At night, the scorched streets resound to solid-shot gunfire and the crack-spit of splinter rifles as negotiations turn sour and rivals are assassinated. Alien mercenaries can be found here in profusion, vying fiercely for the lucrative murder-contracts offered by many of the Kabals.

THE INNER RINGS

As violent as they are, the districts of Low Commorragh are but playgrounds in comparison to the inner rings that surround the Dark City's core. Here can be found the oldest noble houses, which have ruled their demesnes with irresistible force for millennia. Their sweeping wings and towering mansions are crested by citadels full of aristocratic Trueborn warriors, each of whom descend from one of the original orchestrators of the Fall.

Among these inner rings, one of the Dark City's ancient states has literally fallen into shadow. In Aelindrach, shadows thicken and writhe as living things, flowing into one another and crawling up the legs of those that trespass amongst them. Here amongst the velvet domes the dreaded Mandrakes make their lairs, bathing in the darkness. The outskirts of Aelindrach give way to the Bone Middens of the Wych Cults, where the skeletal remains of every sentient species in existence can be found, positioned in grim tableaux and mock battles by the Wyches who slew them.

THE UNDERWORLD

Beneath the core of Commorragh hang vast stalagmite-like structures that jut anarchically into the pocket-realities below the city. Inside these inverted spires lie the labyrinthine lairs of the Haemonculus Covens. Each Coven occupies a sprawling territory of cells and laboratories in which they practise their heinous crafts – spiral-edged torture pits, darklight-warded oubliettes, and galleries through which the screaming choirs of the damned endlessly echo. In many places the superstructure of these nightmare chambers contain remnants of past subjects to whom the Haemonculi have denied death through their dark science. Helical stairwells are lit by lamps sewn into the eye sockets of incautious visitors, and the bodies of countless alien species flensed in successive degrees line the walls as living relief sculptures. The Haemonculus Covens are invaluable to the denizens of Commorragh, dealing in body modification, drug distillation and – most importantly – resurrection of dead flesh. But even the most powerful Kabalites enter the Haemonculi's realm with caution.

THE CHASM OF WOE

One of the newest regions of the Dark City is also one of the most horrific, for the abyss of sub-dimensions known as the Chasm of Woe seethes with Daemons. The warp-creatures were released when Khaine's Gate – the long-held dam

against the immaterium in the heart of Commorragh – burst open. The vile creations of the Chaos Gods tore through the Dark City, feeding on the souls of Drukhari, mercenary and slave alike, but they were eventually corralled into the region surrounding the ruptured Khaine's Gate. Unable to seal up what was now a ragged wound in the fabric of the webway, the Drukhari used their reality-bending technologies to create a series of sub-dimensions between Khaine's Gate and Commorragh proper, transporting dilapidated parts of the city and territories of upstart Archons into the path of the unending Daemon onslaught. In this way, the daemonic incursion is kept from ever reaching the heart of the Dark City, but every day dozens more pocket realities must be added to the Chasm before the surging forces of Chaos overflow and devour Commorragh from within.

DAEMONIC INCURSIONS

Many of the webway's spars and branches were shattered entirely during the Fall of the Aeldari, and have grown ever more dilapidated in the millennia since. The wards once protecting them from the energies of the Realm of Chaos were left broken beyond repair by the Fall; when tensions grow to boiling point within Commorragh, the collective empathic signal of the Drukhari bleeds outward, drawing the denizens of the immaterium to the Dark City like predators to the scent of an open wound. These daemonic incursions are known as dysjunctions, and are disasters without compare in the material galaxy. Fiendish warp creatures pour through cracks in the webway to gorge themselves on the souls of whomever they find, and from the high spires to the slums, all of Commorragh becomes a battleground in a desperate war for survival. A handful of dysjunctions have occurred in the Dark City's history, yet none as immense or destructive as that following the breaching of Khaine's Gate.

KABALS OF COMMORRAGH

The Kabals are autonomous organisations somewhere between criminal cartels, pirate bands and noble households. Though forever set at each other's throats, the Kabals form the primary military strength of Commorragh, and are largely responsible for the constant flow of slaves upon which the Dark City feeds.

The Kabals occupy the upper tiers of Commorragh's power structure, defining the martial aspect of the Drukhari and maintaining a stranglehold on all aspects of the Dark City. Even the most minor Kabals consist of hundreds of Drukhari, though their territories may be confined to hidden locations and scattered hideouts. The largest Kabals comprise millions of skilled warriors. The baleful influence of these monstrous coalitions stretches from one side of the galaxy to the other, plaguing lesser civilizations and inferior races with slave raids and acts of blood-soaked piracy.

THE GENESIS OF THE KABALS

Drukhari society once revolved around a small number of noble houses. The scions of these aristocratic institutions plumbed the depths of hedonism that led to the Fall. The Commorrite nobility jealously guarded their positions, seeking out and killing any who threatened them or questioned their primacy. The central mass of Commorragh – a mind-boggling metropolis of palatial spires, skyscrapers, arch-shrines and pleasure temples – was the province of the noble houses alone. Entry could be gained only by birthright, and elitism was a way of life.

So it was for several millennia after the Fall of the Aeldari. The society of Commorragh remained as stagnant and corrupt as its ancient masters. In all likelihood it would have continued to do so indefinitely, had it not been for a young warrior-slave by the name of Asdrubael Vect, who brought the old order of the nobility crashing down.

Vect's own warrior-clique, or 'Kabal', had prepared for their founder's ascension, seeding their agents into every aspect of Drukhari civilisation throughout Commorragh and beyond. Vect rapidly climbed the ranks of Commorragh's hierarchy. More and more allies were enticed to join his cause, while corpses were made of those who denied his ascension, but it was never Vect's own blade that bore the bloodstains – he was far too prudent for such direct measures. Seeing him as merely an upstart slave, the nobles constantly underestimated Vect's cunning and ruthlessness, only realising the threat he posed when his influence had deeply infested the Dark City. Vect named the ranks of warriors that he gathered to his cause the Kabal of the Black Heart. They were the enforcers of their master's will, and declared Vect to be Supreme Overlord of Commorragh.

In the wake of Vect's uprising, the fickle Drukhari adopted the Kabalite system with an enthusiasm born of self-preservation. Sensing which way the wind was blowing, even the surviving noble houses reinvented themselves as Kabals. Power is no longer inherited in Commorragh, it must be fought for and taken by force. The authors of the Dark City's fate are those who wield the sharpest minds and blades, the precarious nature of their position ensuring complacency can never take root. At the top of this hierarchy sits Vect, the Supreme Overlord, his insatiable hunger for power still carving the path for all of Commorragh. Even death cannot undermine his reign, for Vect was able to use his own murder and subsequent resurrection to eliminate his most dangerous rivals in one fell swoop.

ORDER FROM ANARCHY

In a society as treacherous as that of the Drukhari, a single power-hungry individual soon makes enemies. It is never long before the loner finds a dagger at their throat or feels nerve-searing poison flowing through their veins. Only those affiliated to larger organisations enjoy any degree of security; there is safety in numbers, they say, and even in the shadow-haunted twilight realms of the Dark City this remains true. To kill a Kabalite is to commit a hostile action against their entire Kabal. Regardless of status, sect or species, few Commorrites are prepared to make such an influential enemy without good reason, and those who do must ensure they have powerful friends of their own to protect them against the inevitable retribution.

Competition for Kabalite membership is beyond fierce, despite the varied and often violent initiation rites that must be undergone. The constant supply of fresh aspirants means that the Kabals themselves enjoy a kind of loose immortality. Each has the might to make its displeasure keenly felt should it be threatened or slighted. It is unusual for an entire Kabal to be wiped out altogether. Only the Supreme Overlord can visit such a fate upon his enemies without triggering city-wide outrage or inviting punitive violence on a massive scale. Yet Vect ensures that Commorragh is eternally riven by gang warfare, and not a single night goes past in the Dark City without the streets echoing to running battles between Kabalite factions – the Archons of the Kabals do not care for the notion of peers.

THE KABALS AT WAR

Though all Kabals offer a measure of sanctuary – from outside influences, at least – the true prize for the established Kabalite is to take part in a realspace raid. The war with the material dimension is a never-ending campaign of extreme violence against every other sentient race in the galaxy. A successful raid offers the victors not only the twin bounties of slaves and a feast of pain, but will also do much for the political standing of those who planned and executed it. As such, successful realspace raids are one of the most straightforward ways in which a Drukhari Kabal can rise to prominence over its rivals. The largest and most well-respected Kabals launch raids on an almost constant basis, their sleek attack-craft descending upon one hapless world after another to plunder and enslave.

With their enormous statures and extremely high thresholds for pain, Orks are a dangerous yet favoured target of Kabalite raids. Each of the hulking greenskin warriors can endure far more suffering than most species, meaning the Drukhari can unleash the full extent of their violent tendencies and still return to Commorragh with captives.

It is extremely rare for an Archon to commit the warriors of their Kabal to a battle they have not already meticulously planned. Kabals employ countless spies, mercenaries and informers whose task it is to scout out potential raiding sites in exhaustive detail. Further, the Covens of the Haemonculi can be prevailed upon to provide stranger means of surveillance, be it whisperglass mirrors, flocks of invisible familiars or parasitically invested abductees. These services always come at a price, of course, yet a successful realspace raid will normally justify the cost of such bargains tenfold.

Once a raid is launched, Kabalite forces will work to keep the foe on the back foot at all times, using superior technology and local knowledge torn from the minds of captives to stay one step ahead of the enemy. Stand-up fights are never entered into voluntarily, for the warriors of the Kabals view concepts such as valour or honour as weaknesses to be exploited. Their raiding parties will strike hard and fast where the foe is at its most vulnerable, aiming to cripple command and control structures, undermine logistics and spread terror and confusion. Should an organised response coalesce, the Kabalites will simply fade away and attack elsewhere, aiming

above all else to avoid being pinned down in a war of attrition. Ambush, trickery, the turning of foes against one another, and the bloody quest for personal glory – such are the hallmarks of a Kabalite hunt.

The highest-ranking Archon of a Kabal is often called its Overlord, and serving beneath them are several subordinate Archons – sometimes called Dracons – who oversee the execution of lesser raids. When the Overlord does take to battle, they carve a gruesome path through the enemy whilst favoured retainers ensure that only the most desired opponents are allowed to reach their master. For the warriors in the Kabal, the visceral thrill of seeing their Overlord inflict such pain is exhilarating. Particularly influential Archons may even have several clones of themselves created by the Haemonculi. These duplicate bodies can then participate simultaneously in raids on opposite sides of the galaxy, or they may appear together on a single battlefield should the promise of torment prove especially tantalising. Similarly, some Overlords – ever cautious against the machinations of their rivals – hide their own identities by deploying simulacra of themselves on raids, while others work from the shadows to cultivate champions who believe themselves to be Overlord.

Many Kabals have a bias towards particular methods of warfare; this is often the product of their Archon's personal conceits or origins, or a result of their gangland wars within Commorragh. Some, such as the spaceborne Kabal of the Severed, boast great wings of attack craft that shatter and scatter the strength of their victims before a single Drukhari foot touches alien soil. Others – such as the Kabal of the Storm's Spite or the Kabal of the Bloody Scream – favour the deployment of overwhelming firepower, fielding whole squadrons of Ravager gunships and murderous flocks of Scourge mercenaries who pick the foe apart from a distance. Conversely, a great many Kabals prefer to get in close, fighting where they can feel every hot splash of blood and hear every last death rattle. Kabals such as the Shuddering Blade and the Silver Fang are especially well known for orchestrating such bloodbaths, and competition is fierce to accompany them to the field of battle. Perhaps the strangest of all are the Kabal of the Thirteenth Whisper, whose members keep their faces shrouded at all times and who are reputed to traffic heavily with the Mandrakes of Aelindrach. Raids by this Kabal are nightmarish affairs, tides of shadow proceeding their advance while chill-eyed horrors stalk the darkness with blades in hand.

KABAL HIERARCHY

Each Kabal operates as an independent entity within the Dark City. As such they vary greatly in terms of organisation and can have as few as a hundred members or as many as millions. However, the most common structure sees a single Archon ruling over multiple shards and splinters within a Kabal.

Kabal of the Piercing Eye prior to launching the Vorgan Raid

KABAL HIGH COMMAND
Overlord of the Piercing Eye
Archon
Courtiers
Lhamaeans
Medusae
Sslyth
Ur-Ghuls

OVERLORD'S RETINUE
Kabalite Trueborn
Incubi
Mandrakes
Venoms

SHARD OF THE ABACINATORS

SHARD OF THE MALIGNANT GAZE

SHARD OF THE ENRAPTURED

SPLINTER OF THE BLOOD SIROCCO

SPLINTER OF THE DESICCATORS

SPLINTER OF THE LINGERING MIASMA

MERCENARIES
Along with their own Warriors and raiding vehicles, each splinter maintains multiple pacts with Commorragh's various mercenary organisations with which they can supplement their numbers.

Incubi
Scourges
Mandrakes
Voidraven Bombers
Razorwing Jetfighters

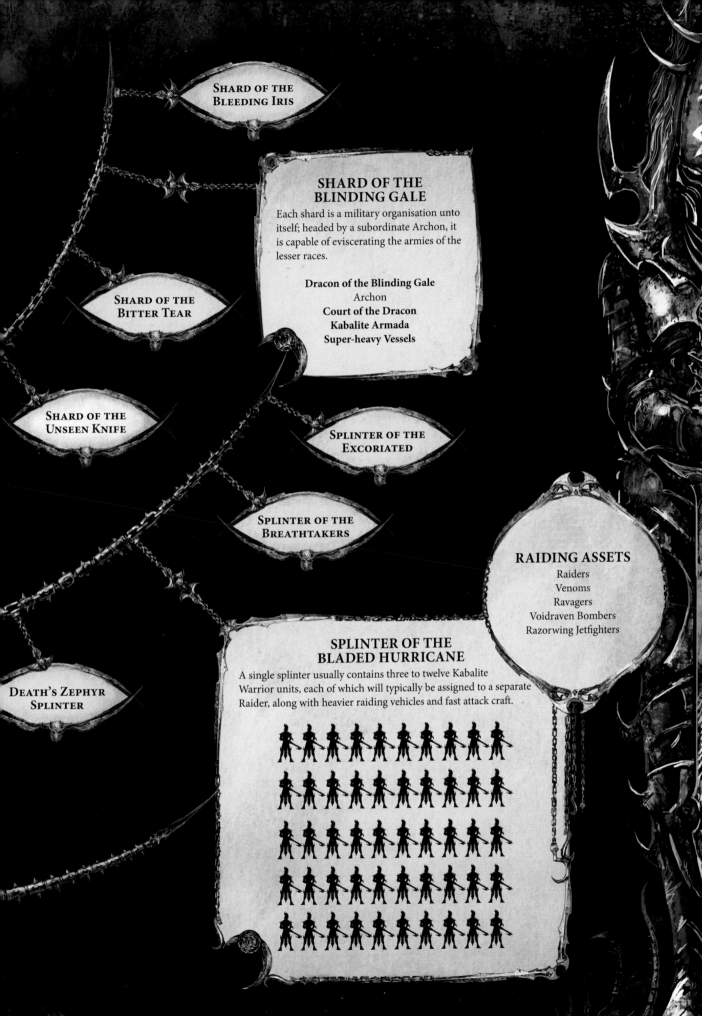

SHARD OF THE BLEEDING IRIS

SHARD OF THE BLINDING GALE

Each shard is a military organisation unto itself; headed by a subordinate Archon, it is capable of eviscerating the armies of the lesser races.

Dracon of the Blinding Gale
Archon
Court of the Dracon
Kabalite Armada
Super-heavy Vessels

SHARD OF THE BITTER TEAR

SHARD OF THE UNSEEN KNIFE

SPLINTER OF THE EXCORIATED

SPLINTER OF THE BREATHTAKERS

RAIDING ASSETS
Raiders
Venoms
Ravagers
Voidraven Bombers
Razorwing Jetfighters

DEATH'S ZEPHYR SPLINTER

SPLINTER OF THE BLADED HURRICANE

A single splinter usually contains three to twelve Kabalite Warrior units, each of which will typically be assigned to a separate Raider, along with heavier raiding vehicles and fast attack craft.

KABAL of the BLACK HEART

VECT'S WILL MADE MANIFEST

The Black Heart is the Kabal of Asdrubael Vect, formed millennia ago to seize control of Commorragh. They are his military arm, the enforcers of his will, and it is through them that the Supreme Overlord keeps the viscous flow of power circulating throughout the Dark City.

Morgat Vykreen, Kabalite Warrior,
Splinter of the Black Chalice,
Shard of the Tainted Blood

The Kabal of the Black Heart is the oldest and greatest of its kind. It is a vast and sprawling organisation, able to support numerous rival Archons within its hierarchical structure. Each Archon controls a separate faction within the Black Heart, and each vies fiercely with his rivals for the patronage of Supreme Overlord Vect. None brave outright murder, however, for only a fool would blunt one of Asdrubael Vect's favourite tools. So complete is his stranglehold upon Commorragh that none of these highly placed subordinate Archons dare challenge the Supreme Overlord's supremacy in anything but the most private dreams or fantasies. Even then, they do so with caution, for it is said that Vect knows well the scent of treachery, and reads the minds of lesser mortals like an open book.

This Kabal's military strength is virtually unassailable. Countless thousands of Kabalite Warriors, Commorrite mercenaries and lethal gunships stand ready to exterminate their foes at the slightest crook of Vect's corpse-white finger. A cast-iron bond with the Wych Cult of Strife puts yet more might at the Supreme Overlord's fingertips, providing him with the closest thing the Dark City has seen to genuine allies. This union – alongside the impossibly intricate web of spies and informers that Vect has scattered through every stratum of Commorragh, standing compacts with multiple Haemonculus Covens, and secreted agents throughout the wider Aeldari race – means the Kabal of the Black Heart holds more power than several of their largest rivals combined.

No action taken by or against the Kabal of the Black Heart is too small to elude Vect's notice, and with fractal genius he subtly influences every outcome. As such, when an Archon of the Black Heart launches a raid into realspace, they do so with the knowledge that Vect's personal spies have assessed the battle to come, and the Supreme Overlord will have prepared counter-measures for each possible eventuality. Every Warrior and Archon in the Kabal knows that they are under Vect's gaze, and that their slightest failings will incur his unquenchable fury. This is an exquisite motivator, and leads to vast soul harvests being carried out with flawless precision by the Black Heart.

KABAL of the FLAYED SKULL
MASTERS OF THE SHADOWED SKY

The Kabalites of the Flayed Skull are instantly recognisable by the stylised blood-streaks that they sport upon their snarling faces, echoing the sinister design of their Kabal's symbol. The icon itself recalls the mutilations the Kabal's Overlord would perform during his time in Commorragh's arenas.

In terms of sheer military force, the Flayed Skull are second only to Asdrubael Vect's Kabal of the Black Heart. Their Overlord, Vraesque Malidrach, began his long and dishonourable career as a low-born Reaver in the arena of Khad Mhetrul, where he was known for his signature brand of high-speed violence. Even after murdering his way to mastery over his own Kabal, Vraesque has lost little of the flare he cultivated in the arena, and is known for slaughtering his foes in swift, shocking raids. When faced with a worthwhile champion, the low-born lord may treat his warriors to a display of the savagery for which he gained his fame – decapitating his opponent, then slicing off their face with a single swing while their head arcs through the air.

'We are the masters of the shadowed sky.

Not for us a grubbing crawl through the mud and filth of battle. Leave that to lesser races.

We shall only set foot upon the soil these vermin call home in order to place our bladed heels upon their throats.'

- *Archon Vraesque Malidrach,*
Murderprince of the Poisoned Crown

The Kabal of the Flayed Skull rule over one of Commorragh's highest and most jagged spires. Known as the Poisoned Crown, the spire is encrusted with docks and grav-moorings beyond counting, and around them hangs a constantly shifting cloud of Razorwing Jetfighters and Voidraven Bombers. Those Commorrites who win their way out of the arenas to own such an attack craft are eager to align themselves with the Flayed Skull, for Vraesque is a renowned master of airborne warfare. Furthermore, he is quick to adopt new aerial strategies created in the arenas, so long as they are sufficiently spectacular and violent. These are often enacted by Reavers and Hellions who clamour to go to war alongside the Flayed Skull, or by flocks of Scourges who have sold their fickle loyalty to Vraesque. So honed are the Kabal's aerial skills that they once famously conquered the world of Thrandium without a single Kabalite setting foot upon the ground.

Exelot Vorn, Kabalite Warrior,
Splinter of the Skinless Finger,
Shard of the Shattered Hand

KABAL OF THE POISONED TONGUE
THE VENOMOUS WORD OF MALYS

The Kabal of the Poisoned Tongue has insinuated itself throughout Commorragh, its agents working like subtle toxins in the Dark City's necrotic veins. They are perhaps the most insidious of the Kabals, yet when their schemes call for it, they are more than capable of flexing their violent might.

Leprio Kalzag'ha, Kabalite Warrior,
Splinter of Deathly Rigour,
Shard of the Last Breath

The Kabalites of the Poisoned Tongue are universally sharp of wit, with a flair for duplicity so pronounced that they can tie their rivals in knots and dissect them with words alone. They have carved their own niche in the Dark City through constantly misleading and wrong-footing their rivals, ensuring their 'allies' bear the cost in blood whilst they plunge the knife into the foe's delicate underbelly. They even use failure and mischance as weapons, elegantly scapegoating and framing others to achieve their means. Many an opposing Archon has been torn to shreds by their own Kabalites due to the campaigns of misinformation spread by the Poisoned Tongue. Nobody trusts the honeyed words of this infamously sly Kabal, but seeing as no Drukhari trusts another in any case, this is not much of a handicap.

During their realspace raids, the Poisoned Tongue put their skills of deceit to deadly use. On worlds where the Kabal have trained their eye, inhabitants are often supplied with false signs of an impending

attack, as well as fragmented messages and fleeting signatures of Drukhari raiding craft. They position their defences as best they can to repel the impending invasion, but when the Poisoned Tongue finally strikes it is inevitably where their victims least expect. The Kabal regularly employs infiltration tactics, assassinations and massed poisonings to ravage their enemies before ever meeting them on the field of battle. The result is that the raiding parties of the Poisoned Tongue are able to swiftly run through the disordered ranks of their prey before spiriting back their captives to Commorragh.

Led by the intellectual titan Lady Aurelia Malys, the Kabal of the Poisoned Tongue enjoys a position right at the forefront of Commorrite society. Their number includes many Trueborn – the closest to nobility in the Drukhari society that Vect's mercilessly enforced Kabalite system will allow. The whispersmiths have it that the Lady has her own mysterious patron, for those bold or foolish enough to eavesdrop

on her personal chambers have reported two distinct voices when only one life-sign registers within. Few such spies survive long, for Lady Malys has her little ways, and she is invariably several steps ahead of the competition.

The accuracy with which Lady Malys can predict her enemies' moves borders on supernatural, leading to the belief amongst many of her detractors that she has a degree of psychic ability. However, the truth is that she simply has a mind like a steel trap. So astoundingly complex is her psyche that she was once taken by Asdrubael Vect as one of his consorts, until the Supreme Overlord eventually cast her out. Outraged, Malys and most of her Kabalite Warriors left Commorragh and struck out into the webway. There it is said she encountered the god of the Harlequins, Cegorach, who banished her followers and challenged her to a duel of wills. When Malys successfully answered all of the Laughing God's riddles, Cegorach vanished with an amused chuckle, leaving behind a semi-sentient blade and a pulsating crystal, which was the trickster god's own heart. Determined to gain enough power to undo Vect, Malys used the blade to cut out her own heart and replaced it with that of Cegorach. The heart has continued to beat within Malys' chest ever since.

Lady Malys returned to Commorragh, where she reinstated herself as Overlord of the Kabal of the Poisoned Tongue. Since then she has deftly led the Kabal through the Dark City's most deadly intrigues, including the great treacheries that have occurred in recent years. Following Vect's murder, many suspected the hand of Malys was involved. Rather than wait around for the reprisal that the Black Heart had inevitably planned, she took the vast bulk of the Poisoned Tongue and ventured out into the webway, there to await the coming storm. Malys' foresight was once again vindicated when those Archons who attended the Great Wake in Commorragh were butchered one and all, and Vect himself arose, alive and triumphant. For now, the Poisoned Tongue are content to watch the Dark City from afar.

KABAL OF THE OBSIDIAN ROSE

SLAVES TO PERFECTION

The Kabalites of the Obsidian Rose are known by the exquisitely crafted instruments of death they take with them to war. Thus armed, even the lowliest of their Warriors is able to fight like a virtuoso, and their champions stride arrogantly across the battlefield to put their perfectly crafted weapons to use.

The Kabal of the Obsidian Rose control the greatest swathe of weapons shops in the Dark City. Through the inventive genius of their Overlord, Aestra Khromys, they maintain a death grip on the Commorrite arms trade, and when they raid the worlds of realspace, they do so armed with the best equipment in Commorragh. Every weapon, suit of armour and vehicle used by the Kabal is a work of art, finely detailed and honed for maximum lethality. A single one of these tools of war would be a prized artefact to one of the minor Kabals, but to the Obsidian Rose the achievement of perfection is not an elusive ideal – it is the benchmark by which success and failure are measured. These same exacting standards are applied to every aspect of life in the Kabal.

Before launching a raid, the Obsidian Rose practise every step, shot and contingency until each Warrior can perform their part blindfolded. It is the duty of each Kabalite to ensure that their splinter rifle and armour are in pristine condition, not only so that they can efficiently inflict torment, but also to proudly display the Obsidian Rose's inherent superiority over their victims. It is not uncommon for Warriors returning from a raid to be hoisted onto the bladed vanes of their craft next to the screaming captives, simply because they have allowed their weapon to become tarnished with enemy blood. Anything less than immaculate is considered an utter affront.

Archon Khromys herself is an impossibly skilled artisan in the field of weapons manufacture, and a blade or pistol bearing her signature mark will sell for a huge price in slaves and souls. Yet she was not always the Kabal's leader. Having failed to bow down and kiss the hand of the Obsidian Rose's previous master, Archon Vhloriac, Khromys was flung into the Kabal's vast weapons shops to suffer death by ennui alongside the other slaves. Here she was forced to monotonously assemble the same parts over and over until her days blended together into a recurring nightmare. For the Drukhari, who are by their nature born hedonists, such a fate is far worse

than death or torture, for in the relentless mundanity their very souls are starved. Many so fated go mad – but Khromys developed a plan that would take many years to come to fruition. The first step was to sate her soul's need for extremes by constructing the most perfectly balanced and accurate weapons imaginable. The results of her prodigious craftsmanship were noticed by the factory overseers, and within a year she was transferred to a graded workshop within High Commorragh. Such was the quality of her weapons that they were soon asked for by name, and a thriving trade in Khromys' weaponry circulated throughout the upper echelons of the Obsidian Rose.

Eventually, Khromys and the team of master artisans she had trained were purchased wholesale by Archon Vhloriac, who had long since discarded any memory of his past encounter with the disrespectful weaponsmith. For him she produced finer armaments than she had ever

before created, and her master boastfully equipped himself and his bodyguard with her wares. When Khromys and her team were summoned before their patron they brought gifts with them, seemingly harmless artefacts and trinkets that in reality harboured dozens of concealed weapons. The shock when Khromys' clique put their hidden armoury to use was compounded by the fact that the equipment borne by the Archon's Court stopped working at that very moment. It was an act of treachery that was meticulously crafted, and executed to perfection.

Since that day, Khromys has ruled as Overlord of the Obsidian Rose, and the Kabal has a flawless reputation for its firearms and blades. In her perfectionism, Khromys does not tolerate any lapse of quality in her weapon shops' produce, or in the members of her Kabal, and will personally descend into the bowels of Commorragh to make an example of those accused of imperfect workmanship.

Phorsa Quex, Sybarite,
Splinter of Darkness Emerging,
Shard of the Jade Chrysalis

KABAL OF THE LAST HATRED
DECADENTS OF DEATH

The Last Hatred are recognisable for the myriad, still-living bodies that adorn the hulls of their raiding craft in different states of necrosis. The twisted grimaces and agonised screams of these unfortunates not only terrifies the Kabal's enemies, but also invigorates its warriors as they ride into battle.

The Kabalites of the Last Hatred have a morbid interest in the forbidden arts. Though they outwardly seek to master the transition between life and death, their aims are far grander than those of petty necromancers. Some say the Last Hatred seek to transcend mortality entirely, others that they wish to exterminate the Aeldari race and enslave whatever entity is born from the ashes. Madness this may seem, but any who have looked into their eyes will never truly dismiss their ambition, nor the depths of depravity to which they will go to fulfil their goals. So it is that they prosecute their kin-strife against the Asuryani and Exodites, but above all it is the Ynnari who are shown the full measure of their fury.

Originally famous for their pain-farms and a talent for keeping their wretched captives alive indefinitely, the drive to drain every last drop of suffering from their 'clients' has led the Kabal of the Last Hatred into infamy. In recent years, the Kabal have mastered the technique of permanently binding a soul to the cadaver from which it would usually depart at the moment of death. Yet the carnival of corpses that accompanies them to war is merely a distraction to draw attention from something far more sinister, for down in the pits under their stronghold, the Kabal practises ever more complex rites. Here the Kabalites unpick the tapestry of life, studying the postponement of entropy in gardens hung with wax-skinned undead arranged in artful but unnatural poses. Should they ever succeed in their quest, the lines between life and death may be irrevocably blurred.

Pheriavex Nastradus, Kabalite Warrior, Splinter of Unanswered Pleas, Shard of Ungiven Mercy

KABAL OF THE DYING SUN
BRINGERS OF TWILIGHT

Proportionally, the Dying Sun are comprised of more Trueborn Drukhari than any other Kabal, and they show open disdain to those lesser born. Even Asdrubael Vect is viewed amongst the Kabal as a usurper who has elevated himself far beyond his birthright.

Those who fight under the symbol of the Dying Sun belong to one of the oldest Kabals, renowned for their overweening pride and disdain for anything that has not endured for millennia. They prefer to raid at sunset, for their Overlord, Archon Vorl-Xoelanth, is obsessed with the transition from light and hope to darkness and despair. The Kabal's wild claims that they retain the ability to extinguish stars are infamous, though their rivals have never quite managed to explain the deterioration of the sun Echillos during the Aleuthan Persecution.

The truth is that the Kabal of the Dying Sun possess ancient fragments of forbidden arcana, heirlooms from the days of the Aeldari empire of old. Their stronghold – the Pinnacle of Disdain – is an impenetrable mountain of elegant, buttressed armour and echoing chambers, within which the Kabal hide their darkest secrets. These timeless artefacts, hidden away in shadowy vaults, possess the power to kill stars, suck the life force from worlds and exterminate whole races of sentient beings. However, they are ill understood and, in many cases, charged with psychic potential. Thus, they are as lethal to their owners as they are to their victims, not least because it would attract the violent displeasure of the Dark City at large should their existence become known. They are therefore used very sparingly, deployed by the Trueborn elite of the Kabal only as a last resort – but knowledge of these trump cards' existence fills the Kabal's upper echelons with justified arrogance.

Maiys of Grovenspire, Sybarite, Splinter of Blooded Alabaster, White Shard of Grovenspire

THE LORDS OF IRON THORN
WRIGHTS OF WAR

The deafening scream of grav-engines heralds the Lords of Iron Thorn as they burst from the webway into realspace. Few other Kabals can boast as great a navy as the rulers of Pandaimon, and none can match their ability to create these machines of war.

Masters of the sub-realm of Pandaimon, embittered remnants of a long-gone aristocracy, the Lords of Iron Thorn are Commorragh's most industrious grav-vehicle crafters. Prowling squadrons of Ravagers and sleek-sailed Raiders fill the skies of Pandaimon, sweeping between its spires in great numbers.

Long ago, this proud and ancient Kabal were brought to their knees after an ill-fated rebellion against Asdrubael Vect by their then-master, Archon Qu. However, in the centuries since, they have rebuilt their power through ensuring the Kabal of the Black Heart remains well supplied with Iron Thorn war machines. This Kabal's weapon factories and grav-docks are so sprawling they would cover the surface of a small moon, and they ring night and day with the hellish clangour of slave-driven industry. It is said that the mark of the Iron Thorn upon a Raider's hull is akin to Aestra Khromys' brand upon the stock of a gun – a mark of quality that is second to none.

The Lords of Iron Thorn are highly active in the raids upon realspace. Every successful attack proves afresh the supremacy of their airborne armada, and also supplies them with the massive force of slaves required to power their ceaseless industry. They believe in the application of overwhelming firepower, and delight in proving the superiority of their finely crafted gunboats over the lumbering war engines of the lesser races.

Dyoz Nazzanct, Kabalite Warrior, Splinter of the Pointing Needle, Shard of the Voyaging Nerve

KABAL OF THE BROKEN SIGIL
WEAVERS OF FEAR

Though uncontrolled fear is a common byproduct of a Drukhari raid, the Broken Sigil ensure that their victims are gripped with terror before a single Kabalite has emerged from the shadows. Perched in the wings of the webway, they wait for the sound of screaming to beckon them to the stage of battle.

The Kabal of the Broken Sigil takes its icon from the ancient Aeldari glyph *Drethuchii*, loosely translated as 'the Shattering of Harmony'. Like its namesake, the Kabal is synonymous with discordance. Wherever order and prosperity abound, the Broken Sigil strike with overwhelming force, bringing confusion and despair to the most idyllic planets in the galaxy. Terror tactics are much beloved by the Kabalites of this sect, so much so that the Broken Sigil's Overlord, Archon Xerathis, is looked down upon by his rivals for the predictability of his strategies. True enough, his Kabalites are not above blanket-bombing with hallucinogenic gas or hijacking communications channels to ensure their victims are frightened half to death before the invasion starts in earnest. Yet the Kabalites of the Broken Sigil maintain that the price they pay in forewarning the enemy is outweighed by the rich feast of fear that awaits them when the onslaught begins.

Perhaps unsurprisingly, the Broken Sigil are amongst the most feared and infamous of the Kabals, especially upon the worlds of the Imperium. Entire conclaves of Ordo Xenos Inquisitors seek their demise, and on multiple occasions Lord Xerathis has found himself the personal quarry of Deathwatch Kill Teams. If this concerns the toweringly arrogant fear-monger, he conceals it well. Instead, Xerathis boasts of the fine slaves such post-human warriors make, and insinuates knowingly that, with the correct persuasion, perhaps Space Marines can be made to know fear after all…

Olascyn Vongoliot, Kabalite Warrior, Splinter of Rictus Immemorial, Shard of the Twisted Visage

WYCH CULTS OF THE ARENAS

The Wych Cults provide their fellow Commorrites with a feast of agonies that, for a while at least, keeps the blades of their kin from one another's throats. Each Cult's arena is unique, every performance more violent and outlandish than the last, for these gladiatorial sisterhoods are locked in constant competition to offer up the greatest show for their hungry-eyed audience.

Commorragh exists in a delicate but well-established balance. Its citizens would gladly stab each other in the back just for the looks on their victims' faces, for to witness another's anguish is the only way the Drukhari have left to feed their withered souls. Yet for the ruling Archons of Commorragh to allow the natural bloodthirst of their kin to go unchecked would be to invite catastrophic civil war.

Because of their kind's unending need to bathe in murderous sensations, the Drukhari have evolved the Hekatarii, known in common parlance as the Wych Cults. Each Wych Cult is a thousands-strong organisation of gladiators that put on frequent displays of the most incredible brutality – not only for the edification of the masses, but also for their literal sustenance. Such is the scale of the carnage staged by these armies of warrior-athletes that their audiences leave the arena with the glow of well-fed predators. In this

way, the populace is kept from full-scale anarchy – at least, those residents of Commorragh wealthy enough to attend the Wych Cults' nightly performances.

BLOOD ON THE STAGE

Each Wych Cult has its own arena, which is as much a display of their wealth and status as it is a stage for their spectacles of violence. Comparing architectural masterpieces such as the Crucibael or Moedh Stair to the primitive amphitheatres of other civilisations would be much like placing a glittering palace next to a mud hut. Likewise, the Drukhari athletes that perform within them make the most gifted human acrobat look like an uncoordinated ape by comparison. Each arena has its own deadly charms and challenges, from staples such as spinning blades and ravenous beasts, to gravity-wells, kinetic inversion snares or even more esoteric and inventive hazards.

Each Wych Cult is constantly in competition to outdo its rivals with the sheer scope and imagination of its gore-soaked games. Many performances spread into the audience in interesting and deadly ways as the excitement builds to fever pitch. Arterial spurts of blood rain down into the rapt crowd as battle takes place over their heads, or even amidst their stalls. The arenas crackle with tension, the viewers leaning forward in their seats with eyes wide and the leers of hungry predators etched upon their faces. Be they aerial ballets of bloodletting, zero-gravity mass murder or carefully selected menageries on the prowl, all Cult performances have one thing in common – the arena is slick with blood and viscera by the show's conclusion.

Most of the Hekatarii are female, for amongst the Drukhari it is they who are more often able to attain the pinnacle of poise and grace their craft demands. Male

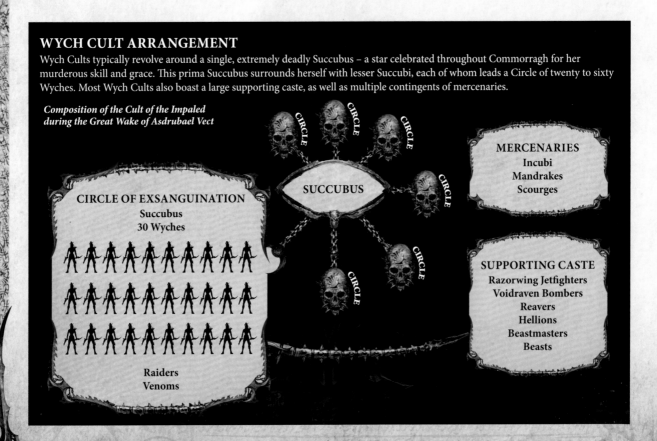

WYCH CULT ARRANGEMENT

Wych Cults typically revolve around a single, extremely deadly Succubus – a star celebrated throughout Commorragh for her murderous skill and grace. This prima Succubus surrounds herself with lesser Succubi, each of whom leads a Circle of twenty to sixty Wyches. Most Wych Cults also boast a large supporting caste, as well as multiple contingents of mercenaries.

Composition of the Cult of the Impaled during the Great Wake of Asdrubael Vect

CIRCLE
CIRCLE
CIRCLE
CIRCLE

SUCCUBUS

CIRCLE

CIRCLE

MERCENARIES
Incubi
Mandrakes
Scourges

CIRCLE OF EXSANGUINATION
Succubus
30 Wyches

Raiders
Venoms

SUPPORTING CASTE
Razorwing Jetfighters
Voidraven Bombers
Reavers
Hellions
Beastmasters
Beasts

Wyches ensure that their Wych Cult is never wanting for strong offspring, yet though they are valued they rarely attain high rank. Certainly the Succubi who rule over the Wych Cults are universally female. Most Cults contain several Succubi, each leading the Wyches of a particular Circle, but a single Succubus possessed of unmatched power and deadly grace typically reigns over them all. So it has been since the earliest days of the Dark City, and so shall it always be.

BEYOND THE ARENA

Almost every Wych Cult enjoys the patronage of a powerful Archon, for there is much glory to be had for the founders of the feast. More than this, however, the Wych Cults are powerful allies. After all, each is comprised solely of trained killers who enjoy nothing more than to demonstrate their consummate skills in battle. This mutually agreeable arrangement ensures that the Wych Cults never run short of slaves and exotic combat stimulants. A good patron is always generous, lest his stable of warrior athletes decides to bite the hand that feeds them. Meanwhile, the Archon gains the allegiance of an organisation of exceptionally trained Hekatarii to lend their blades to his raids upon realspace.

The Wych Cults take every chance they can to prove their martial skills superior to those of the lesser races, both within the arena and without. Though they profess nothing but contempt for the warrior castes of realspace, the Wyches get an undeniable thrill out of matching themselves against any suitably impressive opponent. The trophy halls of a successful Succubus will thus boast the heads of Adeptus Astartes champions, conquering Ork Warbosses and Tyranid Hive Tyrants alike.

There is much more to a Wych Cult than its arena. Below the elegant spires and weapon-nodes of each Cult stronghold's exterior are academies and training complexes devoted to every aspect of the close-quarters kill. Anti-gravity hemispheres and gruelling 'living landscapes' ensure each Wych is at the peak of physical fitness. Each Cult keeps an extensive menagerie, re-stocked by its Beastmasters with an endless supply of alien captives and dangerous species. Different Wych Cults practise their own specialities, endlessly discussed by the arena's crowd. The Bladed Hand, for

To the untrained eye, a Wych Cult raid appears like a barbaric orgy of violence in which the Commorrite gladiators tear into their foes with savage abandon. But in truth, each attack upon realspace is meticulously staged, with every Wych playing a crucial role.

instance, hones the art of the unarmed kill (though they are famous for blurring the line), whilst the Stilled Heart specialise in the use of poisons, venoms and paralytic elixirs.

A Wych Cult will often stage realspace raids purely at the behest of its Succubus. These raids are not only to gather new fodder for the arenas, but also to provide a chance for the Wyches to test their skills against new opponents. A Wych Cult raid is considered high art by many Drukhari, who will pay handsomely to fight alongside the massed gladiators, alien beasts and speeding aerial acrobats that each Succubus unleashes upon her prey. Other raids are quite literally performances in their own right. While the Wych Cult's Raiders and Venoms scream down into the foe's midst and force their desperate victims to fight for their lives, Commorrite pleasure-barges drift high above. Aboard these craft, wealthy spectators swill intoxicating nectars and offer sneers or applause as each bloody slaughter ebbs and flows, while bets are won or lost on the conduct of favoured combatants. Such spectacles are especially popular amongst

the smirking ranks of the Trueborn, who become steadily more exhilarated and revitalised as they soak up the miasma of agonies that rises from battle below.

Yet for all their foppish hangers-on, Wych Cult raids are veritable blizzards of violence. They are direct and unstoppable strikes that – like the Wyches themselves – scorn the cumbersome protection of armour in favour of the safety that pure speed provides. Like a perfectly placed knife-thrust to the heart, a raid by a Wych Cult is swift, deadly and precise, capable of felling even the largest and most dangerous foes before they even realise they are under attack. Amid hurtling squadrons of Reavers and Hellions, swept over by the half-glimpsed shadows of Razorwing Jetfighters and Voidraven Bombers, the Wyches leap and plunge into the midst of their enemies with joyous abandon, fighting amongst the piles of their mangled victims. Only when the foe's numbers become overwhelming, or there are no further enemies to face the fury of their knives, do the Wyches retreat as suddenly as they arrived – leaving absolute carnage in their wake.

CULT OF STRIFE
EXCELLENCE EMBODIED

The Wych Cult of Strife has become the most influential in Commorragh, largely due to the sublime talents of Her Excellence, Lelith Hesperax. This Cult has risen to the apex of power not through treacherous politicking, but through mastering the creed of speed over strength, and elevating their blood sports to high art.

Even outside of the Dark City, the Cult of Strife has become synonymous with flawless cruelty. The Wyches of this Cult are master executioners all, dedicated to perfecting the art of the kill in all its forms. From subtle murders to orgiastic slaughters, no method of death is beyond these Wyches' grasp, and whilst raiding in realspace the techniques of the Cult's victims are keenly observed. If one of the inferior races has devised a new way of killing it shall soon be catalogued by the Cult of Strife, and – if suitably spectacular – may be adopted for use in the arenas.

The Cult's arena performances are more patronised than those of any other in Commorragh, for each time they put their craft into practice they display new styles of violence and expose their crowds to unique methods of bloodshed. Nobility from every fractal corner of the Dark City come to observe these performances, and to imbibe the exquisitely crafted suffering the Cult of Strife produces in their victims. Many Archons pay handsomely to see famous Cult of Strife Wyches fight champions from other Cults, lavishing even more riches on the eventual winner. This constant inflow of wealth allows the Cult of Strife to maintain an unending supply of the best combat drugs available, which they use to further enhance their talents in the arena. The brutal reputation surrounding the Cult breeds in its constituent Wyches an air of superiority that is pronounced even by the standards of the Drukhari, and they take every opportunity to show that this pride is well deserved.

Though the Cult of Strife boasts dozens of the best warrior-athletes in the galaxy, it is their prima Succubus – Lelith Hesperax – who is the flawless diamond at the centre of the crown. Her allure draws in hundreds of thousands of spectators every night, each of whom is prepared to pay a high price for the privilege of watching her perform.

Night after night, Lelith dances her way through massed ranks of stimm-enhanced Orks, gut-wrenching Grotesques, disgraced Archons and more, the crowd roaring its approval as she gifts each victim the kiss of death with a contemptuous flick of her blades. Though the Cult's other Succubi model themselves on Lelith, none have achieved the same heights of infamy.

A POWERFUL PATRON

Amongst Lelith's many admirers is Asdrubael Vect himself, and the Cult of Strife has long been affiliated with the Kabal of the Black Heart to the mutual benefit of both. Whether this is a bond of reciprocal admiration or the wary respect of natural born killers is immaterial, for the alliance has proven as strong as steel, and strength is hard currency in the Dark City. Thanks to the unparalleled power and generosity of their patron, the Cult of Strife's arena, the Crucibael, is the most lavishly appointed and spectacular in all of Commorragh. From the expansive laser-grid of its toroid Reaver arena, to the black-veined living jade of its mighty galleries, the Crucibael is one of the Dark City's greatest spectacles. As Vect himself was once heard to say, Lelith Hesperax is the greatest treasure of the Dark City, and one does not display one's finest emerald amid squalor.

The alliance between the Kabal of the Black Heart and the Cult of Strife brings constant benefit to both. Even the most impulsive and hot-tempered Succubus must recognise that a challenge to the Cult of Strife is likely to incur the wrath of Asdrubael Vect himself. Equally, the Kabal of the Black Heart basks nightly in the reflected glory of Lelith's sublime victories on the arena sands. This unique symbiosis is magnified a hundredfold on the battlefields of realspace, where the followers of Lelith and Vect fight alongside one another with merciless synchronicity. The pitiless firepower of the Kabalites and the point-blank ferocity of the Wyches

mesh to deadly effect. The gladiatrixes of the Cult of Strife weave sinuously through the covering fire of the Black Heart to fall upon the surviving foes in an orgy of bloodletting. Freed from the customary necessity of watching their supposed allies for signs of treachery, both Commorrite factions are able to fight at their full potential against their luckless prey.

On those rare occasions that the belladonna of the arenas deigns to take to the field in person, the spectacle of this alliance at war is raised to the sublime. Such a raid occurs only rarely, for Lelith's first duty is to the baying crowds of the arenas. Yet when it does take place, the competition to join the raiding party is so fierce it has, on occasion, triggered full-blown inter-Kabalite war.

THE GHORVENFAL RAID

One of the more infamous joint endeavours between the Kabal of the Black Heart and the Wych Cult of Strife was the raid upon the world of Ghorvenfal. The planet was a stronghold of the Alpha Legion, a Heretic Astartes faction synonymous with the use of stealth and subterfuge. For decades an Alpha Legion warlord by the name of Jaghathra Vrax had operated out of a fortress in Ghorvenfal's Black Mountains. A noted bladesman, he plagued surrounding systems with piratical raids, evading the Imperium's clumsy reprisals with ease.

Vrax, however, eventually overreached himself. Having discovered that the Kabal of the Black Heart planned to raid the Imperial factory world of Melidrantis, he elected to use the Drukhari as pawns in his own schemes. Vrax concealed Alpha Legionnaires on the planet's surface, ordering them to wait until the raid was well underway. At the battle's height they struck, catching both the Kabalites and their beleaguered Cadian foes by surprise and exacting a heavy toll upon them both. Vrax's forces escaped with a huge stockpile of weaponry, and left the Black Heart to retreat empty-handed. Needless to say, such an insult could not be allowed

to stand. Asdrubael Vect spared no effort in tracking down this mysterious assailant and prepared an attack to make an example of them. This was not to be a slave raid, but a slaughter. It was at Vect's request that Lelith Hesperax herself joined the forces arrayed for the attack, for to her would fall the task of personally humbling Jaghathra Vrax.

The raid began as Ghorvenfal's bloated sun rose red and bloody on the horizon. As a swirling webway portal tore the skies above the Black Mountains, the Alpha Legionnaires were caught completely by surprise. From the portal flew dozens of attack craft, falling like a rain of knives towards the squat immensity of the Alpha Legion stronghold where it nestled amid the mountain peaks. By the time the Chaos air defences cycled up and flak batteries began to pound, it was already too late. Sleek fighter craft streaked overhead, bombs and missiles silencing one quad-gun after another and tearing rents in the fortress' armoured hide.

Through these gaps poured the Kabalites of the Black Heart and the Wyches of the Cult of Strife, leaping straight from the decks of their Raiders into the smoke-shrouded corridors of the fort. Towering traitors strode to meet them with bolters blazing and blades bared. The Hekatarii sprinted and leapt into their enemies' midst, cutting down the armoured giants with no thought for their own horrific casualties. Kabalite Warriors advanced in the Wyches' wake, their gunfire laying low those traitors who evaded the gladiatrixes' blades.

The surviving Alpha Legionnaires were finally surrounded in their primary arming chamber, massively outnumbered and outgunned. It was here that Hesperax met Vrax in single combat, mockingly offering the Chaos Lord and his followers their freedom should he defeat her. A lethal swordsman with daemonic strength burning in his veins, Vrax set upon his slender foe with his hellforged broadsword. Hesperax met him with a simple knife in each hand, standing firm with a slight smile pulling at one corner of her perfect lips. The fight that followed was a storm of blades too fast for the eye to follow, and within moments Vrax's sword struck the floor, his severed hands still wrapped around its grip. Hesperax – bare flesh unmarred but for the Chaos Lord's blood – did not stop there, swiftly truncating his arms and legs to leave him roaring in helpless fury at her feet. Even as the Chaos Lord fell, her followers closed in once more. Only one Alpha Legionnaire left the fortress alive that day, and his limbless form howls its unimaginable agony above the Onyx Gate of Vect's palace to this day.

Evelancia Davenyr,
Circle of the Winnowing Harvest

CULT OF THE CURSED BLADE

SISTERHOOD OF TRAITORS

While all Drukhari celebrate sins such as wrath, pride and malice, the Cult of the Cursed Blade revels in the practice of treachery. The Wyches in their ranks thrive in this culture of mistrust, growing strong in an environment where one's closest conspirators are also one's deadliest adversaries.

In Commorragh the term 'cursed blade' does not refer to a physical weapon, but instead to an individual or organisation that rebels against its masters. The Cult of the Cursed Blade has earned its name many times over, so much so that even for a well-protected Archon to invite Wyches from this Cult into his palace is tantamount to cutting his own throat. Treachery is held as the greatest of all virtues by the Cursed Blade, for by a process of hyper-accelerated natural selection the Wyches of the Cult ensure that only the strongest and most cunning within their ranks survive. Weapons that deceive and wrong-foot the foe are popular within their warrior cliques. Many a harmless-looking ornament worn by the Wyches contains a hidden snap-sword, poison barb or pair of flick-blades, and it is common to see many razorflails wielded among their ranks. In the arena, a favoured performance of the Cult is to feign an alliance with an unwitting alien combatant – giving the warrior hope that they may survive the brutal ordeal – before cutting down their false ally when all other enemies are dead.

The stronghold of this devious Cult is known as the Nhexus Arena, and is far more deadly than its elegant architecture would suggest. Every curve and line contains sprung monofilament nets, venomous dart-launchers, toxin-loaded syringe-drills and a myriad of other lethal surprises. Nor is this cornucopia of misfortune confined to the arena floor, for these deadly booby traps are ever-shifting and as likely to spring up amid the audience as to lacerate or impale the performers. This is merely part of the fun, of course, adding a delicious frisson of very real danger that many Drukhari simply cannot resist.

Since the opening of the Great Rift, the Cult of the Cursed Blade have launched multiple large-scale raids in the Imperium Nihilus, both individually and alongside the Kabal of the Black Heart. Whilst they have ravenously preyed upon Imperial worlds lying isolated within this nightmarish realm, they have also defended such planets from slavering daemonic hordes and warbands of Chaos Space Marines, each time instilling a dim glimmer of hope in the beleaguered defenders before snuffing out thoughts of salvation with their own merciless cruelty.

Vyvax the Untrustable,
Circle of the Broken Promise

CULT OF THE RED GRIEF

THE STORM THAT BRINGS DEATH

Whether in the arena or on the battlefields of realspace, the Cult of the Red Grief use their aerial expertise to swiftly butcher their enemies. Their raiding craft attack with such speed that they are almost impossible to hit, and racks of living bodies hooked under their wings release contrails of blood to mask their manoeuvres.

All Wych Cults believe that the best defence is simply not to be there when the opponent's blade falls, but the Cult of the Red Grief takes this to extremes. Their raiding forces employ whole flotillas of Raiders that fly in close formation towards the foe, escorted by Reavers, Venoms and Hellions. When the aerial formations close with the enemy, the Wyches bound and spring from Raider to jetbike to skyboard and back again with athletic precision, dismounting and mounting so swiftly that the transports barely have to slow. Only the Wyches themselves ever deign to touch the ground, and even then only to deliver the killing blow to enemies who are still trying to adjust to the fact that they are under attack.

Even when they have become full-fledged members of the Cult, many within the Red Grief still actively participate in the gang wars that rage through the skies of Commorragh. For most Cults and Kabals, these unending skirmishes are merely a proving ground for new recruits, but the Red Grief view them as an almost meditative practice that they return to after completing a realspace raid. Like a hunter sharpening their weapons after each kill, the Wyches of the Red Grief continue to hone their skills by preying upon Commorragh's gangland underclass.

The Red Grief's main arena, the Pit, is an especially unforgiving structure built into the peak of a towering spire. Its galleries are made from transparent crystal, revealing that the audience are suspended only moments from a sickening plunge to their deaths. The arena proper truly has no floor – just a yawning gulf prowled by drifting anti-grav platforms. Hellion duels in the Pit are particularly spectacular, as their skyboards trail lines of monofilament wire that unspool in increasingly complex webs around the arena's struts and spars. Aerialists who lose track of their opponents' moves inevitably end up flying at breakneck speeds into the deadly lattice, whereupon the monofilaments slice through their boards, sever their legs from their torsos or decapitate them outright. Such bouts are typically brief, but the promise of seeing limbless, still-living combatants tumbling to their deaths far below draws huge crowds to the Pit night after night.

Jeda Lynx,
Circle of Torrential Anguish

A Space Marine of this type had never before graced the Pit. Though his appearance had been welcomed by only a smattering of applause from patrons trying to maintain a facade of disinterest, now all eyes were firmly fixed on him. Only one combatant could be first to slay the new breed of Space Marine, thought Khresilla – but it had to be done right, with appropriate flair for the occasion.

Khresilla jammed her heel on the thrust pedal and her skyboard screamed around the crystalline spar. Through the translucent facets of the fractal column she could see the Space Marine swing his spent gun at an oncoming Reaver. The Reaver yanked backwards on her controls, pulling up just in time to avoid the blow, but with a burst from his jump pack, the Imperial warrior flew violently upward into the Reaver's underside, shattering the jetbike and sending its rider plummeting to her doom.

This was the distraction Khresilla needed. She rounded the corner of the spar with her target in sight and her hellglaive ready. The Space Marine still had his back turned as she closed the final few yards, but suddenly Khresilla experienced a sharp pain across her midriff followed by total numbness. She felt herself drifting towards her prey, but looking down she saw neither her skyboard nor her legs – only droplets of blood trailing from where her lower half should be. She looked up just in time to see her hellglaive plunge into the back of the Space Marine's skull, and heard the muffled sound of cheering for the Hellion who laid the monofilament trap that had bisected her. It was an exquisite double-kill, and Khresilla's mind was filled with burning jealousy before all went dark.

CULT OF THE SEVENTH WOE
TEACHERS OF DESPAIR

A surge of pale flesh rushes across the battlefield as the Cult of the Seventh Woe close upon their enemies. As the flood of Wyches leap through the opposing battle line, they swipe and slash with practised deftness, leaving a carpet of mutilated bodies that writhe in agony and cry out for death.

Milak Mytar Vos,
the Thirteenth Circle of Misery

The Seventh Woe, in the ancient myths of the Aeldari, refers to the destruction of the maiden-god Lileath's hearth-moon at the hands of Kaela Mensha Khaine. The legend is synonymous with the end of innocence, a tenet that the Cult of the Seventh Woe embraces wholeheartedly by teaching those born into their ranks to wield a blade before they can talk. Each of its members has been learning to fight and kill since infancy, and although a great many of the Seventh Woe's warriors defect from the oppressive and controlling weapon-regime of their masters to join the Hellion gangs, those that remain are counted amongst the most deadly of all Wyches.

These Wyches enact the philosophy of their Cult on the battlefield through a fighting technique they call 'the Teaching of Despair'. Pistols are fired at bone joints, and blade-strikes aim to carve out ligaments and tendons. In this way their enemies are left alive but completely incapacitated, flailing helplessly and in agony as the realisation of their own dark fate crystallises in their minds. Once the entire enemy force has been thus mutilated, the Wyches leisurely stalk the battleground, savouring the screams of their opponents as they are pinned to the prows of Raiders. In the arenas, this fighting style is less showy than that of some other Cults – whose beheadings and disembowelments coat the crowds in showers of viscera – but discerning patrons appreciate the delectable suffering that is wrung from the rag-doll victims of the Seventh Woe Wyches.

CULT OF THE BLADE DENIED
FATE'S EMPTY HAND

Even amongst the myriad horrors that grace the Dark City's arenas, there are few sights more unnerving than seeing the unarmed Wyches of the Cult of the Blade Denied pounce upon the enemy, pry the weapons from their opponents' hands and viciously turn those tools of death upon their former wielders.

Norcellen Agrenyar,
Circle of the Bared Throat

The Blade Denied is an elder Wych House that specialises in the art of using their foes' weapons against them, the irony of a warrior impaled upon their own blade a sight particularly favoured by this Cult. A perennial display in the Blade Denied's Helix arena is an unarmed Wych, seemingly at the mercy of a heavily armed opponent and sometimes even tightly bound or blindfolded beforehand, slipping the noose and gradually turning the tables by systematically disarming and then stealing the weapons of her opponent before the showy – and invariably messy – finale.

The tendency for using the enemy's strength against them is magnified whenever the Cult of the Blade Denied mounts a realspace raid. The Cult deliberately puts itself at a disadvantage against its enemies, taking on superior numbers in heavily armed emplacements with little more than well-sharpened knives, haywire grenades, and the Raiders and Venoms that bear them planetside. When the killing begins, however, the Wyches will improvise, turning the technologies of their foes against them, crippling the largest of enemies with judiciously targeted haywire attacks, and digging out the fleshy bounty inside with the care of an epicure savouring every nuance of his carefully prepared meal. In fact, stories of planetary defenders falling on their blades and killing their compatriots out of fear when a Drukhari raid appears are often just accounts of the Blade Denied practising their grim art.

CULT OF THE WRATH UNBOUND
MASTERS OF THE KILLING TRANCE

When the Wyches of the Wrath Unbound go to war, they do so in a state of consciousness altered beyond what combat drugs can achieve. They are practitioners of the killing trance, and through gruesome meditations they set their minds to the sole task of butchery.

The killing trance – known in the Aeldari tongue as *Khaélas Maenaid* – is seen as a double-edged sword by the Asuryani, a near-berserk state where allies are killed as often as enemies and the tang of blood in the air is the only thing that matters. The Cult of the Wrath Unbound seek to harness this half-crazed state of mind to better become one with the kill. Led by the Succubus Hythnamene Veilblood, the Wyches and Beastmasters of this Cult practise long and gory rituals before each performance or battle, gradually letting their intellect slip away and their hungry instincts take over. Slowly but surely they become creatures of pure bloodlust; their eyes roll back in their heads, and ancient litanies to Khaela Mensha Khaine – the Aeldari god of war – spill out of their painted lips. A Wych in the grip of the Khaélas Maenaid will not just kill her victims but reduce them to bloody scraps of meat, laughing hideously all the while.

Whilst the killing trance is upon them, the warriors of the Wrath Unbound are every bit as savage as the packs of Khymerae and Clawed Fiends that run with them on the hunt. When in the full grip of Khaélas Maenaid, the Wyches of the Cult enter a state of absolute euphoria, and are seemingly unaffected by injury or fatigue. As such, their raids gather more and more momentum as the slaughter increases and the Wyches slip further into their trance. An intended assault upon a single city can easily become an orgy of violence that consumes a continent or even an entire world.

Beestria La'kreen,
Circle of the Ever-Fury

CULT OF THE PAIN ETERNAL
HEKATII'S ICONOCLASTS

In the name of the Dark Muse whom they serve, the Cult of the Pain Eternal commits atrocities throughout great swathes of realspace, defiling the shrines and holy sites the lesser races use to pray to their gods. In this way, the Cult spreads despair far beyond where its raiding fleets reave.

The Pain Eternal are exceptional in that they do not make regular appearances within the arenas of High Commorragh. Instead, they are a spacefaring Cult that dock only once every few years in the Dark City. Unstinting in the service of the Dark Muse Hekatii, Mother of Strife, the Pain Eternal exists to tear down and destroy everything that is holy to the lesser races of the galaxy. Acts of anarchy and despoilment are held as a kind of inverse worship for the Pain Eternal, for they believe in a higher reward than the adulation of the crowd.

The stagnant serenity of worship is a powerful goad to the Pain Eternal. Shrine worlds in particular are preferred targets; the Adepta Sororitas is well aware of the Cult's agenda, and has brought it to battle in countless war zones. Despite the best efforts of the Sisters of Battle, many a religious stronghold has found massed strike forces of Wyches descending without warning, hell-bent on replacing the surety of faith with terror and doubt. The sistrens of Hekatrices that lead the Pain Eternal love nothing more than to snuff out the flame of hope wherever it can be found, taking pains to defile and destroy the saints and venerated nobility of those they see as beneath them. Their detractors often say that the Pain Eternal wreak their own brand of havoc for no greater reason than to prove that nothing is sacred, but the Succubi who lead them to battle profess a far greater aim – where the Wyches of the arenas fight to bleed away the lifeblood of mortals, the Cult of the Pain Eternal wishes to bleed away the lifeblood of gods.

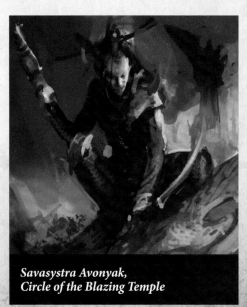

Savasystra Avonyak,
Circle of the Blazing Temple

COVENS OF THE HAEMONCULI

Beneath the Dark City lurk the Covens of the Haemonculi, twisted brotherhoods of ancient torturer-alchemists who are crucial to the continued survival of the Drukhari race. Their unnatural sciences give them power over life and death, yet those who deal with the Haemonculi should be wary, as there is always a price to pay…

The Haemonculi deal in body modification, drug distillation and beauty elixirs. However, the true source of their power lies elsewhere. Every member of Commorrite society must eventually ask for their help, for the Haemonculi are masters of the flesh, be it alive or dead. Those of a like mind gather together into Covens, and each Coven occupies a vast demesne of cells and laboratories under the core. Here these diabolical figures slice and meld the flesh of those that fall into their clutches, savouring their pain as a gourmet would savour a fine meal.

The dungeon-strongholds of the Haemonculi take many forms, each echoing the madness in the minds of their creators. Labyrinths of fractured mirrors, spiral-edged pits with narrow, twisting walkways, towers of living flesh illuminated by millions of glimmering eyes – all of these unspeakable sights and more await the unwary traveller in the darkness beneath the core. The eldest and most vile Haemonculi dwell at the heart of each nightmarish lair, revelling in epic depravities of their own invention. To cross these monstrous beings is considered beyond foolish. Not only is their vengeance terrible to behold, but the Haemonculi have the power to bestow – or withhold – life after death.

THE ETERNAL CYCLE

The Aeldari gestation cycle is much longer than that of many of the lesser races, and conventionally born children are rare symbols of status. Artificially grown Drukhari are far more commonplace. Once fertilised, an egg can be implanted into one of the amniotic tubes that honeycomb the breeding-walls of the Haemonculi's lairs. Using a repulsive, insectile science developed many millennia ago, an embryo's growth can be hyperaccelerated within these tubes, each newly grown specimen wriggling from its chrysalis-sac in a drizzle of fluids before being taken away by Wrack attendants. These 'half-born' are seen with contempt by Trueborn Drukhari, who believe them inherently inferior. Yet the real triumph of the Haemonculi's science is not the ability to create new life, but to

deny death. It is this that affords them such power within Commorrite society.

Most Drukhari warriors, including each Kabal's ruling elite, will at some point enter into a terrible pact with the Haemonculi. This devil's bargain states that the Haemonculi will regenerate the warrior's body after death, and in exchange, the seeker will leave the Haemonculi a permanent portion of their soul. Even a corpse that has been all but destroyed in the crucible of war can be restored to its former glory; the Master Haemonculus Urien Rakarth once crafted a perfect new Archon Vrirech from a single withered hand. Provided this process is enacted within a day or so of the warrior's demise, and his will is strong enough that some of his spirit still resonates within his remains, his animus will slowly regenerate along with his physical form. Hence Kabals on realspace raids take great pains to strike hard and fast, returning before the night is out with the remains of their deceased in order that their strongest warriors – barring the occasional individual who encounters an unfortunate accident – can return to life.

The key to this terrible process is, of course, pain. The Drukhari are rejuvenated by witnessing agony, and if saturated with enough of it, they can heal from almost any wound. As such the mortal remains of those delivered to the dubious care of the Haemonculi are installed into crystal-fronted pods arrayed above the pain racks and torture tables.

These sarcophagi are arrayed in concentric circles that rise up into the darkness, each holding a semi-cocooned Drukhari warrior in a regenerative state. The patients literally drink in the dark energy of the torturer's craft as the Haemonculus works upon his victim below, ably assisted by his Wrack servants and the semi-sentient Engines of Pain. As a cacophony of shrieks rises around the chamber, those installed in the cocoons slowly feast upon the energies, ever so gradually growing back their bodies – skeleton first, then muscle, sinew and skin, until they are whole once more. During times of war, it is common for

every one of an oubliette's regeneration pods to be filled with red-raw fiends that shiver and rattle with every fresh scream.

THE NIGHTMARE DESCENDS

To the Haemonculi, each foray into realspace is not so much an act of war as an exhibition of their talents. Members of a Coven will compete to create the most pleasingly abhorrent monstrosities in the lead-up to a raid, releasing them upon the foe and watching the results with interest. The Haemonculi consider such competition inspiring, and will offer a heartfelt compliment should their rivals' creations achieve some especially impressive act of violence.

Realspace raids by Haemonculus Covens are comparatively unhurried affairs, their leaders having lived for thousands of years and seeing no call for unseemly rushing around. Instead they will strike from unexpected quarters, preferring if possible to use offshoot webway portals that open deep within abandoned mines, shadowed forests or other sites local lifeforms consider to be cursed. The Coven will emerge like horrors from primitive folklore, glorying in the unreasoning terror that spreads before their advance. Engines of Pain drift between iron-masked Wracks and Grotesques as they hack and carve the enemy's soldiery to ruin. With the defenders slain, the Coven gather up the choicest victims then disappear back into the shadowed realm from whence they came.

How an individual becomes a Haemonculus is uncertain. They are all of incredibly advanced age, and their withered and nightmarish appearance speaks of one who has passed well beyond the ability to recapture a youthful physique. Monstrous self-mutilation leaves many Haemonculi unable or unwilling to engage in physically demanding tasks. Indeed, most Haemonculi eschew mundane physical exertion, and instead perform their grand tasks through their supplicants and minions, namely Wracks, Grotesques and various Engines of Pain.

Over their long and abhorrent lives, the Haemonculi have encountered, captured and painstakingly studied almost every race in the galaxy, and in doing so have created tools of death and torture that can afflict any physiology. Whenever a new species presents itself, the Covens are quick to set out and procure specimens.

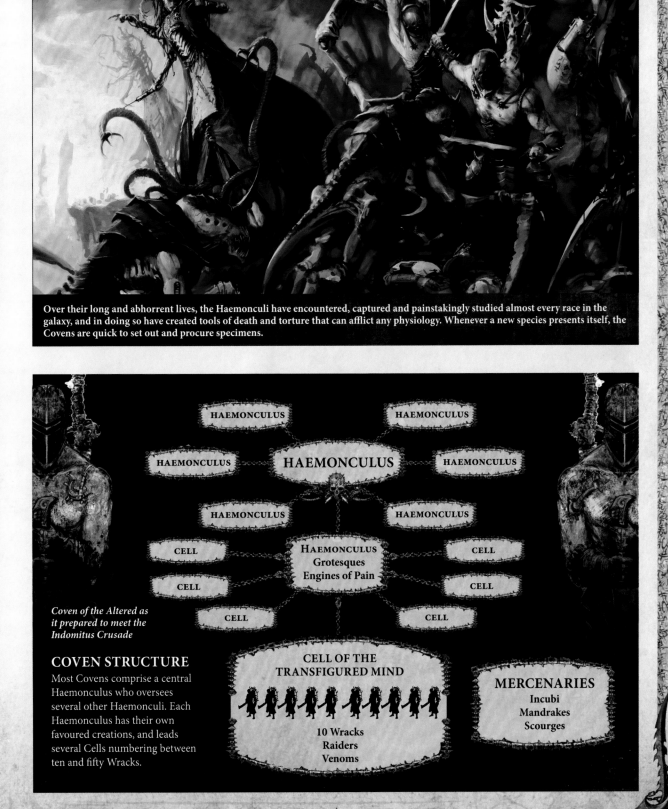

Coven of the Altered as it prepared to meet the Indomitus Crusade

COVEN STRUCTURE

Most Covens comprise a central Haemonculus who oversees several other Haemonculi. Each Haemonculus has their own favoured creations, and leads several Cells numbering between ten and fifty Wracks.

HAEMONCULUS

HAEMONCULUS

HAEMONCULUS

HAEMONCULUS

HAEMONCULUS

HAEMONCULUS

HAEMONCULUS

HAEMONCULUS
Grotesques
Engines of Pain

CELL

CELL

CELL

CELL

CELL

CELL

CELL OF THE TRANSFIGURED MIND

10 Wracks
Raiders
Venoms

MERCENARIES
Incubi
Mandrakes
Scourges

THE PROPHETS OF FLESH
EXEMPLARS OF EXCRUCIATION

The influence of the Prophets of Flesh is felt throughout the Dark City, for they are like a massive cyst buried deep within Commorragh's tissue, swollen with power and impossible to excise. They are a Coven possessed of innumerable mutilated thralls and led by the most infamous of the Haemonculi.

The Prophets of Flesh are the Coven of Urien Rakarth himself. They are considered by many Commorrites to be the apex – or rather the nadir – of the inverted hierarchy of the underspires, and as such they receive more supplicants than any other Coven. To be a Prophet of Flesh is to be respectfully feared amongst the Drukhari, and to cast terror into the hearts of enemies and allies alike. So many aspirants seek a place in the Coven's ranks that each of the Prophets presides over thousands of Wracks. This allows the Coven's Haemonculi to operate dozens of laboratories and abattoir-like surgeries at once, keeping watch as their servants perform the manual tasks of dissecting and reconfiguring the musculature and nervous tissue of their subjects. Furthermore, when they desire fresh specimens from the lesser races over which they can worry, the packed cells of Wracks are sent en masse into realspace in terrifying raids.

Upon induction into the Coven, each Wrack's limbs are extensively branded, tattooed or altered according to their new master's whim. Should they impress their superiors with especially inventive acts of sadism, the Wrack will have one of their marked appendages cut off and replaced with a bare limb taken from the

Prophets' flesh libraries. By the time the favoured few make it to the lesser ranks of the Haemonculi they are entirely free of blemish, having had much of their original bodies replaced with unmarred grafts. Though they become convinced of their own purity, the opposite is true, for in climbing the heights of status, the aspirants invariably stain their souls with depravities that are unimaginable even by the base standards of the Dark City.

Many of the Prophets of Flesh dabble in soothsaying, despite the prohibition of psychic activity that pervades Commorragh. They seek to learn the truths of the universe not through the shaman's technique of reading entrails, but by interpreting the effects of the cruelties they wreak. In this regard they are quite surgical in their approach, divining through careful study how the trauma of one conflict will

form a scar throughout an entire war zone. This is one of the practices that makes the Prophets so sought after by Archons, Succubi and even Haemonculi from other Covens, for their visions extend far into the future and can provide glimpses of atrocities that have yet to be achieved.

Like all Haemonculi, the Prophets of Flesh engage in multiple sadistic arts during their extended lifespans, practicing new forms of cruelty to help stave off the ennui that comes with functional immortality. As they flirt with various methods of torture, fleshcrafting and deathletting, a Haemonculus may find themselves drawn to a particular discipline over all others. These disciplines take many shapes in the undercity, and devotees of each can be found throughout the Covens – those known as Nemesines seek the best ways to kill every creature in the galaxy, whereas Repugnomancers delight in creating artefacts of abject revulsion. Many Prophets of Flesh are Black Cornucopians – expert plunderers and architects of large-scale raids. They model their behaviour on the Sculptor of Torments, Urien Rakarth, and through constant abductions have stocked their oubliettes with enough victims to see them through centuries of isolation.

THE PROPHETS AND THE PRIMARIS

The Prophets of Flesh are undisputed masters of fleshcrafting in the Dark City, the sheer number of their mutilated servants bearing out this fact. Yet this supremacy does not carry with it complacency. The Prophets actively seek out new and alternative methods of shaping their subjects' biology, and will even look to the practises of the lesser races for morbid inspiration. It was from the shamanistic species known as the Mehn-Shi that the Haemonculus Letikuss Ohm adapted the method of rewiring nervous tissue so that dreams – and in particular, nightmares – will have physical effects on living tissue. In this vein, the Prophets have always kept a close eye on the genetic dabbling conducted within the Imperium of Man.

When Roboute Guilliman – Primarch of the Ultramarines – awoke from his eight-thousand-year stasis, the Prophets of Flesh turned their soothsayers' vision upon him. As he launched his Indomitus Crusade to stem the tide of Chaos

surging across the galaxy, they saw the new breed of Adeptus Astartes he brought to battle. The Primaris Space Marines were the product of genetic manipulations that – whilst rudimentary by the standards of the Dark City – were undoubtedly effective in creating resilient warriors. Even Urien Rakarth's curiosity was piqued by the appearance of these augmented Space Marines.

The Prophets of Flesh have since waged an ongoing campaign against the Indomitus Crusade, launching harrying raids against flanks and reinforcing detachments where they are most exposed. While all captured Imperial forces are welcomed into the Prophets' oubliettes, it is the Primaris Space Marines whose lives are most highly valued. Urien Rakarth himself seeks Primaris subjects from every Space Marine Chapter, for each carries a variant of the Adeptus Astartes gene-seed; the Master Haemonculus knows they would provide interesting and unique samples to add to his extensive flesh-libraries.

THE FEAST OF PECH

After capturing not only countless T'au upon Vigos but also the mercenaries with which they bolster their cadres, the Prophets of Flesh discovered that the Kroot are able to adapt and evolve by selectively devouring the dead. The Haemonculi of the Coven immediately began experimenting on the captives in the hopes of appropriating this ability. Before long the Prophets of Flesh required more specimens for their gruesome studies, and so opened up a webway gate upon Pech, the humid jungle home world of the Kroot.

The raid was as protracted as it was brutal, the Haemonculi scouring the tribal centres of their quarry one by one before loading the mangled survivors onto the barbed railings of their Raiders. Although the Kroot put up stiff resistance, the Prophets were able to fill their transports with living flesh while their Venoms and Ravagers laid waste to the jungle from above the canopy. Most importantly for the Coven, their Engines of Pain were able to seize more than a dozen Kroot Shapers, the genetic trailblazers of the carnivorous race.

Before the invasion could consume the entire planet, T'au Hunter Cadres arrived to aid their allies. As the counter-attack was launched, the Prophets of Flesh abruptly withdrew, taking their Kroot bounty with them back to Commorragh. In their wake they left a grim message, spelt out in corpses and translated by the T'au Water caste as 'welcome to the feast'. Since that day, the T'au have encountered many similar messages within their empire on worlds that have been butchered by the Prophets of Flesh.

THEFT OF LETHIDIA

Following their successful experimentations on the Kroot, the Prophets of Flesh turned their attention to the hyper-adaptive capabilities of the Tyranids. Urien Rakarth mustered a number of Covens under his banner, and together they set out for the southern edge of the galaxy. There they descended upon the maiden world of Lethidia, which was infested with Tyranids from Hive Fleet Leviathan. In a desperate attempt to save the Exodite defenders, Asuryani from Saim-Hann had already engaged the xenos swarms – but the designs of the Haemonculi were far less altruistic. After activating warp breachers placed at geomantic sites on Lethidia's surface, Rakarth drew the planet, along with all of its defenders and invaders, out of realspace and into the interstitial space surrounding Commorragh. Having established the world's new orbit, the Prophets of Flesh were free to harvest its inhabitants at their leisure.

Absydius Vyle,
Cell of the Mind Exposed

THE DARK CREED
ARCHITECTS OF TERROR

Though the work of all Haemonculi is the stuff of nightmares, the Dark Creed use fear itself as a deadly weapon. For these Covenites, breaking an enemy's spirits is but the opening salvo, and their terror-based attacks continue until the foe is tearing itself apart from fright.

Monmort Vargehl, Cell of Sanity's Twilight

Specialising in the arts of fear, the Haemonculi of the Dark Creed have a deep reverence for the indirect kill. They love nothing more than seeing their victims debase themselves in horror, and will drive their captives to madness or suicide purely to show they are above such primitive notions as physical intervention. Having long grown bored of traditional murder techniques, the Dark Creed believe it is the height of sophistication to end a victim's life without making a direct attack. An abstract death, perhaps caused purely through heart-stopping emotion, is considered the finest victory.

Aside from the clear aesthetic beauty of murder through terror alone, killing in such a fashion also has the practical benefit of being difficult to trace. As such, the Coven of the Dark Creed are often entreated by Archons wishing to assassinate one of their fellows without inciting a full-blown war between Kabals. Doing so is no easy task, for the Drukhari – and particularly the ruling elite – have become inured over their long sadistic lives to the horrors of pain and psychological torment. But the Dark Creed view this obstacle simply as an opportunity to improve upon their craft. A Haemonculus may toil for months, years or even decades to produce a unique form of terror tailored to the specific psychology of their target. Alongside this, they develop a vector that can surpass even the most mistrustful Archon's defence systems. This may be an odourless, tasteless gas possessed of enough sentience to wend its way directly to the intended victim, or possibly a sub-dimensional parasite that worms undetected into the host's brain to lay its psychosis-inducing eggs. Once infested with the terror weapon, the target is afflicted with waking nightmares so intense that they will claw out their own eyes, rip off their ears or even drive spikes through their brain to silence the horrors they perceive. Truly dedicated Haemonculi craft their inducers to also afflict those parts of the target stored for regeneration, so that upon each rebirth the victim is still stricken with terror and driven to endless and futile suicide.

This preference for esoteric kills extends to the Coven's Wracks as well. Each cell boasts at least one liquifier gun, ossefactor or hexrifle with which to slay their targets from a distance, where the death throes can be enjoyed by all. When not aiding in the creation of their masters' concoctions or gathering living specimens in realspace, the Wracks take up positions in the apertures that honeycomb the inner walls of the Dark Creed's abyssal lair – the Chasm of Echoes. This spire descends lower than any other protrusion of the undercity, delving far into the darkness of the unknown sub-dimensions beneath Commorragh, and is filled with the screams of tortured prisoners and those who will one day be incarcerated in its chambers. As supplicants to the Coven's Haemonculi descend into the yawning blackness, many are driven to insanity and hurl themselves to their death, at which point the Wracks make sport of shooting the plummeting bodies.

'A blade to the chest? How pedestrian. We left behind such base concepts long ago, dear heart. Let me introduce you to a far more interesting demise…'

- Haemogarch Vanthis, Necromaester of the Dark Creed

It is because of their preference for unusual deaths that the Coven has a great many Cronos Parasite Engines in its number. Strung with blooded chains and grisly trophies, these constructs generate so much negative energy that they can kill without striking a single physical blow. Likewise, the Dark Creed's forces are regularly joined in battle by the night-clad denizens of Aelindrach, for that realm too thrives on the fear of the enemy. During their realspace raids, the Coven is often accompanied by packs of Mandrakes that hurl soul-blistering balefire to terrorise their victims before the Haemonculi close in for an elaborate kill.

THE COVEN OF TWELVE

BUTCHERS WITHOUT EQUAL

The Coven of Twelve are masters of close-quarters combat. They must be, for the only way to ascend the ranks of the Coven is for a Wrack to slaughter their master, and each Haemonculus is always on guard against the gruesome scheme that would see their body ravaged beyond repair.

The Coven of Twelve is a conclave of several Haemonculi, each of whom considers himself the foremost practitioner of the dark arts. Membership of the Coven is restricted to just eleven individuals at any time – the twelfth spot is left open for Urien Rakarth, should he ever deign to accept the Coven's invitation. Since Haemonculi have a habit of overcoming death, the only way that a new aspirant can ascend to join the Twelve is to dispose of a current incumbent in a manner so thorough that even a master Haemonculus cannot undo it. Shegmeth Kro was pushed into a mirror dimension the size of a coffin too small for his frame. Khaebrys Xulfur was posed an impossible riddle that, with each wrong answer, turned more of his body into bone until finally he was nothing more than an osseous statue. Zakrodevia was rendered into a sentient soup using acids from captured Tyranids and then imbibed by his peers at a banquet.

Perhaps the most grandiose coup in the history of the Coven of the Twelve was that conceived by Mydilian, an Acothyst who felt slighted after enduring an imperfect regrowth. Mydilian gifted his Haemonculi masters a flock of Aelindrachi Shaderavens – nightmarish fowl that are rumoured to feast on sanity. The avian terrors were well received by the Haemonculi, for not only would it have been seen as an act of cowardice to refuse the gift, but the recipients were more than willing to risk their minds to experience a new and unique sensation. As it was, the inherent depravity of the Coven of Twelve meant that few noticed the Haemonculi masters becoming ever more eccentric.

A year to the day after Mydilian's gift, four of the senior Haemonculi departed the Coven's lair, known as the Pendulum, without warning. They took with them hundreds of Wracks and Grotesques and headed directly into a shattered spar of the webway. Though normally patient when enacting their torturous plans, the Haemonculi surged carelessly through a forbidden gate onto a long-lost crone world, headless of the horrors that may have poured inward towards the Dark City.

In their maddened minds, the Haemonculi thought only of the daemonic specimens they could acquire for use in their experiments.

Upon the crone world, the Covenites found a plain of burning bones packed with Khornate Daemons in far greater numbers than they had anticipated. The Blood God's servants descended upon the Haemonculi and their servants, and in savage battle tore every last one of them apart. This began a never-ending cycle of slaughter as Khorne claimed the souls of the Haemonculi for his playthings, holding them on the blood-soaked world to be butchered again and again in gory yet mundane ways. At that time, back in the Pendulum, Mydilian and three of his fellow Acothysts enjoyed a sudden promotion.

A warped arms race consumes the Coven of Twelve. Their quest to stay one step ahead of each other ensures these Haemonculi bear the deadliest devices their arcane science can yield. These tools of atrocity feature strongly in the arsenals of the Coven during their realspace raids – flesh gauntlets, electrocorrosive whips, null batons, mindphase gauntlets and even stranger weapons abound. As they look for weakness amongst their own ranks, so too do they seek out the slightest opening in the defences of those they would butcher. The same mindset breeds a ruthlessness in the Haemonculi, who are swift to administer punishment to their servants, for they are well aware their Wracks could turn upon them without warning.

Many of the Coven's members are Scarlet Epicureans, their tastes for inventive fatalities so all-consuming they seek to experience them in person. Wracks and Grotesques in service of the Twelve are usually flayed, their muscles left raw and their nerves exposed so they can better appreciate the full spectrum of sensation.

Raizhar of Vayn,
Cell of the Sutured Mouth

THE BLACK DESCENT
SOWERS OF TORMENT

With the patience of a venomous spider, the Haemonculi of the Black Descent lie in wait while their enemies stumble into the web of traps prepared before battle. Only when the foes are ensnared and screaming in agony do the Covenites stalk forward to gather their harvest.

Evinkahr the Ghast,
Cell of the Nightmare Abyss

The Haemonculi of the Black Descent revel in the laying of traps and their lethal denouement. Their plots and snares range from the feigned flights and baited ambushes of their realspace raids, to thousand-year intrigues that see their rivals fully humbled. To cross the Black Descent is to invite a punishment darkly twisted to fit the crime. One who uses brute force against them may later find himself stung by an insect-sized Wrack, the hyperdrenaline introduced into his bloodstream forcing him into a frenzy so severe he literally tears himself apart. One who delays payment for the Black Descent's poisons may awake one morning trapped in a Sslyth venom-nest. Even unintended offense can yield retribution – when an ambassador from the Kabal of the Baleful Gaze wrinkled his nose at the stench of the Coven's dungeons, he soon found himself coughing on transmutative gas. Later that night he sprouted the quivering nostrils of an Ur-Ghul, his eyes sealing over so he could better appreciate the fine bouquet of rot.

When they deign to enter realspace, the Haemonculi of the Black Descent put their skill at snaring enemies to gruesome use. Even compared to other Covens, their raids are meticulously planned, with some of their more merciless excursions taking decades to come to fruition. Rather than assaulting their victims head-on, the Black Descent typically lure them to some predetermined battle site laden with sadistic traps, then watch as their opponents are killed in increasingly inventive ways. Oftentimes the Haemonculi will lace the flora of a planet with time-delayed mutagens, tangled weeds to explode in showers of thorns when the foe arrives. Other favourite traps include storms of neuro-electric lightning that fry the enemies' brains internally, or ruins of past battlefields seeded with biological scabbing agents so that unwary combatants are grafted bodily into the rubble. Archons who wish to prepare the sites of their raids with such traps will often make pacts with the Black Descent, but in doing so they must take care not to inadvertently offend the Coven's overly decorous Haemonculi.

In recent centuries, a particular mode of slaughter has become highly fashionable amongst the masters of the Black Descent. Through numerous experiments on Genestealers and the Hybrids that are spawned on the worlds of lesser races, the Haemonculi have started to weaponise the mutated flesh of these creatures. The biological matter is harvested and distilled into toxic cocktails along with a panoply of growth accelerants, often causing it to rapidly take hold of a host. Once prepared, the bio-weapon is vaporised in a planet's atmosphere or implanted into its water and food stores. The raid is then launched to coincide with the apex of mutation. Defenders are gripped by an insatiable hunger, sprouting fangs and claws which they use to savage their allies before eventually cannibalising themselves.

A large contingent of the Black Descent are aligned with the Apparitians – Haemonculi who delight in capturing the vain and exposing them painfully to their inherent flaws. Some Apparitians practise their twisted cruelty in mirrored cells, inside of which their victims' eyelids are shorn off so that they are forced to see their own mutilation. But the Apparitians of the Black Descent prefer to steer the gaze of their subjects inward to the grim recesses of their own minds. The Coven's lair is a pyramidal labyrinth of glass that hangs inverted beneath the Dark City, and promising captives are thrown into the maze's sensory deprivation chambers whilst the Covenites leer outside. The only way out is to negotiate the labyrinth's trap-strewn confines through touch and instinct, all the while inhaling psychotropic gases that heighten every sense of fear and self-loathing. The vast majority of those that undertake this journey are killed, caught in paradox cubes or falling eternally into Moebius pits as they try to avoid the labyrinth's bladed convolutions. Many simply succumb to the internal torment of their own mind and hurl themselves into the eviscerating devices laid out by the Haemonculi. But those that manage to pass through safely are rewarded with a new life as a Wrack, becoming a part of the Coven forever more.

THE HEX
SCULPTORS OF REALITY

When the Covenites of the Hex go to battle, they do so surrounded by nightmares of their own creation. The Haemonculi of this Coven take pride in creating ever more devastating minions and weapons, each more esoterically cruel than the last.

The Haemonculi of the Hex consider themselves to be the pre-eminent artists of flesh, with the entirety of realspace as their canvas. To construct truly impressive works they employ large cells of Wracks and Grotesques, mind-bound in much the same manner as hive organisms so they can be better suited to enact their master's artistic vision.

Ever since their creation in the dark days that followed the Fall, the Coven has specialised in the fabrication of curses. Most of these are the product of baleful technologies, the effects of which have been refined to the point where – in the eyes of the primitive races – they are indistinguishable from magic. However, some of the Coven's favourite curses truly border on the supernatural, and they have slaughtered whole species to obtain the ingredients needed to craft such technomantic maladies.

In 926.M36, the Covenites of the Hex harnessed the Plague of Glass that had been released by the sculptor-fraud Jalaxlar. Their studies of the plague's deadly potency led to the invention of the rifle that bears their name. To this day, hexrifles are the preferred weapon of many would-be assassins, their payloads turning those hit into transparent statues.

It was the Haemonculi of the Hex that learnt of the aberrant Cursed Founding of the Adeptus Astartes. The Covenites were taken by one Chapter in particular – the Black Dragons – whose corrupted gene-seed forced sharp protrusions of bone to grow from its warriors' skeletons. The Hex attacked the Chapter in the Donorian System, capturing a dozen of the most mutated Black Dragons and bearing them back to Commorragh, where – over the course of an agonising three-year period – the Adeptus Astartes were experimented upon endlessly. The Covenites eventually isolated the osseovirus affecting the gene-seed of the Black Dragons. They then refined the macro-steroidal effects of the bone mutagen to create the ossefactor – a weapon favoured by the Acothysts of their employ.

The Coven of the Hex were even responsible for creating the fabled Orbs of Despair – heavy black spheres so saturated with raw negativity that they can reduce a grown man to a gibbering wreck in a heartbeat. Though the technology behind these orbs is closely guarded by the Hex's Covenites, it is believed to function through a similar process to that of a black hole. Where a black hole draws matter into itself, growing larger and hungrier the more it absorbs, so too do the Orbs of Despair feed off the sorrow they inflict to become ever more potent.

The glee with which the Hex unleash their carefully cultivated curses upon an unsuspecting universe is palpable in its intensity, and the Haemonculi's thin lips curl back over their sharpened teeth as they drink in each fresh nightmare. However, the unbridled use of curses leaves its mark on the wielder as well as the victim. Those that deal with the Coven's most arcane weapons are often pale to the point of albinism, covered with inkblot discolouration, or possessed of a slight greenish pallor. Regardless of form, the servants of the Hex are always unsettling, their leers somehow obvious even behind their masks.

Many of the Haemonculi of the Hex are adherents of the Nadirist discipline. They seek to attain godhood by bleeding darkness into the fabric of reality, believing they themselves will transcend the mortal plane once it has been corrupted beyond recognition. It is this school of thought that drives their curse-craft, for with every horror they bring into existence they draw closer to the nadir of experience – beyond which lies true immortality.

'Each tormented soul experiences unique nightmares. It is our duty to share these nightmares with others.'
— Xethretic the White,
Haemonculus of the Hex

**Morpex Kras'vand,
the Cursed Cell of Norvahk**

REALSPACE RAIDS

The Kabals, Wych Cults and Haemonculus Covens of Commorragh are wholly separate entities whose goals are often in direct opposition to one another. Yet they set aside their thinly veiled animosities when raiding the worlds of realspace, working in unison to reap the suffering of their shared victims.

KABAL OF THE BLACK HEART
Splinter of the Open Wound

Alovok Grette, a lesser Archon of the Kabal of the Black Heart, leads this raiding party. Through centuries of navigating the deadly intrigues of Commorragh he has garnered enough influence to draw support – however ephemeral – from the Cult of the Cursed Blade and the Coven of the Dark Creed.

Archon
Court of the Archon

30 Kabalite Warriors

3 Raiders
2 Ravagers
2 Venoms

WYCH CULT OF THE CURSED BLADE
Circle of the Throat Exposed

The Succubus Lethrael the Pale and her Wyches in the Circle of the Throat Exposed join Grette's raiding force, providing the Archon with high-speed shock troops as well as a significant aerial presence. They also bring their own transport craft, which they will decorate with the flayed bodies of their victims.

Succubus

30 Wyches

10 Hellions
6 Reavers
1 Raider
3 Venoms
2 Razorwing Jetfighters

ALLIANCE OF AGONY

Every step of a raid is planned in meticulous detail. In most cases such a raid is championed by an Archon, though on occasion a Succubus or Haemonculus will be its chief architect. Regardless of who leads, a raid brings together the most deadly factions of Commorrite society – the splinters of a Kabal, the circles of a Wych Cult and the cells of a Haemonculus Coven – to fight as a single terrifying force, whilst affording each the opportunity to pursue their own twisted proclivities on the battlefield.

HAEMONCULUS COVEN OF THE DARK CREED
Cell of the Ever-dreaded

Representing the Coven of the Dark Creed is the Haemonculus Sectilius Vyle. His flesh-sculpted servants in the Cell of the Ever-dreaded will sow terror amidst the enemy army whilst his Engines of Pain harvest the choicest victims and provide the Drukhari with invigorating agonies throughout the raid.

Haemonculus

20 Wracks

1 Talos Pain Engine
1 Cronos Parasite Engine
3 Grotesques
3 Raiders

MERCENARIES

Each of the forces comprising the raiding party are bolstered by mercenaries from the Dark City. Ever wary of those with whom he is conspiring, Grette has brought a personal bodyguard of Incubi as well as a flock of Scourges, whereas Lethrael and Vyle have each formed pacts with the shadow creatures of Aelindrach.

5 Incubi (in covenant with the Kabal of the Black Heart)

10 Scourges (contracted to the Kabal of the Black Heart)

5 Mandrakes (entreated by the Cult of the Cursed Blade)

10 Mandrakes (entreated by the Coven of the Dark Creed)

PATHS OF TERROR

Ordo Xenos map AV 996/4CM – map compiled by Inquisitor Balek Narn comprising confirmed Drukhari sightings

SEGMENTUM OBSCURUS

HALO STARS

SCARUS SECTOR

CALIXIS SECTOR

FINIAL SECTOR

GOTHIC SECTOR

NAOGEDDON

DIMMAMAR

STORM OF THE EMPEROR'S WRATH

VALHALLA

THE EYE OF TERROR

MORDIAN

2

1

CADIA

BELIS CORONA

PISCINA

ALARIC

BAAL

NACHMUND GAUNTLET

AGRIPINAA

NECRON MEPHRIT DYNASTY

FENRIS

MOLOV

HYDRAPHUR

ARMAGEDDON

ELYSIA

THE ROCK

CICATRIX MALEDICTUM

SEGMENTUM SOLAR

LASTRATI

PROSPERO & PLANET OF THE SORCERERS

GOLGOTHA

SEGMENTUM PACIFICUS

VORDRAST

TERRA & MARS

RYZA

CATACHAN

THE MAELSTROM

GATHALAMOR

NECROMUNDA

BADAB

ULTIMA MACHARIA

MACHARIA

KRIEG

LUTHER MCINTYRE

TALLARN

6

CHIROS

OPHELIA

NOCTURNE

BALOR

UHULIS SECTOR

V'RUN

SIREN'S STORM

SEGMENTUM TEMPESTUS

ALEUSIS

BANE'S LANDING

SOLSTICE

RYNN'S WORLD

NEPHILIM SECTOR

5

REDUCTUS SECTOR

AGRAX

GRYPHONNE IV

BAKKA

ANTAGONIS

SAN LEOR

ILLUSTRIS

The Map (Ultima Segmentum)

SISTEC PRIME

NEW DREKPORT

MALFACTUS

LUNAPHAGE

3

MACIA III

ANGELIS

COELIA

DESPERATION

GHOUL STARS

ASTRO TELEPATHIC DUCT

NEXUS III
ASTRO STATION

ASYLUS

SOMNIUM STARS

SABLE

ULTIMA
SEGMENTUM

HEXOS

FORMUND

4

KAR DUNIASH

CORINTHE

ATTILA

THE EASTERN FRINGE

CIRILLO PRIME

TEMPORARY
RIFT CORRIDOR

THE YMGA MONOLITH

VENGEANCE

SCHINDELGHEIST

T'AU
EMPIRE

NECRON
SAUTEKH DYNASTY

HADEX ANOMALY

ICHAR IV

THE SCOURGE STARS

7

MACRAGGE

PERDUS

BLACK REACH

NECRON
NIHILAKH
DYNASTY

FALSE HOPE

SALEM

SPREADING FEAR

Drukhari raids appear across the galaxy, often leaving only a few screaming survivors to tell the tales of the horrors that occurred.

1. On the western border of the Eye of Terror, the Cult of Strife fight alongside other Aledari against Chaos forces. At first the Aeldari alliance avoid Imperial planets, but soon the Drukhari begin butchering the populations of every world in their path.

2. In the howling blackness of the Imperium Nihilus, the sanctuary world of Vigilus becomes a hub for refugees who wish to traverse the Nachmund Gauntlet. The Kabal of the Black Heart flock to the area, annihilating whole flotillas of escape craft and spiriting their human cargo back to Commorragh.

3. The Coven of Twelve find their raiding ground Macia III wracked by Tzeentchian Daemons, so much so that its primary hive city has congealed into a mutated organism comprised of its inhabitants. Whilst driving back the Daemons, the Coven's Wracks set about the grim task of peeling each fleshy layer from the abominable living city so that it can be transported back to the Pendulum and reconstituted.

4. A string of maiden worlds are enveloped within a nebula of impenetrable gloom. As the cloud moves past each planet, Biel-Tan Rangers descend only to find them completely barren and their Exodite populations eradicated. On each world, a constant scream pierces the air, crying the names of Haemonculi from the Coven of the Hex.

5. While raiding the Cinder Stars, the Cult of the Red Grief crosses paths with a colossal Ork Speed Kult, racing from planet to planet through a series of erratic warp tunnels. The Wyches turn their blades upon the greenskin convoy, but each time battle is about to erupt, the Orks are hurled to a new world. To trap their quarry, the Cult tears a rent in reality and lures the speeding armies into a dislocated segment of the webway, causing the Orks to continually loop back around to the same location.

6. As Roboute Guilliman's Indomitus Crusade presses forward to reinforce beleaguered Imperial worlds, the Prophets of Flesh develop an increasing interest in the new breed of Space Marine. Wrack cells, indebted Kabals and mercenary Commorrites are sent to intercept the Adeptus Astartes advance, with orders to maim but not kill the Primaris warriors.

7. The Kabal of the Broken Sigil launches a massive offensive against the Sautekh Dynasty. The Necrons soon bring to bear techno-arcane devices powered by enslaved C'tan, but on each war-front the Broken Sigil focuses all of their efforts on destroying the captive star gods before fading from battle.

A TALE OF ETERNAL SIN

The history of the Drukhari is one of unrelenting horror. Much of it is hidden in shadow, recorded only in allegory and fable by those races whose worlds they have ravaged. Records are kept, however – tomes scribed in still-living flesh using bladed quills of bone. These histories divide the tale of Commorragh into four ages – ill-defined and overlapping though they are – each more redolent with cruelty and evil than the last.

M18-M31 THE AGE OF DARK GENESIS
The Port of Commorragh
Commorragh establishes itself as the primary nodal port of the webway, growing larger with every passing decade. Built entirely within the labyrinth dimension and hence outside the jurisdiction of the Aeldari councils, Commorragh acts as a magnet for those who wish to avoid attention.

The Twilight Cults
Those leading the new paradigm of total self-indulgence rise in status and power until they can secede entirely from the physical plane. They take up permanent residence in the webway, from which they can plumb the depths of decadence undisturbed by puritans and weaklings. Over time, their sovereign estates grow into entire sub-realms, many of which are powered by the energy of stolen suns. The solar systems plunged into darkness by the Aeldari's star-theft wither and die in the freezing cold of the void, but the Aeldari care not.

Darkness Rising
The depravity of the Aeldari race plumbs terrible new depths. Cults of pleasure and pain flourish in the hidden reaches of the webway, and even the core worlds of Aeldari society become obsessed with ever-greater acts of excess. As the lines blur between sensation-seeking and outright evil, a new force stirs in the warp.

Exodus
Sensing the end, portions of the Aeldari race combine and modify their spaceships into craftworlds, gigantic living vessels able to accommodate an entire planet's population. One by one they begin to escape the corruption that plagues their empire. Hundreds of craftworlds sail into the sea of stars in search of the relative safety of the untrammelled void.

The Fall of the Aeldari
A new god is born, collapsing the entire Aeldari civilisation – Slaanesh, the Dark Prince, whose birth-screams tear out the heart of the empire and leave pure Chaos in its place. The shock wave of the new god's apotheosis plunges a vast section of realspace into the warp. Most of the Aeldari craftworlds are destroyed in the psychic backlash. Only the Exodites, the Aeldari of the farthest-flung craftworlds, and those hidden in the sub-realms of the webway survive. The Aeldari race is shattered forever in a single apocalyptic instant.

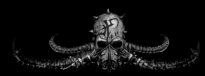

M32-M35 THE RISE OF VECT
A Legacy Begins
A half-born slave – known at the time only as Vect – vows to rule the Dark City, even if it takes an eternity to do so. Vect founds the Cult of the Black Heart, the first organisation to openly refer to themselves as Drukhari, or 'Dark Aeldari'. The Thirteen Foundations of Vengeance are laid down at this time, an intricate code of dishonour destined to spread through the society of the Dark City in the centuries to come. The impact of Vect's rise to power will resonate through Commorragh's history for millennia to come.

The War of the Sun and the Moon
The solar cults that control the Dark City's stolen suns rise in power and influence, declaring war upon the noble houses that would see Commorragh plunged into permanent night. An aerial war rages for centuries, but ultimately the noble houses emerge victorious. Vect's Cult of the Black Heart transforms to become the first true Kabal, and is instrumental in the final defeat of the cults of old during the Battle of the Seven Shrouds.

Vect Ascendant
Asdrubael Vect launches a series of punishing raids against the Imperium's shipping lanes in the Desaderian Gulf. True to his plans, this triggers a punishing counter-attack from three Chapters of the Adeptus Astartes. Vect manipulates the invasion to cripple the power bases of the patrician Archons and, in the aftermath, takes their place as ruler of High Commorragh. Shortly after, the Desaderian portal is forcibly collapsed, triggering a massive implosion and annihilating Imperial naval elements mustering for a second attack.

M35-M41 THE AGE OF PAIN
The Battle for the Thaxar Rift
The Severed begin to plunder the region of space known as the Thaxar Rift. They find their efforts hindered by Chaos-worshipping renegades, who have a substantial presence in the region. Rather than face the renegades directly, Archon Ariensis ensures that his foes come to the attention of the Imperial Navy and Adeptus Astartes, and a grinding war ensues. The Severed haunt the edges of this conflict, tales of murderous ghosts and xenos pirates spreading like wildfire in their wake while they test and study the Imperium's way of war. Eventually the Imperium's forces are reduced to a shadow of their former might, resorting to selective Exterminatus to annihilate what remains of their traitor foes. While the doomed worlds still smoulder, the Severed descend in full force. They annihilate the surviving Imperial Navy ships left behind to watch over Thaxari space, before proceeding to plunder and pillage at will.

Vect's Gift
Asdrubael Vect tricks his would-be rival Archon Kelithresh into opening a casket that has ostensibly been presented as a tithe. Held precariously in the collapsing field of the casket is the unstable essence of a black hole. Kelithresh's entire realm is plunged into a howling, yawning vortex.

The Black Conquest of Yaelindra
Yaelindra of the Blackened Tear uses her preeminent grasp of the arts of Shaimesh

to poison an entire hive world. As the populace of Tybor III are withering into desiccated husks, Yaelindra is granted a boon by Asdrubael Vect. She chooses to take a spire of her own in High Commorragh, founding the Cult of Lhamaea and training an army of courtesan warriors to further her works.

The Plague of Glass
The noted Commorrite artisan Jalaxlar is feted for his incredibly lifelike black-glass statues of Drukhari. His rivals soon discover that he is using an isolated viral helix to create his masterpieces from living victims. In the fight to control this deadly virus it is accidentally released, running rampant through several districts of the Dark City. The Plague of Glass is eventually contained and weaponised by the Hex.

The Breaching
Vect causes the hidden portals that link each satellite realm of the webway to be revealed, forcing them open and building the Great Gates: huge edifices that are permanently guarded by Vect's elite garrisons. Over several millennia of violent strife, Commorragh expands into these once-independent regions until they become integral to the Dark City. Only the realm of Shaa-dom remains autonomous.

War in the Webway
A cabal of the Thousand Sons conducts a great ritual in the webway, hoping to gain access to Commorragh. At the ritual's climax, hundreds of Drukhari pour from an invisible portal into their ranks, led by vaulting troupes of Harlequins. Battle is joined as the Chaos Space Marines counter-attack. The fabric of the webway is breached in the process, and the backlash strands the combatants in a shattered pocket reality with no way out. It is rumoured in Commorragh that they fight there still, locked in an endless cycle of war and rebirth for the rest of time.

The Tower of Flesh
The Haemonculi stronghold known as the Tower of Flesh is created – a living, breathing fortress, made of the bodies of those who defied the Coven of the Thirteen Scars. The renegade Space Marine Fabius Bile is tutored in the dark arts within its blood-slicked halls. Bile is accompanied to the Dark City by Lucius the Eternal, who is declared by his 'hosts' – the Wych Cult of the Wrath Unbound – to be endlessly entertaining both in and out of the arena.

The Blade of Vect
The sub-realm of Shaa-dom grows steadily in affluence until Archon El'uriaq, the self-proclaimed Emperor of Shaa-dom, declares himself more worthy of rule than Asdrubael Vect. Vect publicly vows that all of Shaa-dom will feel the edge of his blade, much to the amusement of El'uriaq's famously well-funded and elite forces. Three days later, a warp rift opens above the satellite realms and a burning Imperial Navy battleship thunders downward, plunging deep into the hidden city's heart before its warp drive detonates. The palace-fortress of El'uriaq is torn apart. The warp rift allows Daemons to invade the city, and within a single week the devil-haunted realm of Shaa-dom is reduced to cinders. Vect is reported to have allowed himself a rare smile at the moment of its fall.

The Last Act of Lord Korscht
Inquisitor Lord Korscht of the Ordo Xenos second-guesses the Drukhari raid upon the industrial world of Demoisne. The moment the Kabal of Immortality Denied blink into existence above Demoisne's capital, they are all but annihilated in a thunderous firestorm. Korscht's absence is keenly felt at the post-action debrief, however, and the Inquisitor Lord's underground fortress complex is investigated. His remains are found, spread thinly upon every page of every occult tome in his library.

Pandaimon Betrayed
The trans-dimensional satellite realm of Pandaimon declares independence from Commorragh, instantly triggering a great war between Archon Qu of the Iron Thorn and the Kabal of the Black Heart. Qu is ready for Vect's attack, but not for the treason of his own daughter, who reveals herself as one of Vect's many courtesans. Civil war rages for weeks but ultimately the realm of Pandaimon is delivered unto Vect.

The Dancing Dead
The insane Archon Thyndrak of the Last Hatred launches a raid on the hive world of Tamantra's Folly. During fierce fighting between her Kabalite forces and the Tallarn 8th Infantry, Archon Thyndrak abducts

the planet's tyrannical governor and his entire sadistic household. The luckless abductees are fitted with neural restraints, dressed in improbable and torturous finery, and installed in life-support tubes built into the ceiling of Archon Thyndrak's grand ballroom. Trapped in an agonising half-life, the nobles can be lowered down to the Archon's dance floor at will on brass armatures, their mere presence leaving the hall awash with an aura of pain and misery that the Commorrites find most refreshing. Needless to say, Thyndrak's new toys are something of a coup, her guests delighting in dancing and frolicking with the whimpering humans amid the mocking laughter of their peers.

The Plague of Becoming
A narcissist without equal, Archon Vhane Kyharc of the Black Myriad releases the Doppelganger Virus on the planet of Phlogiston VI. This transmorphic plague rewrites the biology of every living creature on the planet, forcing their features to reform in the likeness of their alien conqueror.

Fear the Shadows
The Kabal of the Black Heart strike at the hive world of Lapradus, but are hurled back in disarray by the intervention of Titans from the Legio Castigatum. Mere days later, Princeps Gendath – the author of Castigatum's victory – is murdered on his own bridge, hacked to shreds within his amniotic tank by hissing horrors that slither into being. The murky shapes disappear as suddenly as they struck, leaving only a half-frozen mulch of blood and shattered armaglass in their wake.

Just Beyond the Door
Word reaches Asdrubael Vect of a disturbance at Khaine's Gate. Something has begun to pound slowly – rhythmically – impossibly – on the other side. Vect stations five hundred Incubi to watch over the Gate chamber as a delaying measure. He pays exorbitant sums to secure their discretion, while simultaneously ensuring all those hired hail from brotherhoods who have defied or hindered his machinations in the past. As further insurance, Vect deploys several of his more esoteric arcane weapons within the chamber itself, ingenious fail-safes that include temporal flux-mines, the Seventh Shard, and a tri-prismic dimensional mirror keyed to hurl anything reflected in its surface into the heart of a sun.

The Harvest of Chogros

The Kabal of the Broken Sigil begins a series of raids on the planet Chogros, capturing the Ogryn natives for the arenas. When Astra Militarum regiments arrive to intervene, the conflict escalates into a planet-wide engagement. Though they fight hard, the soldiers of the Imperium are eventually defeated. The Crucibael is thronged for many nights to come as the captured Guardsmen are forced to fight the very Ogryns they were sent to save.

The Enemy Beyond

The Incubi standing guard over Khaine's Gate report new and disturbing developments to Asdrubael Vect. In accompaniment to the slow, relentless pounding, the Gate has begun to vibrate at the microscopic level. Worse, those who stand too close to the portal report hearing whispered voices. Though he shows no outward signs of concern, Vect continues to devise new schemes.

The Shadow-Hunt

The Kabal of the Baleful Gaze and Wych Cult of the Wrath Unbound cripple the infrastructure of the industrial world Durondas II using sustained haywire bombing. The Cult then lands great packs of Khymerae and Clawed Fiends, the beasts loping through the darkened streets and tearing the planet's defenders to shreds. Buried in darkness, weapons fried and transportation crippled by the haywire bombs, the terrified Astra Militarum and their civilian charges are forced to fall back time and again. The hunted survivors are finally herded together in the Grand Templum district of Durondas' capital city. Here the Drukhari Beastmasters loose their feral pets en masse, beginning a horrifying massacre that takes several long and bloody days to conclude, and from which no human emerges alive.

The Panacea Wars

Vect sets his Archons a seemingly impossible task: 'poison the Imperium of Man, and bring proof of the deed'. Lady Malys proves equal to the task. Through the Harlequins she has learned that the Tech-Priests of Verdigris IX have recovered an STC codenamed the Panacea, a miracle cure that could save billions of human lives. Using hit-and-run raids, Malys' Kabal of the Poisoned Tongue lure the might of an Ork Waaagh! down upon the heavily defended forge world. The Ork fleet literally ploughs headlong into Verdigris

IX, one massive ship after another slamming into the world's surface to cause untold destruction. As waves of Orks disembark from their wrecked spacecraft, the planet's surviving defenders find themselves embroiled in a desperate war for survival. Malys and her Kabal swoop into the midst of the resultant havoc, cutting down anyone who stands between them and their prize. After prying the Panacea template from the gnarled fingers of the Ork Big Mek who had stolen it before her, Malys returns to the Dark City, leaving Verdigris IX to burn in her wake. Asdrubael Vect is reportedly impressed with this audacious raid – even as Malys is setting the Imperium's miracle cure atop a pedestal in her personal trophy hall, she receives an invitation from Vect to dine with him by way of congratulations.

The Nobility Resurgent

Descendants of the noble houses deposed during Vect's ascension, Archons Xelian, Kraillach and Yllithian attempt a coup. They successfully resurrect the ancient Archon El'uriaq, once Emperor of Shaa-dom and the last individual to present a genuine challenge to Vect's supremacy. However, their schemes go horribly awry, leading the Dark City into a period of strife unlike any it has seen for thousands of years. As a result of their actions, a powerful daemonic dysjunction shakes Commorragh to its very foundations and forces Asdrubael Vect himself to take drastic action lest his city slip into oblivion altogether.

The Long Midnight

The Last Hatred ravages the hive world of Persya in a six-cycle-long siege, using arcane technologies to bring pitch darkness to its principal hives and sending Mandrakes and Ur-Ghuls into its confines. Many hive workers go mad with terror, but are taken back to Commorragh nonetheless. It is claimed that during this siege, Kheradruakh the Decapitator selects an unprecedented seven worthy skulls for his macabre lair.

The War of Dark Revelations

T'au forces defending Vigos against the onrushing might of Hive Fleet Kraken make the fatal decision to ally themselves with Urien Rakarth. Despite initial victories alongside their twisted allies, the T'au soon become alarmed by Rakarth's demands that they engage in ever more costly 'cultural exchanges'. They finally resolve to strike back when he transforms T'au warriors into monstrous Grotesques, and begins demanding a tribute of their sacred Ethereals. The T'au muster their reserves from the world of Rubikon, yet when their blow falls they find Rakarth's fleet already gone, having left only holograms and sensor-ghosts in its wake. Panicked distress calls begin to issue from the defenceless Rubikon mere hours later. These gabbled reports tell of twisted, pale-fleshed invaders calling themselves the Prophets of Flesh. Yet it is far too late for the woefully outmanoeuvred T'au forces to respond, and they can only listen in anguish to the death-cries of their world.

The Bane of Commorragh

After being defeated by Lelith Hesperax in the Crucibael, the Aeldari known as Yvraine passes through the veil of death only to be reborn as the Emissary of Ynnead, the God of the Dead. Her violent apotheosis sees the alien combatants of the arena unleashed upon the spectators. In the ensuing anarchy, Asdrubael Vect recedes into the shadows.

The Gate Opens

Yvraine's possession by the macabre god Ynnead shakes the very fabric of the Dark City. Psychic energy bleeds uncontrollably from her, leading to a hyperspatial quake. Millions die in the first shock wave alone, and as the ripples continue, Khaine's Gate – which had held fast for millennia – is torn violently open. For months daemonic entities surge through the breach, ravenously devouring Drukhari souls as they press forward. Despite desperate attempts by Commorragh's nobles to stem the tide of Daemons, Asdrubael Vect is mysteriously absent. Only when the warriors and slave armies of the Dark City are stretched to breaking point against the invasion does the Supreme Overlord finally play his hand. Vect calls upon the Incubi, citing pacts and debts of old, and the bodyguards of every Archon present in Commorragh are recalled from their duty in order to fight the Daemons. In battle after harrowing battle, the Incubi – along with myriad other warriors – corral the Daemons into the sub-realm containing the gaping hole that was Khaine's Gate. This sub-realm is then severed from the rest of Commorragh, plunged into a nether-abyss which comes to be known as the Chasm of Woe. But the Daemons keep coming, rising from the massive abscess created within Commorragh. More of the Dark City's sub-dimensions are plunged into the Chasm, and armies of warriors and slaves with them, in an attempt to keep the Chaos entities from reaching the heart of Commorragh once more.

M41 THE AGE OF THE LIVING MUSE

The Feast Awaiting

The Chaos incursion that savaged the Dark City is also felt throughout the galaxy as the Great Rift yawns open. A bow-wave ripples throughout realspace and the webway, shattering countless portals and gates that lead to and from Commorragh. Whole sections of the labyrinth dimension become dislocated, and through the fractures in the interstitial plane more Daemons come pouring inward. Meanwhile, the Imperium of Man is bisected by the warp-maw and one half – the Imperium Nihilus – is plunged into shadow, their ability to travel and communicate between systems all but lost. Each world stands isolated in the darkness as the servants of the Chaos Gods begin their campaigns of slaughter. The watchers in Commorragh see these worlds that are ripe for plunder, but must first contend with the cataclysms in the webway and the Dark City. Those raids that are launched in the Imperium Nihilus, while brutal, are but a fraction of the Drukhari's terrifying potential.

The Assassination of Vect

With every Incubi bodyguard within Commorragh deployed to stem the tide of Daemons, long-stifled rivalries between the Dark City's elites erupt into bloodshed. Assassinations become commonplace, and the threat of civil war looms ever closer. Yet right when the denizens of Commorragh seem set to tear themselves and their city to shreds, the impossible happens. Asdrubael Vect himself is murdered, cut down by Mandrakes in service to an unknown master. Furthermore, every receptacle that contains a fragment of the Supreme Overlord's essence is destroyed simultaneously, ensuring that he cannot be regrown by the Haemonculi. The

internecine conflicts that have ravaged the Dark City are quickly replaced by an uneasy stillness as every Commorrite assesses their alliances. If Vect can be killed, then who amongst the Drukhari can be assured of their own survival?

The Great Wake

Harlequins of the Veiled Path prepare a wake for Vect to be held in the Nhexus, the arena of the Wych Cult of the Cursed Blade. Many begin to suspect that it was the Cursed Blade who orchestrated the Supreme Overlord's demise – others suspect the hand of Lady Malys, for she and her Kabal of the Poisoned Tongue have withdrawn from Commorragh into the fractured spars of the webway. Nonetheless, the Great Wake is attended in great numbers, both by those loyal to Vect and by those who come to gloat before beginning the war to divide up his territories. At the crescendo of the proceedings, the arena is saturated with potent airborne hallucinogens, and the Harlequins unleash their full fury on the Archons in attendance. Joining the fray on the side of the Veiled Path are the Wyches of the Cursed Blade, as well as the Prophets of Flesh and warriors from Vect's own Kabal. The blood of Archons flows in great rivers, and amidst the screams of agony and terror, Asdrubael Vect rises from the centre of the arena, his body perfect in form and his eyes filled with wrath. When the slaughter has finished, those Archons who remained faithful to Vect are resurrected by the Prophets of Flesh, as are some of his enemies – though they are remade as twisted monstrosities whose only purpose is to serve the Supreme Overlord by their suffering. Having culled the upper echelons of Commorragh, Vect's position is rendered nigh-unassailable, and he declares himself a living Dark Muse.

The Price of Beauty

An enormous raid on hive world Vorgan in the Imperium Nihilus returns to Commorragh with hundreds of thousands of captives. Whilst poring over the still-living specimens, Haemonculi of the Hex identify the slave population as being host to a Genestealer Cult. Hybrids are singled out and pumped full of growth accelerators, causing dormant mutations to blossom in their flesh. Once word spreads, a trend arises whereby the alien growths are harvested and grafted onto the bodies of high-paying Drukhari elites. The Vorgani, as these beautified individuals

come to be known, form tight-knit cliques within High Commorragh in which they revel in their augmentations. Furthermore, they develop a collective obsession with Lethidia – the Tyranid-infested planet that had been drawn into the webway and still orbits the Dark City.

The Obsidian Circlet

A dark, glassy substance is found during raids on worlds held by both Necrons and the Adeptus Mechanicus. Within the Covens of the undercity it is soon discovered that this material can be used to repel daemonic entities. After more raids are launched against Necron and Adeptus Mechanicus planets, the plundered blackstone is arrayed around the ever-deepening Chasm of Woe. The captives from these raids are also sent into the Chasm, where their anguished deaths feed the souls of the Drukhari.

Tortured Throne

Following the apparent abduction of several Custodian Guard, Inquisitors of the Ordo Xenos pursue the Coven of the Twisted Spiral to a wandering moon deep in the interstellar void. Hopes of catching their quarry soon vanish, but on the moon's barren surface the Inquisitors find what appears to be a simulacrum of the Golden Throne, covered in blood and viscera. Just as they are sending word of their discovery, the Twisted Spiral appear and butcher the Imperial agents.

United by Hatred

A great number of the Asuryani of the craftworlds, along with many Harlequins and denizens of the Dark City, unite behind Yvraine as she seeks to destroy She Who Thirsts. It is the first time in millennia that such close military bonds have existed within the fractured Aeldari race. Yet not all share the vision of the Emissary of Ynnead. Within his palatial spire in High Commorragh, the Supreme Overlord and Living Muse Asdrubael Vect makes plans to end the Reborn prophet…

Those who do battle with the Drukhari and are taken alive face a fate far worse than death. They are hooked or impaled on the hulls of raiding craft and taken back to Commorragh where they are plunged into the slave pits, thrown into the arenas or – for the most unfortunate – taken to the oubliettes deep beneath the Dark City. In the hands of the Haemonculi, they enter an eternity of torture.

ARCHONS

The Archons of the Drukhari Kabals are the true monarchs of Commorragh. They sit at the pinnacle of the pyramid, the apex of the hierarchy that controls their twilight domain. Each wields influence enough to collapse portions of realspace, stall an Imperial Crusade or steal away the populations of entire planets. Though a Kabal's Overlord is always a terrifying opponent to face in battle, they have attained their lofty heights not merely through prowess in the arts of war or the brute suppression of the weak, but through consistently emerging victorious in the most convoluted contest of all – the game of intrigue at the heart of the Dark City, sometimes known as the *thyllian ai-kelethril,* or 'path of shards'. Only the most ingenious survive long enough to kill their way to the top.

In both word and deed, each Archon is as poisonous as a serpent, their mind as labyrinthine as the darkest reaches of the webway. Such traits are a necessity, for to sit at the very peak of power is to make oneself a prominent target indeed. Though the Archons are conceited megalomaniacs certain of their own superiority, they will retain rulership only for as long as they can stave off the coups and assassination attempts of their rivals and Dracon lieutenants. Placing even a single foot wrong in the upper echelons of the Dark City will inevitably lead to a fatal fall. Because of this, Archons have an uncanny ability to predict the schemes of others, and take a cold delight in turning the traps laid out before them upon their heads.

Despite the elaborate network of allegiances within the Dark City, the Overlords of the Kabals run rings around those who seek to beat them at their deadly game. The endless ambition of their underlings keeps their paranoia razor-sharp, and hence it is at the business of treachery that the Archons truly excel. Their strategies stretch across the millennia, wheels turning within wheels as centuries-old ploys finally come to fruition. Some of the Lords of Twilight, who govern from the highest spires of Commorragh, even claim to have seized their thrones in the times before the Fall. These elder Archons look upon the rest of their race as squabbling children, and do not suffer fools gladly. A single syllable out of place may rouse an Archon's deadly wrath, and in matters of Kabal hierarchy, Archons will seek solutions that work to the detriment of all other parties purely out of spite.

'You think to challenge me, pitiful human? I, the bane of empires, the father of pain? Let me educate you; I need a new pet…'

- Archon K'shaic, Kabal of the Bladed Lotus

Revelling in the depths of the abyss always has a cost. Over the years in which they have clawed their way up the precipice of power, the Archons of the Drukhari have become something altogether more otherworldly. They have fed upon the pain of others for so long that it takes a true atrocity to invigorate them. Archons regularly lead full-scale planetary raids, for drinking in wholesale excruciation is the only way they can properly rejuvenate. Thousands of slaves are sacrificed before the oldest Archons each night, and still this might not be enough to grant them a youthful sheen. Hence, elder Archons sometimes cover their black-veined visages with masks – some stylised and beautiful, some fashioned from the flayed faces of rivals whose schemes were not as foolproof as they liked to think.

Before going to battle, an Archon will visit their weapon museum, savouring the process of selection as they choose between the most arcane and lethal of all the technologies of Commorragh. Some Archons choose a different array of armaments for each engagement, indulging in the variety at their disposal. Others have used the same tools of slaughter for years, decades or even centuries, and continually find new ways to induce suffering with their favoured implements. One such weapon – the huskblade – is a favourite of many Archons, for it evaporates the internal fluids of those it slices, causing their flesh to shrivel and crumble to dust in a most spectacular fashion. Other, more esoteric items are also taken to war by Archons, such as eldritch soul-traps, whip-like agonisers, and force fields that shroud the wearer in tendrils of darkness.

Thus accoutred, the Archon strides haughtily onto the battlefield, eyeing their enemies with utter disdain. Their most favoured retainers and pets, each of whom specialises in bestowing the gift of death in its own fashion, accompany the Archon, butchering those to whom they are directed to by their master. Even the least of a Kabal's Archons can move like the wind, seeming almost to vanish from sight and reappear again when their blade has done its bloody work. Few mortal warriors have set their eyes upon an Archon and still kept them within their sockets.

COURT OF THE ARCHON

Archons surround themselves with a coterie of favoured retainers and bodyguards. Depending on the personality of the Kabalite lord, these can be as varied as the tools in their torture chamber. However, certain breeds of creatures have proven to be eminently useful to Archons, and are seen frequently by their sides both within the Dark City and upon the battlefield.

MEDUSAE

The visored slave-beings that Archons use to record the roiling emotions of the battlefield are hosts to strange creatures of the webway, known as Medusae. These highly empathic parasites look like a collection of brains and spinal cords one atop another, and they float through the ether like jellyfish, feeding on daydreams and nightmares. Medusae can latch onto a host that intrudes into their realm, absorbing their emotions directly and providing a means of motive power in realspace. Though meeting the gaze of a Medusae's host can cause instant emotional haemorrhaging, these hybrid creatures are highly valuable in Commorragh, for they absorb and store extreme sensations. Consuming one of the Medusae's brain-fruit brings back all the vivid and anarchic emotions of a raid as if they were happening then and there.

LHAMAEANS

An Archon's entourage will take many strange forms, its members as varied as they are deadly, but the mysterious sisterhood of Lhilitu are desired above all others for their skill in crafting and administering poisons. Descending from the original Cult of Lhamaea, they draw from the knowledge of Shaimesh, Father of Poisons, to concoct the most potent toxins used in Drukhari society. Whether these poisonous creations are used on the Archon's enemies within the Dark City or in realspace, the results are equally horrific. A mere scratch from a Lhamaean's shaimeshi blade can cause a victim's flesh to begin eating itself, their brain to swell until it bursts through the skull, or their blood to acidify and melt bones and organs internally. It is said that even a kiss blown upon the wind by a Lhamaean can kill in seconds.

SSLYTH

Most Drukhari make rather dubious bodyguards due to their treacherous nature and unquenchable selfishness. Archons therefore often employ the more reliable alien mercenaries that inhabit Commorragh to protect them from inevitable coups. Though these bodyguards hail from all across the galaxy, favoured amongst them are the Sslyth, hulking serpent-bodied warrior-fiends whose race fell to the temptations of unbridled excess millennia ago. Having two sets of arms, Sslyth mercenaries sport enough guns and blades to easily make a mess of any assassin or would-be usurper, and their insensibility to pain makes them slow to give away secrets should they be captured by one of their master's rivals. But their greatest assets are their quick reflexes, which allow them to pounce in front of an attack that would fall on their employer.

UR-GHULS

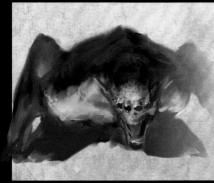

Archons keep all manner of deadly alien creatures in their courts, from worm-like Haemovores to greater Shaderavens, whose croaking caw drives those who hear it insane. Though innumerable species of atavistic bloodbeasts prowl Commorragh, perhaps the most hideous of all is the Ur-Ghul, a sightless but agile troglodyte that hails from the labyrinthine ziggurats of Shaa-dom. Once one of these whip-thin horrors has scented its prey with its rows of quivering scent-pits, there is no escape from the violence that follows. Ur-Ghuls are regularly used as entertainment at high society functions, where an Archon will allow his pets to gruesomely savage a captured rival. Those who provide the most visceral maulings are rewarded by their owners by being taken into realspace, where they can feast on new types of flesh.

INCUBI

The Incubi are an order of Drukhari that hone themselves for war and war alone. Warriors of the highest calibre, they dedicate themselves to the perfection of the killing strike. Despite the Incubi's monk-like asceticism, no shred of virtue exists in their bloodstained souls, for though they profess a desire to achieve perfection in every aspect of their existence, their true goal is simply to kill as often as possible.

Everything about an Incubus accoutred for war conveys menace. His armour is spiked and segmented from top to toe, and his horned helmet is framed by a pair of great razored blades. He walks with the measured surety of a stalking sabrecat, and despite his formidable armour he makes no sound as he does so, for each Incubus warsuit is so perfectly designed it barely inhibits his dexterity. The ornate plates slide as fluidly as silk over one another as the Incubus moves in for the kill, yet they are as rigid as ceramite when struck by a blade or blast of energy.

Mercenaries all, the Incubi will fight for anyone, at any time, and will even impart their skills to those that prove themselves worthy. Their forbidding obsidian shrines, each presided over by a Hierarch, are thronged with patrons and aspirants eager to steep themselves in the murderous arts. Through long and gruelling practise, the strong prosper and learn, whereas the weak are cut down and their bodies burnt as an offering to the iron statue of Khaine at the heart of each shrine. The only known path of entry into the order is to best a proven Incubus and take his armour. Should an aspirant live long enough to achieve this murderous feat, then the final training can begin. The initiate is given a singular, spiteful task – to kill an Aspect Warrior of the Asuryani in single combat, shatter his quarry's precious spirit stone, and return it to the Hierarch. When this task is completed, only then can he be fully inducted as an Incubus. The sundered spirit stone is then rebuilt into a psychic torture device known as a tormentor and mounted on the Incubus' chest, where it exudes an aura of terror and malice that penetrates the minds of even the most dauntless foes.

The Incubi lead rigorously disciplined lives; some whisper they can even be trusted to keep their word. They are highly valued as bodyguards and shock troops, and they take a cold joy in proving their deadly skill in times of war. As such, their services are regularly sought after by those who dwell within the Dark City, and the Incubi are never short of opportunities to ply their deadly trade in realspace. When their services are put to use on the battlefield, they race forward at the head of the assault, carving a path straight through the enemy's front lines and leaving a bloody trail of severed limbs and bifurcated torsos in their wake. Alternatively, a particularly wealthy Drukhari warlord may hold his Incubi back as rearguards, though the mercenaries must be handsomely compensated for delaying their indulgence in violence.

Despite their prowess as duellists, even Incubi scorn a fair fight, and will concentrate solely upon killing in the most efficient way possible. Though they train in multiple forms of combat, their preferred weapons are great powered swords they call klaives. Their martial style with these enormous blades allows them to strike swiftly from various angles, with killing blows that can penetrate the hides of monstrous beasts and hulking vehicles alike.

KLAIVES

A klaive is a masterpiece of balance and form, considered by the Incubi to be the one true weapon. Able to be held in one hand or gripped with both, the weapon is impossibly light for its size and can be swung in tight, controlled arcs just as easily as in grand, beheading sweeps. The blade itself is wreathed in dark energy that molecularly separates all matter through which it passes, rending armour, flesh and bone with elegant brutality. The leaders of the Incubi are known as Klaivexes due to their unparalleled skill with the klaive. Each shrine has a different ritual for how a Klaivex is chosen, but all revolve around displaying absolute mastery of the ritual weapon. In the Shrine of Naked Hatred, those who would become leader must first disable an incumbent Klaivex in single combat. They must then show their skill by flaying the defeated in but four strokes of the blade – if they fail, they themselves are skinned with their klaive.

DRAZHAR
MASTER OF BLADES

Even amongst the insular ranks of the Incubi, the enigmatic Drazhar remains a mystery. All that is known of his origins is that he entered the Great Shrine of the Incubi unannounced and unbidden, clad in the segmented armour of a senior member of the Incubus creed. He cut his way into the inner sanctum, leaving those who tried to stop him clutching bloody stumps as their blades clattered to the flagstones, and saluted the shrine's enthroned Hierarch in challenge. Incensed at this upstart newcomer's contempt for proper protocol, the Hierarch rose from his throne, entered the candlelit duelling circle and took up the battle stance. The Hierarch's self-assured superiority soon evaporated when his challenger blurred into action, moving so quickly that it was hard to follow him in the flickering tallow-light. The duel was over within minutes, and the newcomer stepped over the Hierarch's dismembered body. By rights the challenger was entitled to take the throne then and there, but Drazhar merely cleaned his blade and sketched a simple bow.

Drazhar's mysterious appearance gave rise to many wild theories and unanswered questions. After weeks of rumour and gossip, it was confirmed that none of the Incubi shrines across Commorragh had ever heard of Drazhar, or recognised his unique and ancient battle gear. Some say he is Arhra, the fabled Dark Father of the Incubi incarnate, others that his armour is filled with nothing more than bone-dust. What was soon confirmed beyond a doubt was that no matter how skilled the challenger, Drazhar always emerged victorious from his duels. Though he has never shown any inclination to take up the position of Hierarch or Klaivex, his merciless skill in the battle arts of the Incubi is unparalleled. So it is that Drazhar occupies the post of Executioner, the champion of his order, lethality personified.

Though Drazhar has become an integral part of the Great Shrine since his dramatic appearance, he has famously never spoken, nor removed his helmet, not even to eat or sleep. Even the name Drazhar is ceremonial, meaning 'living sword'. The most that can be expected from Drazhar by way of conversation is an occasional slight nod or tilt of the head, and it is only the most senior Incubi that are accorded even this scant courtesy. The lords of other Incubi shrines treat the Master of Blades with extreme suspicion, for despite their revered position each was once a lesser warrior, flawed and mortal. Though their original names and identities have been left far behind, a small flame of ambition flickers yet in their black hearts. Drazhar alone remains incorruptible by emotion or pride. He simply exists to kill – nothing more, nothing less.

Regardless of any suspicions that may be held against Drazhar, in him the Incubi ideal of violent perfection is exquisitely personified. His every strike exemplifies the tenets of his order, and each life he claims serves as a gruesome liturgy for his dark brethren. Those Incubi who fight in the presence of Drazhar set aside their deep-seated jealousy, and are driven by his unquestionable skill to even greater extremes of martial expertise. Drazhar invariably becomes the locus of murder on the battlefield, the calm centre in a storm of beautifully enacted violence.

Taller and more lithe than even other Incubi, Drazhar has a deadly mantis-like speed, and he strikes with his grimly filigreed demiklaives at any that so much as raise a weapon in his direction. He has an uncanny ability to move like lightning, darting through even the most chaotic melee to cut his chosen foe down before their blade can fall or their trigger-finger twitch. Those chosen as Drazhar's prey have few options other than to commend themselves to the gods they hold dear, for once they are marked by the Master of Blades they have only seconds to live.

Drazhar is one of very few Commorrites whose atrocities are widely admired within the Dark City. The deeds of this enigmatic bladesman are often spoken about, particularly by those Drukhari who managed to secure his services on a realspace raid. There are countless stories of his macabre work, such as the time he personally butchered every Imperial defender in the spire of Hive Tarson, or when he single-handedly dispatched a trio of Custodian Guard at close quarters.

'Though his aptitude for murder is legendary, my interest in Drazhar lies elsewhere. None of the Drukhari whose minds I have seen know what he is or where he came from. But they do fear him, and rightly so. I suspect even the mighty Vect questions what this silent executioner is capable of. Could it be true that he is but dust encased in armour, like my own accursed brothers – and if so, is there a way that I can bend him to my will? I must be patient in this regard, but time will tell.'

- Ahzek Ahriman, Arch-Sorcerer of the Thousand Sons

KABALITE WARRIORS

The Warriors of the Kabals form the beating heart of each Drukhari strike force. They are the cruellest and most rapacious of their caste, hungry for power and thirsty for the suffering of others. Each Warrior will have carved out a fearful reputation for himself in the war-torn halls of High Commorragh, and has proven himself time and time again as a merciless fighter. The more vicious and ruthless a warrior is, the better their chances of advancement within the Kabal. It takes a born killer to thrive in the constant strife of the Dark City after all, and still only a chosen few enjoy the privilege of striking at the heavily defended worlds of realspace and returning with the living, screaming bounty their Kabal requires for survival.

The most martially gifted Drukhari of each sector are selected to become Kabalite Warriors. Male or female, Warriors are tall and athletically built, more powerful in stature and violent of temperament than their city-bound peers. When going to battle, each Warrior girds themselves with a sophisticated bodysuit of segmented armour. These suits are donned during lengthy and unnecessarily painful pre-battle rituals, the better to ensure their wearer's psyche is honed to a single point of murderous intent. Much of the bodysuit is held in place with long metal barbs and hooks that penetrate deep into the wearer's nerve bundles, sharpening their senses with the constant sting of pain. It is pain that energises the Kabalite Warriors, and pain they seek to inflict upon their quarry – the more agonising the better.

To this end, Kabalite Warriors carry a wide array of exotic and fiendish weapons. Foremost amongst these are the dreaded splinter rifles, long-barrelled and elegant guns that fire a stream of jagged crystalline slivers. Each needle shard is impregnated with a wide spectrum of virulent hypertoxins. A splinter rifle slays its targets over several excruciating seconds, allowing the grinning wielder to savour their agonising demise as a connoisseur savours a fine wine.

Though the distilled poisons of the splinter weapon can bring down even the monstrous biological terrors of the Tyranid hive fleets, it is of very little use against enemy vehicles. A squad of Kabalite Warriors will usually carry a far more destructive weapon for such a purpose – the blaster is a particular favourite, for it can cripple even a Rhino with but a single squeeze of the trigger.

Though all Kabalite Warriors are expert combatants at close quarters, few have the influence needed to ensure regeneration in the lairs of the Haemonculi. As a result, Warriors frequently employ heavy weaponry that can slay the foe from afar. The sightlinks built into their splinter cannons and dark lances not only improve accuracy, but also allow the wielder to see the agony-wracked look on his victim's face when each salvo hits home. Enterprising operators use mnemonic scopes to record such moments, replaying the resultant hologhosts upon their return and basking in the envy of their peers.

Each squad of Kabalite Warriors is led to war by a Sybarite, typically the most experienced of their number. Sybarites are not only veteran realspace raiders, but also the Kabalites who initiate each Warrior into the violent mysteries of their sect. Though their seniority engenders not a shred of loyalty from their charges, the Sybarites' orders are obeyed to the letter upon the battlefield, for they are masters in the craft of war.

SPLINTER WEAPONS

Along with the splinter rifle, which is found everywhere from the slums to the high spires of Commorragh, there are many other patterns of weapon that utilise the same magno-electric pulse technology to fire toxin-coated crystalline shards. The splinter pistol is an elegant sidearm that possesses the same deadly potency as the rifle, and is favoured by assassins and street fighters alike. The shardcarbine boasts a punishing rate of fire, yet is still lightweight enough to be fired while moving at breakneck speeds, making it the preferred weapon of the winged Scourges. Even the heaviest splinter weapon in common use – the splinter cannon – can be carried into battle by infantry, though it is at its deadliest when mounted on a fast-moving vehicle such as a Venom or Razorwing Jetfighter.

VENOMS

The Drukhari rely heavily on surprise and raw speed, and hence their skycraft are all fast and manoeuvrable. The most deft of all Commorrite transports is the Venom, an arrow-swift skimmer that carries an elite cadre of warriors into battle to strike like a poisoned dart at the heart of the foe.

Rather than present a single obvious target, a Drukhari strike force will attack in waves, with a dizzying number of craft pouring out of the fractured skies in order to confound the guns of the foe. Although a few Drukhari vehicles may be intercepted by the flak of particularly lucky enemies, even a disciplined gun battery cannot hope to stop the entirety of the malignant swarm that descends upon it. Furthermore, as any experienced Drukhari commander knows, it is the largest and most populous transports that are the target priority of well-drilled enemy soldiers. So it is that the most devious Drukhari ride to war upon craft no larger than the Vypers of the Asuryani, or the sky-chariots of the ancient Aeldari empire that preceded them.

Speed is paramount – should even a single Venom penetrate the foe's defences it can be enough to sow the seeds of destruction. Those embarked upon its open deck are free to shoot at opponents as they fly past, and the Venom itself bears a frightening amount of firepower as well as bladevanes to slice through enemies in its path.

Though the Venom's booster engines and anti-gravitic ribbing are similar to those of other Drukhari craft, the transport is so deft and sensitive to the commands of its pilot that it can jink through a storm of incoming fire, its holographic flickerfield confounding enemy marksmen. It is said that a skilled Venom pilot can even traverse the parts of the webway designed only for the passage of single individuals. For this reason Venoms are very popular with Commorrite hunters, and also those aristocrats of the upper spires who enjoy running their enemies down for the sake of sport.

Despite its small size, the Venom is the ideal craft for carrying a small clique of hand-picked warriors who are well used to fighting as a coordinated unit. Though most Drukhari lords and champions will lead their Kabalite Warriors into battle from a personalised Raider, this does not always sit well with those who prefer not to consort with mere footsoldiers. Many Archons ride to war surrounded by the deadliest members of their court, and for them the fast and compact form of the Venom is ideally suited. Sometimes Venoms are even used to transport but a single warrior to battle in style – usually those Drukhari nobles too arrogant or paranoid to trust even their own bodyguards. Those who have seen the denizens of the Dark City in action know that a single warrior is sometimes all it takes, and that a Venom's true poison is in its passengers, not its guns.

THE DARK MUSES

Though the Drukhari typically do not worship anyone apart from themselves, they do pay homage to those they respect. Vaunted warriors or dark artists may become revered amongst their own kind; not to honour their skill, but purely in order to learn more of their power.

In this way truly mighty Drukhari from ages past have become almost folkloric figures. Many epitomise a particular form of vice, whose clandestine worship led to the weakening of the ancient Aeldari gods and, indirectly, the Fall. They are known collectively as the Dark Muses, and they are figures of terrible power. Favoured by assassins and murderers is Shaimesh, Lord of Poisons, the treacherous brother of Saim-Hann the Cosmic Serpent. The courtesan elite of the Cult of Lhamaea pay homage to Lhilitu, Consort of the Void, whereas powerful Archons are more likely to follow the tenets of Vileth, a figure synonymous with immense arrogance. On the eve of battle many traditionalist Wych Cults invoke the Red Crone Hekatii, or make sacrifices to Qa'leh, Mistress of Blades.

Though many suspected Asdrubael Vect would join the ranks of the Dark Muses upon his death, none foresaw that he would take the title for himself in such a spectacularly sadistic fashion.

RAIDERS

The first sign of a Drukhari realspace raid is a glimmer of unlight that appears in the sky, unfolding and spiralling outward to become a shimmering portal ablaze with green flame. Through this ethereal gateway come dozens of bladed skycraft, arrowing towards their bewildered quarry with the single-mindedness of sharks that have scented blood. The most common of these anti-gravity skimmers are known as Raiders, the favoured transports of Drukhari across the galaxy.

Lightweight and extremely manoeuvrable, Raiders epitomise the Drukhari belief that velocity triumphs over durability. Unlike the sluggish vehicles of the Imperium, Raiders do not hold their passengers within metallic shells. Instead they are more like the gliding pleasure boats of the ancient Aeldari – albeit adapted for extreme speed, and fitted with sword-sharp bladevanes and jagged keels with which to cut apart the foe.

The primary motive power of the Raider comes from compact turbo-engines, and they are held aloft by anti-grav ribbing that allows them to skim over rugged terrain, defensive walls and masses of land-bound combatants at a tremendous pace. Though each of these craft is customised by its owning Kabal, Wych Cult or Haemonculus Coven and adorned with the body parts of conquered victims, all have certain key features in common – a repulsor keelblade manned by a talented steersman, aethersails to harness the energies flowing from the portal from which they descend, and a prow-mounted heavy weapon to sow terror amongst the enemy. The curved hull of each Raider is sheltered by sweeping fairings, and its metal deck is pierced through with tessellating designs to lessen the craft's weight. Sickle-blades, electroshock rams and gun racks are also frequently mounted upon Raiders, for the Drukhari will gladly use any weapon at their disposal.

At first glance, the Raider is so pared-down and streamlined that it appears to be more of a racing craft than a troop transport. True enough, when its engines are at full burn it is capable of keeping pace with even the miraculous skimmers of the Asuryani. Nonetheless, troop transport is the Raider's primary function – such is the surety and confidence of its Drukhari passengers that they can hang onto the balustrades and trophy-hooks of the Raider with ease, rejoicing in the thrill of the hunt as shrapnel bursts all around. The bulwarks offer just enough cover to protect those embarked upon the Raider from incoming shots without blocking line of sight to their prey. As such, a fully loaded Raider becomes a terrifyingly mobile base of fire, ferrying those within to where the fighting is thickest whilst they level ceaseless streams of death at those they fly by. After a punishing salvo has been loosed, it is the work of but a second to leap from the Raider and drop down into the enemy's midst, teeth bared in anticipation of the bloodletting to come.

Once victory is secured, any surviving enemies will be lashed or chained to the Raider or simply impaled upon its trophy hooks. Those Drukhari who have died in the raid – as well as those whose injuries have removed them from the fight – are also carried back to Commorragh with a marked lack of dignity, heaped in a gory tangle of limbs or hung like rag dolls from the Raider's spiked hull. So it is that Raiders have gained a grim reputation across the galaxy, their arrival signifying torture, dismemberment and death.

Private Malko's earliest memory was of Goodwife Ingrid yelling at him.

'You! Child! Listen to me!'

She yelled at all the children in that corner of the hab-block, grabbing them by the wrists and squeezing until it became painful. He remembered that she would hold him so close that he could see every crevice of the cruel scars that zigzagged across her face and around her neck. Her lip would tremble as she spoke, and he would recoil in fear at her outpouring of terror.

'Don't let them take you alive,' she would say. 'The changelings – they come from the sky. They'll try to steal you away, but don't let them take you alive.' Then she would describe the blade-like craft and sickly jade light that came before the nightmare creatures she was describing. It wasn't until he was drafted that Malko learnt many of his fellow Guardsmen had heard similar stories when they were young, told by old and mutilated veterans.

Only now – as the hooks pierced his flesh and the Raider carried him into the sky – did Private Malko fully comprehend Goodwife Ingrid's fevered warnings. The Drukhari had come like lightning, annihilating the gun emplacements and butchering the stationed platoons. Worst of all, Malko had let them take him alive.

RAVAGERS

The Ravager gunship is just as arrow-swift as its brother craft, the Raider. In place of a transport capacity, however, the Ravager mounts three devastatingly powerful heavy weapons. Upon the battlefield it fulfils the role of armoured fire support, engaging the heaviest of enemy targets, but comparing the Ravager to a gun-tank of the Imperium is like comparing a swift-winged raptor to a lumbering beast of burden. Ravager gunships are so fast and manoeuvrable that they can ambush an enemy tank and destroy it in a single devastating pass, disappearing again before the enemy knows what hit them.

Ravagers can be said to fulfil the role of assassins in the war against realspace, though their assigned targets are armoured vehicles instead of flesh-and-blood individuals. Each Ravager crew will have a priority target allocated to it that it must take down, and if it fails to do so it will face dire punishment upon its return to its parent Kabal in the depths of Commorragh.

The targeting arrays of the Ravagers are outfitted with as much information about their quarry as their Kabal can muster, and each grav-skiff's crew are briefed as to the best way to annihilate the enemy vehicle in question. This ensures that the Ravager's capricious gunners focus on a particular task, such as crippling the enemy's prized war engine, bringing an armoured column to a shuddering halt or denying the foe their means of escape. Once this task is achieved, the Ravager crew have carte blanche to swoop around the battlefield causing whatever carnage they see fit and pitilessly obliterating whoever happens to fall under their gunsights.

It is perhaps indicative of the wider mindset of the Drukhari that the Ravager, the most ubiquitous of their gunship designs, bears even less in the way of armour plating than the personnel transports of Mankind. Speed is prized above all. The Ravager's crew reason that if they are already elsewhere when retribution is sought, their chances of survival are far higher than those who wallow around waiting to be hit. This tactic is frustrating to the officers of the Imperium, where war is waged with the sledgehammer rather than the thrust of the rapier. But the proof of its efficacy is undeniable. A Ravager squadron is fully capable of appearing from nowhere, delivering the death blow to a God-Machine of the Adeptus Mechanicus in a single volley, and disappearing over the horizon before the behemoth has even toppled to the ground.

DARKLIGHT WEAPONS

The weapon shops of Commorragh make many implements of war that seem to cheat the laws of physics, the most destructive of which are the darklight weapons. From the blast pistol and blaster to the dark lance and dark scythe, these weapons fire devastating streams of an esoteric substance known only as 'darklight'. This material reacts catastrophically with its target, boring massive holes in vehicles and vaporising infantry soldiers in an instant. Some claim that darklight is harvested from black holes, warp storms or other celestial phenomena; regardless of its origin, its effects on the battlefield are utterly devastating.

Amidst searing light, yet another trio of sleek, blade-keeled vehicles burst into existence less than a hundred metres from the Ork lines. A great roar went up from the ramshackle greenskin encampments arrayed about the walls of the fat-bellied Ork fortress – this was looking like a proper fight after all. As one, the Orks took the bait.

A flood of Greenskins poured out from the shanty towns around the fortress as a huge Battlewagon with rusted metal jaws and 'Da Gobbla' sprayed across its blunt nose hurtled over the entrance ramps, leading an armoured column straight towards the night-shrouded invaders. Nine beams of unlight seared out from the gathering gloom, each a pinpoint lance that struck a vital point on the metallic behemoth. Da Gobbla came apart in an explosion so powerful it flipped two eager Ork Trukks end over end, wreckage hurtling under the massive spiked treads of the Battlewagons behind them. The remaining Ork vehicles careened through the confusion, groups of Boyz sprinting forwards into the darkness in their haste to spill the blood of the invaders. Those still within the fortress could hear the din of battle in the unnatural mists, though the sounds were fading. When the rest of the Ork horde finally arrived, the invaders were long gone. Of the several hundred battle-hungry Orks that had rushed to intercept them, there was no sign.

SCOURGES

'You think that's summer rain falling? Ha! It is the blood of those who crossed the Scourges, boy. You cannot see them, but your foolish kin adorn the spires and crenellations of High Commorragh like grisly fruit upon the bough. Up there they bleed out their last, moaning and helpless, impaled through and through. No! Do not look upward! Catch a Watcher's eye and it will be your blood that rains down next…'

- Edric Shiverhand, Slave-Elder of Gomor Sump

If a trespasser were to climb amongst the jutting spars of upper Commorragh and stare past the highest peaks, he might just make out winged figures flitting and soaring upon the hot thermals of the city. Should he watch carefully, he might recognise them as the Scourge, Drukhari who have been refashioned into something far more deadly. If his gaze lingers too long, he will find those same figures arrowing through the flame-lit clouds toward him, seizing him and impaling him bodily upon the spires of their eyries.

Scourges are an intrinsic part of the lifeblood of Commorragh. The intrigues of the Dark City thrive on information, without which even the greatest Kabal is soon rendered impotent. Even the most secure transmission can be intercepted, and psychic communication is utterly forbidden. Instead the nobility of the Drukhari pay handsomely for the Scourges to take their missives to their destination by hand. Each communiqué is sealed with tailor-made toxins, the antidotes to which – in theory at least – are possessed only by the recipient. The Scourges are so vital to the intrigues of the Dark City that to kill one is to invite retribution from the upper echelons of Commorrite society, followed by a very painful demise.

Considered the pinnacle of body modification, the metamorphosis from Kabalite to Scourge is a lengthy and painful process. A rich and daring Drukhari may surrender themselves to the Haemonculi, requesting that their bones be hollowed out by the cold metal drills of a Talos, that bands of new muscle be grafted onto their torso, and powerful wings and adrenaline dispensers be attached to their shoulders so that they are capable of true flight. Even should these procedures be successful, the individual is still not considered a Scourge, for they must then fly all the way up to the trophy-strewn eyries to join with their new

brethren. Raw and bleeding wings carry the newly transformed from the oubliettes of the Haemonculi to the topmost spires in which the Scourges make their home, and the aspirant must fight through deadly fatigue, warring Hellion gangs, vicious Reavers and all manner of unnatural airborne terrors to get there. Those who make this vertical pilgrimage and still survive earn the right to call themselves a Scourge, one of an exclusive mercenary clique of sky warriors that look with disdain upon the earthbound kin they left behind.

Many Scourges – especially the veterans known as Solarites – are so far removed from their former lives that they grow quills from their skin, feathers in place of hair, or elongated skulls. No matter their appearance, they all relish the gory feasts of full-scale war. Because of this, and because of the wealth they earn from the Kabals, all Scourges equip themselves with highly advanced wargear. Their ghostplate body armour is supple and porous, made from hardened resins and shot through with pockets of lighter-than-air gas, which affords Scourges a substantial amount of protection without impinging upon their mobility. This armour also projects a small personal force field around its wearer, allowing the aerial predators to withstand even the most withering fire as they fly. Many thunderous flak salvoes have fallen silent only for a flock of Scourges to descend from the skies unharmed.

Scourges prefer to engage the foe at range, for they are protective of their expensively altered bodies. They lay down punishing barrages of fire, drinking in the screams of their enemies with their sharpened senses before redeploying and striking again. The weapons of the Scourges are hence devised to be fired on the wing. The most popular is without doubt the shardcarbine, an advanced iteration of the splinter rifle with a far higher rate of fire. A flock of Scourges armed with shardcarbines can swiftly lay down a hail of toxin-coated projectiles, mowing through infantry or toppling towering biological monstrosities in moments. When equipped with shredders, the winged mercenaries can release nets of barbed monofilament wire to slice through packed hordes of infantry. However, when facing a heavily mechanised foe, Scourges have a variety of other armaments with which they can sow destruction. The haywire blaster releases the electromagnetic energy of Commorragh's captive suns in a powerful burst, and the heat lance emits a scorching beam that can atomise a foe where he stands.

MANDRAKES

Within the shrouded corners of the labyrinth dimensions lurk all manner of nightmarish entities and subconscious terrors given form. Yet nowhere in the webway is more shrouded in dread than Aelindrach, where darkness itself has gained a sort of horrifying sentience, for it is the home of the creatures known as Mandrakes – a vile breed that is secretly feared even by other Drukhari. A Mandrake can pull itself into reality straight through another being's shadow, emerging with a hiss to sink its ice-cold claws and teeth into warm flesh. Their inky skin writhes with forbidden runes and their faces shift and flow, one moment sealing over into an expressionless mask, the next parting like a reopened wound filled with needle teeth.

Mandrakes exist both in reality and a cursed otherworld, and to fight them is to fight living shadow, for they are not fully corporeal. As their tangibility ebbs, shots pass harmlessly through them, though the same is not true of the Mandrakes' own attacks, which always land with visceral physicality. They are able to manifest anywhere that shadows gather in the gloom, and as such are a malevolent bane on night worlds and in war zones that are veiled in darkness. The planet Mordian – home to the Iron Guard regiments of the Astra Militarum – has endured multiple Mandrake attacks, the fiendish creatures appearing to butcher high-ranking officers before receding from reality once more.

The origins of the Mandrakes are shrouded. Some claim the Mandrakes descend from Aeldari who engaged in heinous union with unholy entities when their empire was at its most decadent. Others maintain that the mysterious stalkers are the successors of a forbidden cult that found its own way to escape the Fall, passing into shadow and emerging as something altogether more alien. Younger Drukhari call the Mandrakes 'creepers', whispering that they can slink from one shadow to another or crawl their way out of reflections to emerge in the real world. They believe that Mandrakes are unlight given life and, in many ways, they are right.

All these wild theories do not seem so far-fetched when one considers the Mandrakes' appearance. Their flesh is coal-dark and seems to absorb rather than reflect light, their features shift like oil, and their lank hair is as pale as splintered bone. Surrounding them is an aura of darkness and cold that saps the strength of those nearby – often the first sign of a Mandrake attack will be a thin rime of ice hanging in the air. The twisting shapes set into their flesh are sigils of destruction that pulse brightly whenever the Mandrake feeds upon the pain of its prey. Mandrakes are capable of channelling these stolen energies, shaping blasts of cold fire that roar out from their claws to freeze their victims in place. When they fall upon their shuddering prey they do so with not only talon and fang, but also with blood-encrusted glimmersteel blades that are reminiscent of the surgical tools of the Haemonculi.

Like all the denizens of Commorragh, the Mandrakes thrive on the malevolent infliction of pain, and because of their unsurpassed stealth many a Drukhari Archon has sought their services when mustering his forces for a realspace raid. The Mandrakes usually ask for slaves as payment, but sometimes they will ask for something far more esoteric, such as a heartbeat, a true name, or a voice. Few Kabalite lords know the real price that they are paying, yet such requests are rarely denied, for Mandrakes go to war clad in the patchwork skins of those that have jilted or betrayed them. They are infamous for their ability to track down their quarry, and when a cold claw closes upon an ankle or wrist in the darkness, the icy bite of the Mandrake is never far behind.

Even Asdrubael Vect was not safe from the reach of Aelindrach. Mandrakes penetrated every ward and sub-dimensional barrier guarding the Supreme Overlord's inner sanctum, emerging with blades in hand to butcher the most powerful Archon ever to have lived. When Vect appeared once more and declared himself the Living Dark Muse, he enacted swift and merciless retribution against every Commorrite who had shown even a hint of disloyalty – yet his wrath was not visited upon the Mandrakes. Perhaps it is because they were knowing players in his grand manoeuvre, or perhaps it is because they strike fear even in Vect's black heart.

> 'There is a very good reason why so many of the galaxy's cultures and societies are afraid of the dark.'
>
> – Inquisitor Bastalek Grimm

RAZORWING JETFIGHTERS

Through the vortex-torn mists of each Drukhari raid come the twin contrails of Razorwing Jetfighters, aircraft so fast that their fusillades of missile fire hits home at the instant the air is rent by the flyer's thunderous sonic boom.

Even the most conceited Archon knows that the armoured vehicles of the lesser races, though thuggish and unsubtle, are still potentially dangerous. A fleet of Raiders that is intercepted by well-directed artillery fire can often find itself repelled with unacceptable losses. To ensure that the foe cannot call upon such support, the Drukhari employ Razorwing Jetfighters to sow destruction and panic in the midst of the foe, for while the pilots of Razorwing Jetfighters are capable of running aerial interception, they are specialists in the wholesale slaughter of ground targets. There is little that these pilots like more than roaring through an inferno of their own creation whilst mowing down the terrified survivors scurrying below.

There are few enemies in realspace or beyond who are fast enough to outpace these aggressive and consummately skilled fighter craft. Each of their pilots was once an elite member of the Reaver jetbike gangs of Commorragh, and to them fighting at breakneck speed is second nature. Veterans of the Dark City's death races, they have earned through countless acts of spectacular violence enough wealth to escape the arenas forever, and now seek to maim and destroy everything they can find without risking their own skins. The Razorwing Jetfighter is the perfect tool for achieving this desire, a nigh-untouchable instrument of death and darkness.

Razorwing Jetfighters boast an array of diabolically effective missiles. When a squadron of Razorwings looses a salvo it often appears as if the ground is being raked by monstrous invisible talons. Most surgically efficient of all is the dreaded monoscythe missile, remotely steered by the fighter's pilot into the thick of the foe. The secret to their terrifying reputation is in their warheads; when detonated, they emit not a conventional blast but one that is constrained to a specific plane by complex inbuilt power-shields. A great horizontal sheet of force explodes outward at a certain height, decapitating or even cutting in half everyone caught in the blast zone. Such a clinical multiple kill is very satisfying to the jetfighter's pilot, for all Drukhari appreciate a well-administered death.

Necrotoxin missiles have a similarly devastating effect against hordes of lightly armoured enemies. Within the warhead of each missile is a large reservoir of virulent poisons; the warhead shatters upon impact, sending shards of toxin-coated shrapnel tearing through the flesh of huddled masses of victims. Those not instantly killed by the lacerating shower quickly succumb to the effects of brain-eating viruses and necro-dermal pathogens.

'They come for your souls, I've seen it. They've come to feed on your souls…'

- Oelle Blackwinter, Primaris Psyker

Perhaps the most morbidly inventive payload is that of the shatterfield missile. This warhead actually houses two separate detonation cores. The first of these drains the detonation zone of all thermal energy, transforming those caught in the blast to brittle statues; the second core then sends out a shock wave of percussive force that shatters its frozen victims into thousands of pieces.

Along with its missiles, each Razorwing Jetfighter also bears an array of other armaments with which it can reap the souls from its prey, including a pair of cannons mounted on the wings. Those pilots who take sadistic glee in mowing through ranks of infantry tend to favour disintegrator cannons. These highly sophisticated guns fire particles of unstable matter harnessed from stolen suns to swiftly atomise even heavily armoured targets. Other Razorwings are instead fitted with a pair of dark lances, allowing their pilots to impale rumbling war engines and monstrous beasts with beams of darklight energy. But all of these craft bear nose-mounted twin splinter rifles, which afford the perfect vantage point for the pilot to see their victims torn to shreds.

In silhouette, Razorwing Jetfighters appear like jagged, double-edged blades, their crescent wings and sword-sharp curves conveying their lethal power. Due to their deadliness, they are also a symbol of elevated status, and pilots have been known to adorn their craft with the skins of enemies they have slain, both in realspace and within Commorragh.

VOIDRAVEN BOMBERS

Though the Drukhari consider the Voidraven Bomber to be the ultimate in heavy weapons deployment, it is still capable of outstripping even the more agile fighter crafts of the Imperium with ease. The Voidraven shares many similarities with the Razorwing Jetfighter, having distinctive sickled wings and comparable aerodynamic design, but it carries a far larger and more deadly payload than its smaller cousin – the dreaded void mine.

Much like the pilots of Razorwing Jetfighters, Voidraven Bomber pilots are veterans of the death races that take place amidst the tall spires of High Commorragh. Speed is in their blood, and they think nothing of breakneck aerial manoeuvres that would kill a lesser steersman. It is not the pilot of the Voidraven Bomber that defines its role, however. It is the gunner at its front that is the true maestro in the symphony of mayhem that the Drukhari inflict upon their prey.

At the fore of each Voidraven is a crystal pod housing a saddle much like that upon a Reaver's jetbike, surrounded by targeting holographs and crosshair runes that flicker and dance over the gunner's unwitting prey. Ensconced within this lavishly appointed cocoon, the Voidraven's gunner will unleash searing fusillades from the craft's primary guns – either dark scythes that rake the foe with darklight, or void lances that fire pulses of energy harvested from beyond the shattered spars of the webway.

Unlike the Razorwing Jetfighter, whose pilots rejoice in the ear-splitting crack-boom of its passage, the Voidraven Bomber mounts complex sonic dampers that completely obscure the sound of its engines. Often the first an enemy emplacement will know of a Voidraven's presence is when twin beams sear great scars into whatever defensive artillery they might have employed against it.

Once the gunner has ensured that they can work without interruption, they will deploy the craft's void mine from the Voidraven's weapon nacelles. The void mine, delivered with pinpoint accuracy, detonates not one but two warheads, one a split second before the other. The first has no direct effect, for it merely establishes a sphere of force, a bubble in reality that protects everything outside and condemns everything within. The second contains a particle of purest darklight, released from its containment field by the primary detonation. The effects of introducing even a tiny amount of darklight into realspace are catastrophic. If it were not for the force sphere established by the primary detonation the resultant implosion would destroy not only the enemy but also the Voidraven into the bargain. As it is, though, anything trapped inside the crackling sphere is annihilated. All that is left is a smoking, hemispherical crater scooped out of the earth and the contrails of the rapidly disappearing Voidraven high above.

Even after it has deployed its devastating void mine, a Voidraven is still more than capable of annihilating the enemy with its arsenal. Shatterfield missiles employ similar twin-detonation technology to that of the void mine, whereas implosion missiles cause those caught within their blast to collapse inward at a molecular level. Meanwhile, the Voidraven Bomber itself is kept safe from return fire by its night shield, which projects a broad-spectrum displacement field around the craft, shrouding it in inky darkness and confounding enemy auto-targeting augurs.

DRUKHARI BOMBARDMENTS

Though unquestionably effective, the armaments of a Voidraven Bomber are in some ways counter-productive to the needs of a raid. For the Drukhari to sustain their withered souls they must drink in the suffering of their victims, yet weapons such as the void mine obliterate their targets so completely that the bounty of anguish is squandered. However, by annihilating defensive structures and heavily armoured targets, a Voidraven Bomber allows the rest of its raiding party to close upon the enemy's position, where they can revel in a degree of close-range slaughter that more than makes up for the initial loss of torment. Against some armies, though, the void mine itself is the perfect tool for extracting agony. The Adeptus Mechanicus – ever eager to harvest data from battle – often marches columns of Skitarii warriors directly into the path of bombing runs in the hope they will glean some morsel of information from within the void mine's reality bubble. These hopes are, of course, in vain. Furthermore, despite the Tech-Priest's beliefs that their creations are free from the frailties of flesh, the destruction of so many living bodies creates a haze of latent pain that the Voidraven Bomber pilots find delectable.

SUCCUBI

The Succubi are the ruling elite of the Wych Cults. Impossibly elegant and beautiful, they stalk through the mayhem of battle as if born to it, surrounded by cliques of their lethal handmaidens who search out worthy alien opponents for their mistresses to slay. Long-limbed and athletic, each is famous across Commorragh for the grace and flair of her kills. The Succubi are the true icons of the gladiatorial arenas, and when they are in full flow they enjoy an envy as close to veneration as the Drukhari ever get.

Sometimes informally referred to as archites, arena queens or pain maidens, Succubi are collectively known as the *ynnitach*, or 'brides of death'. Each Wych Cult is traditionally ruled over by a council of three such figures, though certain Cults have a dozen or more Succubi comprising their upper echelons. One Succubus tends to hold the true power, whilst those below her constantly try to outdo each other in the magnificence of their gladiatorial spectacles, always seeking to increase their dominance and popularity. Competition is fierce between them, though unlike the immortal games of the Archons, the queens of the Wych Cults are far more likely to resolve their feuds with a perfectly executed decapitation than with a twist of the political knife. But as with all the Drukhari elite, the Succubi temporarily put aside these rivalries when leading their Wych Cults on realspace raids.

Succubi are intensely vain, and not without good reason. With each appearance they make in the arenas of Commorragh they draw enormous crowds who come to see their elegant butchery. Yet the crowds demand not only a bloody spectacle, but one that is pleasing to their perverse aesthetic. Wyches with one too many scars will often find themselves up against insurmountable odds, their fellow combatants turning in unison on them as the crowds clamour for them to die first, purely for the crime of being imperfect. Only those who epitomise hypnotic allure and deadly skill ever make it to the ranks of the ynnitach.

The Succubi of the Wych Cults aggressively guard their beauty, and as a result are ravishing in their physical appearance, with supple alabaster flesh clasped within bladed corsets and high-necked bodysuits of liquid silk. Their every movement is entrancing, and their sinuous, serpentine grace is almost hypnotic as they flow through the battle towards their prey. A Succubus will do almost anything to preserve her stunning aspect, including putting dozens of lesser warriors to a gruesome death moments before she enters the arena, feeding on their last gasps of anguish in order to better present a youthful sheen.

When she descends from her lush aerial quarters onto the field of battle it is with the arrogance and majesty of a cruel-hearted queen. Though each Succubus may be delicious upon the eye, theirs is a cold and haughty allure, and one who observed a Succubus with witch-sight would like as not see a shrivelled abomination instead of a merciless beauty of the flesh.

Many of the greatest Succubi seek to transcend the earthly violence of the arena and become one with the act of the kill itself. It is these most exemplary of warriors that follow in the wake of the Dark Muses, hoping to become synonymous with a certain style of murder in their own right. Currently amongst their ranks are the lethally amorous Helica Venomkiss, Yctria the Flayer Queen – whose flaring temper is legend – and of course Lelith Hesperax, who once famously decapitated a dozen rival Wyches with her signature bladed pirouette.

No Succubus is secure in her position without constant and undeniable proof of her skill. They regularly take the lead in the war against realspace, not only for the feast of plunder but also to hunt the champions of the lesser races and defeat them in showy displays of sheer skill. Though the Drukhari generally look upon the defenders of Humanity with contempt, a Succubus would gladly duel a Chapter Master of the Adeptus Astartes, for even in Commorragh such a kill carries serious prestige. It is not unusual for the trophy collections of a Succubus to boast the head of an Ork Warboss, a synapse-beast of the Tyranid hive fleets or, most coveted of all, an Autarch of the craftworlds. Aside from the sheer adrenaline-pumping thrill of it, each such personal conquest is an opportunity for a Succubus to prove her supremacy with a trophy kill – the more witnesses the better.

LELITH HESPERAX

QUEEN OF KNIVES

Lelith is the undisputed champion of the gladiatorial arenas. Most deadly of all her kind, Lelith's skill in the arts of combat bear all the hallmarks of true genius. Lelith is grace embodied, her movements hypnotic, sensual and spellbinding – watching Lelith go about her blood-soaked business is a privilege that only the wealthiest Drukhari can afford. To see such a superbly talented Succubus perform first-hand is a dream come true for most Kabalites, for the agonising beauty of her kills energises and reinvigorates even the eldest of their kind.

Though the purr of her voice has been likened to honeyed velvet, Lelith rarely speaks, for she is an artiste, not a politician. Nonetheless, her pronouncements are always carried out to the letter by her handmaidens in the Cult of Strife, who look in jealous awe at their mistress's flawless form and supernatural physical dexterity. On the eve before a realspace raid, Lelith will often pad like a hunting-cat into the halls of an Archon preparing for battle, flanked by dozens of hand-picked Wych acolytes. Lady Hesperax blesses raiding Kabals with her presence in this manner only in order to search out unusual prey; she loves to match her abilities against the most formidable elites and champions in the galaxy. She has yet to return without blood upon her blades and a new clutch of grisly trophies for her private museums.

Alone amongst the Wych Cults, Lelith does not use combat drugs to enhance her performance. The Succubus prefers to fight up close, and considers the use of narcotics to be for the weak, for they corrupt the instant where the killing strike hits home and the lifeblood flows out. How can one properly appreciate the delicate nuances of a victim's dying breath when one's senses are polluted by intoxicants? For Lelith, the purest way to enhance the sensory exhilaration of slaughter is by her own hand, and as such her every strike is unique, an improvement upon the last so that the dose of agony she is afforded from her victims is ever increased. To forsake the use of chemical enhancement in this way is usually suicidal in the lightning-fast world of the arena, yet such is Lelith's prowess that her pristine flesh remains scarless – almost.

The harpies of the rival Wych Cults whisper that Lelith's incredible skill is from an unnatural source – that she has somehow persuaded the Haemonculi to replace her blood with hyperdrenaline; that as a child she suckled upon a steroid-syringe; that she sleeps in a baryonic sarcophagus filled to the brim with stimulant serum. The truth is far simpler – she is a born predator with a singular drive to perfect the art of murder.

Lelith's disciples in the Cult of Strife maintain that their mistress needs nothing more than a piece of edged steel to outclass her foes. Sure enough, although she is expert in the use of all the exotic weapons used by her kind, Lelith can most frequently be seen fighting with two simple but perfectly weighted knives. As she darts around her opponents, her blades moving in a blur, she uses her mane of silky hair – sewn through with barbs and hooks – to snare the blades of her foes much in the manner of the shardnets of the Yraqnae. Her long legs and bare feet are edged with spurs, the better to tear open a throat with a perfect pirouette kick, and her fingernails have been reinforced and honed to scalpel sharpness. Lelith can kill a dozen lesser warriors in the space of a few seconds, her knives tracing a spiralling path between each fatal slash, before finishing with flourish and poise. Indeed, vid-steals of her doing so are traded throughout Commorragh and beyond by those with a twisted taste for violence. Perhaps, her spectators say, it is not only mortals who gaze with rapt attention as Lelith weaves her deadly dance.

After battling and defeating Yvraine in the Crucibael, Lelith has gone on to join forces with the Reborn leader, committing much of the strength of the Cult of Strife to the war against Slaanesh. The Queen of Knives and her Wyches, along with allies from the craftworlds and Harlequin Troupes, fight alongside the Ynnari, allowing the Succubus to showcase her exquisite blade-work against the Chaos hordes infesting the Imperium Nihilus. Although this confluence of Aeldari ostensibly has a singular goal – the annihilation of She Who Thirsts – Lelith has her own reasons for stabbing out into the galaxy. Her greatest desire is to locate and capture Lucius the Eternal, the Chaos Lord of the Emperor's Children famed for his martial prowess and repeated resurrections. Were she to return Lucius to the Dark City and strip him of his Slaanesh-cursed armour, she could face him one-on-one in the Crucibael in what would be the greatest duel Commorragh has ever seen.

> *'It is true there has never been one like her before, and by her blades Lelith will ensure no other Drukhari will ever attain more admiration than she within the arena. Yet she has sided with Yvraine – that prophetess of a false god – and in doing so has committed her Cult to a dangerous course. But I have planned for this eventuality. It has always been Lelith's way to seek the path most challenging, and as much as she vexes me, I find the Queen of Knives a useful subject. Let her follow the Emissary. It suits me for now.'*
>
> *- Asdrubael Vect*

WYCHES

The Wych Cults of Commorragh are second in prestige only to the Kabals that sponsor them. The Drukhari thrive upon expert displays of bloodletting, and in the craft of murder the Wyches are talented indeed. Gladiatorial fighters and athletes without equal, the Wyches are true artistes of physical combat. Although most of the Hekatarii, as the Wyches call themselves, are female, few Cults actively discriminate by sex – any Drukhari possessed of enough skill and agility may be trained for arena combat. The weak are thinned soon enough from the ranks of a Cult, and their brutal deaths serve as useful training for more worthy combatants.

Close-range kills are invigorating to the Drukhari, for the pain that comes at the point of a blade provides a feast of energy to sustain their withered souls. This tendency is magnified in the Cults of the Wyches, whose curved knives flicker out like the tongues of serpents as they bathe in the proximity of each wound. The knife is symbolic to the Wych Cults; each is artisan-crafted and kept in a sheath with an inbuilt sharpening field to ensure it stays eternally keen. Wyches are typically bestowed knives of a weight and shape unique to their Cult, the subtle specificities of curvature and resonance serving as a type of signature. Known in the arenas as Hekatarii blades, each is a symbol of its bearer's bond to their Cult, and each Wych is capable of slaughtering great swathes of enemies armed only with this most pure of weapons.

Though Wyches are driven to achieve perfection in combat, it is rare that a given Wych will adhere to a single style of fighting for more than a decade or two before adopting a new method of murder. The Drukhari hunger constantly for new experiences to excite their senses, and mastering ever more extreme forms of combat prevents Wyches from becoming inured to the atrocities they inflict. The manifold fighting styles of the Wych Cults are all based on cunning and deception. They wield a variety of outlandish weapons that can whip out, extend, enmesh, retract, split in two, or snap an opponent's blade with the twist of a supple wrist. Many Wyches have weaponry that they continually return to. Amongst their number are the Lacerai, who use segmented razorflails that can split apart and lash out like whips; the Hydrae, who use crystal gauntlets of extra-planar origin that can sprout and regrow a deadly profusion of blades; and the Yraqnae, who use electrified shardnets and extendable twin-bladed impalers to ensure their quarry cannot escape alive.

Despite their penchant for close-quarters executions, most Wyches carry splinter pistols and plasma grenades with them when they embark upon a realspace raid. In this way they are able to quickly cut through the rank-and-file troops the foe places in front of them before closing ground with more desirable opponents, such as warlords or towering monstrosities. To prove one's skill against such an enemy is the desire of all Wyches, and they will fight amongst each other to land the killing blow.

All Wyches take great pride in their appearance. They enter the fray dressed with as much care as if going to meet a lover, for each battle is a chance to parade their art. Regardless of their Cult, Wyches wear the bladed armour of the arena over one side of an impeccably elegant and skintight bodysuit. The other side has sections cut away to expose naked flesh, bared as if to tempt death himself. Aside from creating a striking aesthetic, this affords the wearer a great deal of manoeuvrability, allowing them to easily outpace foes who wear more cumbersome armour.

Wyches use a variety of distilled combat drugs that galvanise them to ever-greater heights of balletic dexterity. Depending on which intoxicating cocktail is coursing through their veins, a Wych may display sudden bursts of strength or become all but impervious to pain. So enhanced, a gladiatrix of the Cults can roll, backflip and pirouette out of harm's way, stabbing through visors and neck-joints, slicing open a throat here and piercing a heart there. They flow around the blows of their opponents like water, their expressions of aloof disdain melting away into savage smiles as they feed upon each fresh scream of pain. Even when an enemy squad attempts to run from the carnage being meted out by the Wyches, they will often find themselves blocked off at every turn and unable to escape their own slaughter.

Each squad of Wyches is led by a Hekatrix, who in turn reports to the Wych Cult's Succubi. Rivalry between these Hekatrixes is fierce, as each strives to outshine their peers with ever-more inventive acts of murder, and they ruthlessly punish the Wyches they lead for the slightest imperfections in their deadly art. On occasion, several Hekatrixes will gather together into a single malevolent clique. Calling themselves Bloodbrides, they anoint themselves with the blood of the foe in a dark testament to their own prowess.

REAVERS

The Reavers of Commorragh are fascinated by the art of war at speed. They ride to battle upon the most streamlined and pared-down of all skycraft – the anti-grav jetbike, a perfect fusion of raw motive power and finely honed lethality.

The Aeldari experience sensations to a far greater degree than any other race, and their psyches are easily given to obsession. Reavers, having cultivated a taste for high-speed violence during realspace raids, are Drukhari consumed with the act of the maximum-impact kill. It is not enough for them to end a life, or to fly through the air at breakneck velocity – these black-hearted gladiators must accomplish both at once to be truly sated. The instant of a well-placed and fatal blow delivered at obscene speed is a spike of murderous joy that the Reavers consider the ultimate thrill.

In the toroid arenas that girdle the highest spires, the Reavers duel amongst themselves for supremacy. Here these vain and ultra-competitive riders engage in nightly death races, their craft screaming round each arena in running battle for the edification of the bloodthirsty crowd. No quarter is asked for nor given in these races, for to come last is literally a death sentence. Reavers will pull every trick they can to secure even a millisecond's advantage. The arena champions endlessly modify their craft's vanes and blast-engines, fit targeting holograms for their in-built weaponry, pierce their craft's fairings so that the shriek of their passage is a different pitch to that of their peers, and wear flexible 'second skins' to cut down on air resistance.

All Reavers use stimulants to enhance their performance in the death races. They are cheats and liars all, and respect only the 'elegant kill' – it is considered gauche to merely maim a fellow driver, whereas a well executed drop-down inverted decapitation can warm the icy heart of even the most jaded Archon.

Because of their no-holds-barred approach, weapons are used extensively in the death races. Some of the most celebrated Reavers employ underslung grav-talons to push their rivals into the artfully bladed contours of the arena, or release clusters of proximity-sensing anti-grav caltrops that detonate in spectacular chain explosions behind them.

The Reavers are so attuned to their beloved jetbikes that in battle they use them as extensions of their own bodies. Though the Reaver jetbike typically houses a splinter rifle, the craft itself is the rider's favoured killing tool. The Reavers pilot their jetbikes with such uncanny precision that they can take off a head or even slash open a throat with a single pass of the keel blade. A favoured tactic is to dive down from the clouds above the battlefield in a streak of dark metal, corkscrewing the craft at the last moment so that the razored edges of their bladevanes dismember those unfortunates they zoom past – or, in some cases, straight through.

Those who survive the arenas take the tricks they have learnt and put them to deadly use on the battlefields of realspace. Compared to the high-speed opponents they are used to facing, most soldiers from the lesser races seem slow and lumbering. Reavers will always find ways to add excitement to the combat, however, often competing with one another to see who can achieve the swiftest or most spectacular kill.

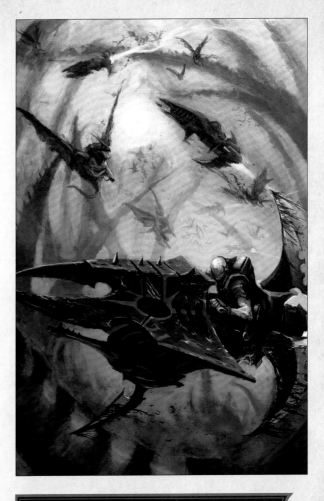

THE CORELOOP GAUNTLET

The aerial arenas in which the Reavers race are designed to enable a wide variety of horrific deaths. Each is laced with all manner of barbaric traps, such as pyro-mines or hives of lung-wasps, into which pilots can shunt their foes. The Coreloop Gauntlet is no exception. Its track consists of a massive vertical loop extending from the high spires of Commorragh down to the filth-ridden slums, passing through several pocket dimensions which – in reality – are located in far distant corners of the webway. Until recently, the highlight for most racers and spectators was when the track reached its nadir, where the Reavers had to navigate a series of spars composed of fossilised corpse-matter. Those Reavers who crashed into the pillars were not always killed outright – instead they tumbled down the osseous cliffs to the floor below, where their broken bodies were torn limb from limb by the soul-starved ghouls who lurked there. The desolate sub-realm containing this portion of the track has now been added to the Chasm of Woe, though this has not halted the races. The gates to and from the bony canyon still open when Reavers approach, but now when they fall they are consumed not by withered Drukhari, but by ravenous packs of Slaaneshi Daemonettes.

HELLIONS

Commorragh's bruised skies are home to war zones that are just as perilous as its barrios and shrouded spires. Through the acrid mists soar arrogant lordlings and winged killers on the hunt. The most savage of these airborne terrors are the Hellions, gangs of feral Drukhari that descend upon their prey in a flurry of hooked blades before hurtling away to safety.

Hellions are reprobates and miscreants without exception. Their numbers include aspirants not yet old enough to be chosen as Kabalites, those who have been cast out or exiled by their Archons, and those who have rejected the Kabals in favour of a lifetime of independence. Packs of Hellions haunt the desolate regions of the Dark City, existing on their wits alone, and they take pride in the scars and bruises of their savage lives. To increase the chances of survival, Hellions gather together into large gangs, some of which are as numerous as a minor Kabal.

Hellion gangs have fierce rivalries with the Reavers and Scourges of the upper levels, for they resent above all those who flaunt privilege and status. Though Hellions might outwardly maintain that they live for the terror and anarchy of the mean streets, each secretly burns with ambition to become a power in their own right.

Hellions ride to war upon skyboards, single-pilot anti-gravity platforms that are highly prized as symbols of independence. Each skyboard is personalised with trophies and glyphs, though most have changed hands several times, won in ritual knife-fights or claimed as bounty. Often they will be bedecked

with the severed heads of several previous owners. Skyboards are sensitive to the slightest pressure; because of this, and for the sheer thrill of it, Hellions take combat drugs that enhance their reactions still further until they can flip and jink at incredible speed, their reflexes as sharp as their artfully filed teeth.

Unpredictable and wild, Hellions attack the Kabals just as often as they participate in realspace raids. It is unusual for the Archons to bring their wrath to bear in return, for they consider such street scum beneath their notice, and a bounty hunter skilled enough to bring a particular Hellion to the torture chambers of his employers is rare indeed. Nonetheless, Hellions make for valued terror troops, and the Helliarchs that lead them are not above dealing with the Kabals and Wych Cults – for the right price, of course. Many realspace invasions are led by waves of howling, drug-crazed Hellions.

When not participating in realspace raids or their own aerial turf wars, Hellions can often be found fighting in the arenas of the Wych Cults. Every night the Cults scout out the sky-battles, looking for Hellions whose skill and panache could draw an audience. Those chosen are given the opportunity to hone their dogfighting skills against all manner of alien enemies. The skyboard riders are a perennial favourite amongst spectators, for invariably they either dispatch their opponents in some spectacular fashion or are themselves torn screaming from the sky.

For heightened excitement, the Wych Cults supply Hellions with all manner of deadly weaponry: barbed grapnels known as stunclaws that are used to yank other riders from their boards, toxin-soaked whips called agonisers that drive their target's sensorium haywire, and duelling blades sheathed in power fields that can slice through the thickest armour or chitin. However, the signature weapon carried by almost all Hellions is the hellglaive, a double-bladed polearm with recurved hooks that allow a skilled wielder to latch onto nearby objects and change direction in a heartbeat. Each hellglaive is kept murderously sharp – it is common for Hellions to 'call' a particular part of the body they intend to cut off with each pass. Such is their skill that a swarm of Hellions can fall upon a knot of enemies and lop off limbs and heads before scattering once more, carrying between them a single choice victim who is borne into the skies to be taken apart at the Hellions' leisure.

BEASTMASTERS

In the millennia since Commorragh's founding, its sand-filled arenas have drunk the blood of millions. Each site has played host to countless spectacles of perversity and death, as the Drukhari have worked their cruelties on hundreds of thousands of alien species, including their own. But there is one gladiatorial favourite that never fades in popularity – the wild hunts of the Beastmasters.

The Beastmasters themselves are technically part of the Wych Cults, though in contrast to the Hekatarii the majority of their number are male. Some suspect they are part of a shamanic tradition, for when the Beastmasters go to battle, they wear totems and masks echoing the nature of the alien predators under their control. It is partially because of these artefacts that they enjoy such mastery over their ferocious beasts, for their masks harbour complex sonic emitters and pheromone traps that augment the wearer's ability to subjugate savage creatures. But even unmasked Beastmasters have a natural ability to dominate, and the most senior of their number can subdue a rampant Megasaur with little more than a baleful glare.

When accompanying a realspace raid, Beastmasters gladly involve themselves in the business of bloodletting. They hover above the gore-spattered ground upon skyboards modified to automatically swoop around hazards, leaving the Beastmasters free to goad their charges into the fray with whip and lure. Splinter pods slung beneath the skyboard spit hails of toxin-coated shards, cutting through the closest enemies before the hunting pack even reaches them, and when the Beastmaster finally crashes into the staggering ranks they lay about themselves until their enemies are torn to shreds. Only when the prey has been thoroughly butchered does a Beastmaster allow their slavering pets to devour the dead and dying.

The arenas of the Dark City have played host to a broad variety of dangerous creatures, including blade-legged Helspiders, hyper-violent Bhargesi, and even captured Adeptus Astartes warriors. Only a handful of species have remained in continual use, however, their natural savagery making their every kill a spectacle worthy of the audience's attention. It is these creatures that are driven to battle in packs by the Beastmasters.

The largest of the perennial beasts is the Donorian Clawed Fiend. Long ago the main webway portal into the Donorian System split under the pressure of a warp storm, and the tunnels that spread out from it became infested with Fiends. The Clawed Fiend is a towering hulk of muscle and fur that has extremely advanced senses, able to see in several spectrums at once. A Clawed Fiend enters a berserk state when it is wounded, its hex-valved hearts pumping vast quantities of blood to its muscles so that it can eviscerate whatever creature injured it. Despite their hulking size, these monstrosities are also terrifyingly swift, and few warriors are quick enough to evade a raging Fiend that has scented the rotten tang of its own ichor.

The warp-beasts called Khymerae are living proof of the Beastmasters' skills as a spirit-hunter. Each Khymera is a denizen of the chaotic dimension known as the empyrean, borne from the stuff of a Daemon world. These strange non-creatures coalesce around vivid nightmares as a pearl forms around grit, taking the shape of a long-fanged, many-eyed, sinewy beast riven with juts of bone and horn-tipped tentacles. Beastmasters must hunt down and harness their own Khymerae in perilous fugues or dream-quests. Should they fail, their soul will be devoured by the malefic entities of that realm – but if they are successful, they can draw entire packs of Khymerae back across the veil to the physical dimension to do their bidding. Khymerae set loose onto the battlefields of realspace can wreak utter havoc, and Beastmasters know to funnel that savagery towards their enemies before the empyric creatures fade out of corporeality once more.

Of all the alien terrors employed by the Beastmasters, the Razorwing remains one of the most popular. These raptors are swift of wing enough to catch all but the quickest enemies, and they are possessed of an insatiable hunger for bone. When encountered individually these carnivorous raptors are only moderately deadly, but when grouped together in flocks – as is their natural instinct – Razorwings can pick apart whole squads of foes, falling upon them with sharp feathers and razored beaks, stripping flesh from frame in a hurricane of frantic motion. Nor do they stop there, for a well-trained Razorwing flock will parade their blood-slicked and skeletal prize around and above their masters before tearing it apart in one final, savage feeding frenzy.

HAEMONCULI

Ancient and horrific, the Haemonculi are deranged flesh-sculptors that dwell in the dark bowels of Commorragh. They are master torturers, true connoisseurs of pain that revel in every nuance of the suffering they inflict. To while away the centuries, they craft long symphonies of agony from those unfortunates held captive in their oubliettes and dungeons. All Drukhari secretly fear the Haemonculi, for they are alchemists not just of the body but also of the soul.

The Covens of the Haemonculi are integral to the survival of Commorrite society due to their mastery of regenerative practices, yet they remain objects of terror and suspicion. All know that to earn the ire of the Lords of Pain is to end up on the slab oneself. Haemonculi specialise in body modification and alteration, and they delight in getting their claws into fresh new subjects. A client may desire barbed quills upon their shoulders, the scaled face of a snake, or to have their eyes replaced by those of a Viridian wraithspider – no request is too bizarre for these inhuman surgeons. The Haemonculi are only too willing to show off their skills with scalpel and hyper-steroid, teeth bared in glee all the while.

Though they take great pride in their creations of flesh, each Haemonculus draws even more pleasure from the pain they inflict through their work. For their purposes, suffering is the fire that allows them to mould their subjects' psyches into new and twisted shapes, and the Haemonculi know full well how to delay the death that would ordinarily culminate from such extreme levels of pain. It is possible that amongst the elder Haemonculi are those who initiated the very first cults of pleasure and pain, yet each Haemonculus has altered themselves so drastically that they no longer resemble those they mockingly call their people.

Despite their peculiar modifications, Haemonculi are always attenuated and twisted. Their sparse alabaster frames have not an ounce of fat upon them, quite unlike those of their more wild creations, and their waspish waists are devoid of internal organs to better present a fashionably disturbing appearance. Some Haemonculi harbour their viscera, lungs and heart in a muscled hunk of meat that sprouts from their shoulders, a rich repository for stimulants and elixirs that often boasts secondary limbs of its own. Others replace their blood so that searing ichor or even acid flows through their modified veins. Their spines are elongated and extended – from the lower back, their vertebrae meld into whipping prehensile bone-tails that can curl around the throats of their prey. From the upper backs sprout antler-like protrusions of bony matter that often frame the Haemonculus' head, hung with peculiar syringes and drug dispensers that channel directly into their spinal sump.

Being functionally immortal, the Haemonculi feel no need for the undignified rushing of younger Drukhari. They move with an ethereal grace, sometimes held aloft by powerful suspensor crystals, sometimes slithering along on elongated spine-tails. Unhurried and patient, they know that to grant a truly interesting death takes time. Over the millennia their tastes become increasingly exotic – a Haemonculus might dine only on the left hands of his victims, or sup with withered lips from a fluted glass full of tears. Having transcended common notions of wealth, they prize unusual ingredients for their alchemical elixirs – the heart of an Arbites judge, distilled into a few drops of liquid, may yield a striking flavour of pure resolve, whereas the essence of a once-proud planetary governor gives a tang of vainglory that thrills on their black, pointed tongues.

In battle, the sinister Haemonculi orchestrate the carnage around them with the passion of an artist. They drift across the landscape with a macabre elegance, gifting those too slow to escape with one unimaginably painful death after another. The wargear they use is taken straight from their oubliettes, and is capable of causing uncontrollable growths with a single touch or desiccating their foes in an instant. Other Haemonculi carry even more esoteric weapons, such as the crucible of malediction – a receptacle filled with the essence of tortured psykers. Should a Haemonculus die, they do so with a leering grin etched upon their face, for they will soon be back to seek an inventive revenge.

URIEN RAKARTH

SCULPTOR OF TORMENTS

Twisted beyond measure, the being known as Urien Rakarth has such a mastery over the arts of the flesh that he has died and risen back to life time and time again. A depraved genius in the fields of bodily manipulation and anatomical sculpture, Rakarth's skill as a fleshcrafter is legendary. Though he once played key roles in many of the intrigues that bind Commorragh, he has transcended the need to involve himself in such petty squabbles over power and prestige. Now, only the most grandiose transmogrifications of Commorrite society pique his interest – those that allow him to revel in the depravity of his twisted imagination.

Urien's wizened body has long passed the ability to regain the glory of a recently fed Drukhari, for he is several thousand years old. Over that great span Urien has perished to bolt, flame, blade, bullet, toxin, eviscerator and more grisly fates besides. Each time he dies, Urien's remains are used to slowly grow another iteration of the Master Haemonculus, through the regeneration process of which he is the progenitor. Each of his surgically altered bones holds the key to a dark resurrection; Rakarth has crossed the veil so many times that he savours death like a fine wine, revelling in the peaks of agony and the transcendent knowledge that comes with each new demise.

In recent centuries, however, something seems to have been corrupted across his repeated renewals – either accidentally or by Urien's own design – and his latest incarnations have each borne unintended vestiges of the one before. So it is that Urien is now a truly horrific sight, his compound spines sprouting from his back in baroque profusion and his leering face tied onto his skull with cords of leathery flesh. Rakarth boasts many sets of limbs: some stripped, silvered and re-strung as fully functional appendages, some atrophied and disturbing, pushing out of his many-spined sump to beckon weakly at those nearby. So profoundly have these constant regenerations affected Urien's metabolism that his artificially toughened flesh is able to reknit and heal at an incredible rate. Rakarth welcomes all forms of injury, especially upon the battlefield, for it forces him to adapt his body to accommodate the wound.

Like all Haemonculi, Urien has an undying enthusiasm for crafting symphonies of pain. He carries a variety of strange weapons to war, including a gauntlet that can inject his own highly mutagenic ichor into his foes and a blade that can kill with the slightest scratch. Rather than covering his amorphous body in bulky armour, he simply abstracts it further by using a clone field to project multiple overlapping hololight images of himself onto the battlefield. Thus obscured, he is able to avoid his enemies' attacks, allowing him to concentrate on harvesting choice subjects for use in his torturous experiments. To aid in the harvest Urien carries the Casket of Flensing – an impossibly intricate puzzle-box that, when opened, unleashes a swarm of evil spirits upon his victims. The souls rip the flesh from the heads of their prey with needle-like fangs, before tearing skulls from spinal columns and carrying them back to Urien with the still-conscious brains left writhing inside.

Despite the panoply of cruel artefacts that Urien possesses, the true weapons of this demented fiend are the repugnant creations that shamble out from his flesh-pens – a menagerie of horrors that strains the sanity of all who behold it. Blood-spattered Wracks and towering Grotesques stalk between living sculptures that moan and stagger as rapacious Haemovores writhe in the gore beneath. At the head of this gruesome procession comes Rakarth himself, theatrically conducting the carnage about him like a ringmaster at some hellish circus. Such a masterful performance demands an appreciative audience, and to this end Rakarth often deigns to enter realspace accompanied by a Kabal or Wych Cult. To set his creations loose upon the field of battle is not just to ensure the demise of his enemies, but to display his latest masterpieces to his fellow Drukhari, and ensure he continues to be regarded as a true artist within the Dark City.

To his faint amusement, competition is extremely fierce for the honour of the Master Haemonculus' presence. Few spectacles are as extreme as the gnashing, thrashing carnival of pain Rakarth unleashes upon his prey. For this reason, Commorragh was abuzz when the Sculptor of Torments announced he would display his craft openly at the wake of Asdrubael Vect. Archons from every corner of the Dark City came to view the grim spectacle, little knowing it was they who would become the subjects of Urien's latest masterpiece.

> 'I have long taken an interest in humans and their crude dabbling in fleshcraft. The Adeptus Astartes are powerful warriors, but their creators have always been too restricted in their vision. This Primarch, Roboute Guilliman, occludes his mind to so many possibilities, and as such will never achieve the perfection he seeks – the perfection that I define through the practise of my craft. If he wishes to learn from the master, let him come to me. I will gladly make room for him in my grandest oubliette.'
>
> - Urien Rakarth

WRACKS

Each Wrack is an abhorrent example of his master's surgical craftsmanship, an individual cut apart and refashioned into a walking instrument of torture. Masked and modified to better instil fear into those they encounter, they act as the hands of the Haemonculi in the world outside, and upon the field of battle they will defend their creators with their lives.

Every ruler needs obedient servants, and Wracks are literally fashioned for the task. Known in some circles as Haemacolytes, each Wrack's sole duty is to dutifully serve their master, whether at the slab or upon the battlefield. To this end they are physically modified to better perform their gory duties. Within the Wrack's surgically enhanced frame lies a shocking strength, and in combat they lay about themselves with a variety of sickled blades, corrosive whips, stun-rods and silvered hooks.

Because Haemonculi tend towards megalomania or even delusions of godhood, they surround themselves with supplicants and minions to enact their orders. In fact, most Haemonculi prefer not to sully themselves with physical labour of any kind, and consider themselves somehow polluted if they have to exert themselves in any way. Instead, the dirty work of each Haemonculus is performed by his Wracks. Most Wracks hope to one day transcend their previous lives entirely – a Wrack will endure almost any degradation in the hope that they may eventually ascend to the ranks of the Coven lords. A typical scene in the oubliettes and laboratories of the Haemonculi is a single figure looming over a partially dissected victim whilst hunched Wracks scrabble to enact every disturbing command.

Wracks often have heavy metal gauntlets grafted in place of their hands that can inject or withdraw fluids from their subjects with the flex of a wire-taut tendon, or be coated with searing venom when accompanying their master on a raid into realspace. Spinal grafts and rampant bone growth is common in these disturbing composites, often forming baroque exterior racks and hooks from which samples and serums can be suspended so they are readily at hand when their Haemonculus needs them. They will also be further modified to ensure that they can defend their creator in battle, or pillage a community in order to gather fresh specimens for their master's pleasure. The nails of their fingers and toes are severed and replaced by razor-sharp talons that skitter and scratch on the cold stone floors of their underground needle-lairs, and their faces are covered by inscrutable metal masks, for identity has no place in the Wrack's existence. Wracks wear only the most rudimentary of clothing in their day-to-day lives, going about their business in stained butcher's aprons and tabards, twilight glinting from a bewildering variety of torturer's tools hung from their belts.

Perhaps the most sickening aspect of the Wrack's strange plight is not their hideous appearance or simmering bloodlust, but the fact that they have chosen this fate for themselves. It is a peculiar trait of the Drukhari psyche that after a few centuries they often request to be modified into a form other than that of their birthright, for such voluntary surgery staves off ennui and gives up a whole new suite of experiences and debaucheries to savour. For this reason a Drukhari who has nothing to lose will give themselves to the Haemonculi, emerging from their foul metamorphosis as something far more frightening than ever before.

The subject to whom Gretius had been assigned hung from the gibbet in the dimly lit chamber. His arms were pinned in place above his head, skewered to the cross-beam to prevent any unnecessary twitching. The skin on his face was flush and full, his eyes bright with anticipation of the transformation he was about to undergo. Gretius remembered the same sensation of ecstasy that had preceded his own making.

'You are to be my brother soon,' said Gretius, locking eyes with the subject. 'I shall teach you how to use our tools so that Master will not be displeased.'

'Yes, brother,' said the subject, the pain and excitement palpable in his voice. 'Teach me your craft'.

Gretius splayed the Haemonculus tools on the table between him and the gibbet, arranging them so that the subject could see each edge and point distinctly.

'This we use to flense,' said Gretius, holding up a brutally curved blade. He flipped the blade over exposing the jagged barbs on its back edge. 'And these we use to pry open joints.'

The subject's mouth split into a crazed grin. 'More. Show me more tools, brother!'

'Patience,' said Gretius. 'We must first finish our studies with this tool.'

He raised the curved blade to the subject's flesh and whispered, 'This will hurt a lot.'

GROTESQUES

Towering and monstrous, Grotesques are insane creations that are employed when their Haemonculi masters have need to commit extreme physical violence. One does not become a Grotesque voluntarily. Though they generally begin existence as Drukhari, these tragic and repulsive constructs have been reborn in the most hideous of ways as punishment for some real or perceived slight to the Haemonculi.

The process by which a captive becomes a Grotesque begins with a series of painful and humiliating body modifications. Drukhari are narcissists at heart, and the cruel Haemonculi take a sinister joy in distorting the flesh of those that have angered them. Though the process often takes years to complete, the hapless victim is constantly pumped full of growth elixirs, macro-steroids and muscle stimulants until their form has swollen grossly out of proportion. Bone growth is driven into hyperactivity by injections of osseovirals, resulting in external spines that curve over the meaty back of the tortured recipient. Their thick, muscled forearms are augmented with blades and toxin-dispensing gauntlets, and their hands are replaced with grasping claws or dripping tubes that can eject a great spray of the victim's own blood. At this point the Grotesque is usually clinically lobotomised, though some are left dimly aware of their surroundings, the better to understand the full horror of what has befallen them. Either way, the Grotesque becomes mindlessly obedient, able to comprehend and execute only the simplest of tasks. Their slack and terror-etched face is sealed forever behind a mask of black iron, and they lumber dripping from the Haemonculi flesh-pods a new and entirely subservient creature whose only desire is to serve their dark master.

On the march to battle, these meat-hulks shamble forlornly after their macabre keepers, but when given the command to kill, they transform into engines of destruction. Racks of syringes depress in their spinal sumps to dump potent stimulants into their ichor-stream, ridged bellow-pumps connected to primary lungs wheeze and contract at triple speed, and veins throb near to bursting as tube-punctured hearts are forced into overdrive. With a great muffled roar the Grotesques thunder into battle, butchering all within reach with hook, claw and cleaver. They absolutely will not stop until they receive their master's command to cease. If this command is not heard, perhaps because their master is temporarily deceased or the din of war is too great, the Grotesques will continue to kill everything within reach – including other Drukhari. Whether the tiny spark of the individuals left within the Grotesques take a measure of satisfaction in this unbridled carnage can never be known, but one thing is certain – a Grotesque has plenty of pent-up aggression within its bruised and muscular frame, and it is not a good idea to be nearby when it is released.

TALOS

The Engines of Pain, of which the Talos is the most widespread, are seen as the pinnacle of the Haemonculi's art. Creations of mad genius, each one is part organic and part mechanical, festooned with surgical apparatus and horrible-looking weapons of war. Though they vary greatly in construction, each Talos is always well equipped to visit hideous retribution upon those that earn their master's ire. From the clanking Chainghoul favoured by the Prophets of Flesh, to the drill-legged Shriveners that guard the Everspiral, each is an unholy terror many times the size and strength of its creator. These semi-sentient constructs drift along with menacing slowness, the whine of their anti-gravitic motors in counterpoint to the flicker-clack of silvered blades as they close with their prey.

The Talos performs several roles in the oubliettes of the Haemonculi, for it is both a guard-creature and a mobile torture chamber that can inflict a dizzying variety of agonies upon those it catches in its steely grasp. A Talos is valuable to the Haemonculi not only as a shield – its metal shell and twisted mind make it all but impervious to harm – but also as a tool, for it allows its master to punish the slow and the impudent without lifting a crooked finger. The forelimbs of a Talos can be mounted with a variety of cruel implements, such as macro-scalpels that can scissor even an Ogryn into bloody chunks, chain-flails that can rip flesh and metal

with equal ease, or ichor-spewing funnels that siphon fluids from a Talos' thorax to reduce lightly armoured victims to primordial ooze. Additionally, the creature bears ranged armaments on its scorpion-like tail. But it is the manipulators and scalpel-keen claws that hang underneath a Talos' segmented carapace that are truly to be feared. When a Talos catches an enemy warrior, it holds them tight with a pair of grasping steel limbs and begins a rapid and efficient disassembly of its victim with the rest. Motors hum and drills whine as it works away with its surgically sharp implements, drawing each constituent part into itself, stripping and rendering down the physical form of its prey layer by layer until nothing is left but a few drops of blood.

In battle, this gruesome process is immensely pleasing to the Haemonculus owner, for not only does it provide an entertaining spectacle but it also affords the Talos even greater motive power as it harnesses and consumes its fleshy bounty. Clacking and twitching as if revelling in the kill, the Talos advances with renewed vigour, its high-tech weaponry spitting indiscriminate death into the ranks of the foe. When it catches its next quarry the process begins anew, but the fate of one caught by a Talos does not end in death – upon the Engine's return to its Coven's oubliettes, the constituent parts of its victims will be siphoned out from within its metal shell and used to create yet more potions and elixirs.

FLESH COLLECTORS

When Haemonculi send their Talos Engines to accompany a raid in realspace, the monstrous servants are often tasked with collecting specific samples for their masters. Typically this involves devouring certain types of creatures from a planet's populace or subsuming a specific individual such as a planetary governor. However, at times the demands of the Haemonculi are far more nuanced. When raiding in T'au space, the Talos known as Marrow Giver was once instructed to consume only those Fire Warriors who had witnessed the rest of their Strike Team slaughtered before them. Failure to complete such a task – or worse still, deviation from instructions – inevitably sees the Talos dismantled and discarded. To outside eyes such stringency may seem wasteful, but in their craft the Haemonculi require absolute precision. Different types of harvested material carry different properties, each of which has a unique purpose. Musculature and nervous tissue are combined in ways unimagined by nature, and the emotions absorbed in flesh at the time of a creature's death are extracted, enhanced and fashioned into weapons. To pollute such work with impurities – meat from the wrong species, or blood permeated with the wrong emotion – would be to spoil the Haemonculus' work, which they may have slaved over for decades, and would deny a new morbid creation to the entire galaxy. Furthermore, the Haemonculi often wish to reconstitute the soupy remains of a Talos' victims and instil them with life so that they can be questioned in the oubliettes. More than one general has died only to end up in the torture chambers beneath the Dark City, bleeding secrets to the Haemonculi in a vain attempt to end their torment.

CRONOS

The Cronos – also known as the Parasite Engine – resembles a giant biomechanical insect or spined deep-sea abomination, its burnished shell covered in bristling antennae and twitching vanes. Though it is employed to the same end as the Talos and other Engines of Pain – to torture and destroy – the Cronos is an even more extraordinary machine. Through the blend of alchemy and science practised by the Haemonculus Covens, the Cronos is able to drain the very life essence from its victims using a variety of esoteric apparatus. What remains of its prey when the vile creature has drunk its fill is a testament to the diabolical skill of its creators, for in its wake a Cronos leaves little more than grey and shrivelled husks.

The Cronos has earned a grim reputation amongst those members of the lesser races who have fought against it and survived, for this horrific product of the Haemonculi's art can generate a feedback loop of negative energy that syphons the life force of those caught in its field. To the onlooker, a victim of the Cronos' invisible attention seems to age at an incredibly rapid rate, their body wrinkling and rotting until nothing is left but an ancient-looking cadaver. In addition, each Cronos has multiple tentacles wrought from metal, flesh and nervous tissue dangling from its forelimbs and underside, which are similarly capable of draining the animating essence of those they strike.

Some Cronos are further modified by their Haemonculus creators to bear other soul-draining weaponry, such as a spirit vortex or spirit probe. The spirit vortex is a spiral-etched device that hurls out massive amounts of negative force across great ranges, ensuring those who try to keep their distance from the Cronos do not avoid their grim fate, while the spirit probe takes the shape of a fluted and crystalline device that hangs from the Cronos' head like the proboscis of an alien insect. The Cronos drives this hollow tube directly into those it has grasped in its tentacles, ingesting their life-force through more direct means. The stolen vitality of the machine's victim is then magnified within its shiny carapace, fed through its ribbed capacitor-valves and projected from its resonator vanes once more. Pulsing waves of spirit-essence flow outward to those Drukhari standing near the Cronos – usually its Haemonculus master and his ghastly carnival of monstrosities. In this way the metallic monstrosity nourishes and rejuvenates those nearby, driving them on to ever-greater feats of destruction. It is this ability that has led the superstitious denizens of the Imperium to refer to the Cronos as 'time-thieves', for they steal youth and vigour from their prey and gift it to their sadistic keepers.

'Down from the skies it came, buzzing and clicking, a bristling profusion of antennae and a glinting carapace the colour of dried blood. We thought we had more pressing concerns, for to repel a Commorrite invasion is to fight against a hurricane of blades. Bolters spat fury. Then my brothers began to fall, soundlessly, to the ground. Brother-Captain Alkon was unresponsive. I wrenched off his helmet to find a wizened skull leering back. It was then the xenos attack doubled in its force…'

- Epistolary Thule of the Silver Skulls,
Yria Massacre

These beneficial effects are by no means confined to the Covens, however; all Drukhari can absorb the life forces purloined by the Cronos, becoming stronger and more vital every time the beast successfully feeds. Archons who expect a raid to become protracted will pay handsomely for such an Engine of Pain to accompany their mission, for should their warriors become bogged down in a roiling battle, a nearby Cronos can not only sustain them through grievous injuries, but drive them to such heights of murderous passion that the scales are quickly tipped in the Drukhari's favour. Even within the Dark City, it is not uncommon for a wealthy Overlord of a Kabal to permanently keep a Cronos close by, so that it can be set upon disloyal servants and potential usurpers.

When a Haemonculus enters realspace to gather living fodder for their oubliettes, they will regularly take a Cronos with them – not only to bolster their own vim in battle, but also to observe the effects different harvested souls have on their other fleshy creations. Indeed, countless sentient species have been eradicated over the millennia for the simple reason that their spirit essence proved especially invigorating to a particularly genocidal Haemonculus.

PAGEANTRY OF COMMORRAGH

A Drukhari army presents an exciting challenge for modellers and painters alike. The wide range and broad scope of models available makes for a varied collection, with ranks of Kabalite Warriors standing alongside lithe arena-fighters and twisted monstrosities, each with their own array of swift and savage vehicles.

Archon with splinter pistol and huskblade

Sslyth

Medusae

Ur-Ghul

Lhamaean

A massive Drukhari raid descends upon the Genestealer Cult that has taken over this Imperial world. Blasts of darklight fill the skies, while in the shadows below, the nightmare creatures of Commorragh set about their butchery.

Blaster

Dark lance

Kabal of the Black Heart Sybarite
with agoniser and splinter pistol

Kabalite Warrior with
splinter cannon

Kabalite Warrior with
splinter rifle

Kabalite Warrior
with shredder

Archon Velestraad of the Kabal of the Black Heart bathes in the tormented screams emitted from the enemy army as his own
Kabalite forces lay down a shredding hail of splinter rifle fire.

Kabal of the Poisoned Tongue

Kabal of the
Baleful Gaze

Kabal of the
Obsidian Rose

Kabal of the
Broken Sigil

The Lords of
Iron Thorn

Kabal of the
Flayed Skull

Kabal of the
Last Hatred

Drazhar,
Master of Blades

Highly disciplined mercenaries, Incubi wield the towering
weapons known as klaives.

The Mandrakes of the shadowy realm of Aelindrach
wield a variety of deadly glimmersteel blades.

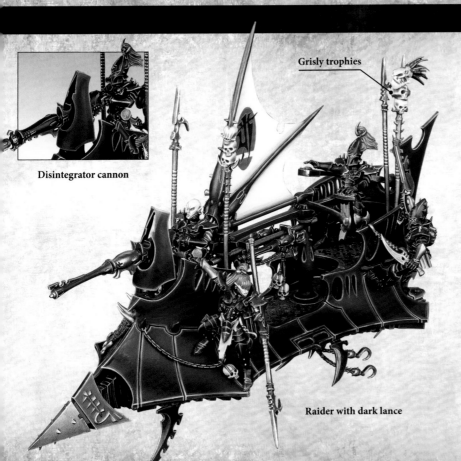

Disintegrator cannon

Grisly trophies

Bladevanes and chain-snares

Splinter racks

Shock prow

Raider with dark lance

**Lelith Hesperax,
Queen of Knives**

**Hekatrix with blast
pistol and agoniser**

**Wych with
shardnet and impaler**

**Wych with
hydra gauntlets**

**Succubus from the
Cult of Strife with agoniser
and archite glaive**

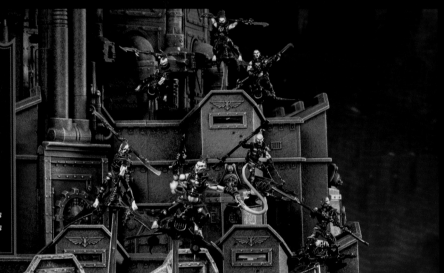

'Accounts of Drukhari presence on Odecima Tertius remain uncorroborated, though 4th, 5th and 7th platoons have not yet reported in. They are all overdue. Recommend censure for their Platoon Commanders. I have reviewed the Journal of Boyen Mossiel, who purports to have faced these xenos before. If he is right, we can't be too careful, and we can't let them-'

*- Master of Ordnance Boyen
Sazzaar, final transmission*

A gang of Hellions from the Cult of Strife swoops along the battlements of the Imperial fortification, reaping the heads of the defenders as they fly by and disabling the comms relays before the full brunt of their raiding party arrives.

Scourge with haywire blaster

Some Reavers ride to battle on jetbikes equipped with a heat lance.

**Cult of the
Red Grief**

**Cult of the
Seventh Woe**

**Cult of the
Blade Denied**

**Cult of the
Cursed Blade**

After cutting off the Astra Militarum artillery's escape route with aerial bombardments and dark-lance blasts, the Cult of Strife send an outflanking force skimming over the debris to annihilate the trapped heavy vehicles.

Having isolated the Genestealer Cultists, disabled their communications and assassinated their leaders in short order, the Wyches of the Cult of Strife charge towards their enemy, bringing their raid to a crescendo of perfectly performed brutality.

Wracks from the Coven of Twelve disembark from their Venom amidst the creeping industrial sprawl on Macia III. They know there is great pain to be harvested on this planet, and many choice subjects to be taken back to Commorragh.

Haemonculus of the Prophets of Flesh

Wrack with Haemonculus tools

Acothyst with hexrifle and scissorhand

Wrack with ossefactor

Venom blade

Liquifier gun

Flesh gauntlet

After long decades toiling with his Wrack servants, the Haemonculus Estrak Krael brings forth his latest flesh-creations, loosing his Talos, Cronos and bulking Cotesea upon the battlefield so that they may halt and dategript the examine a freely

Grotesque with liquifier gun and flesh gauntlet

Wrack of the Black Descent

Wrack of the Coven of Twelve

Urien Rakarth, Sculptor of Torments

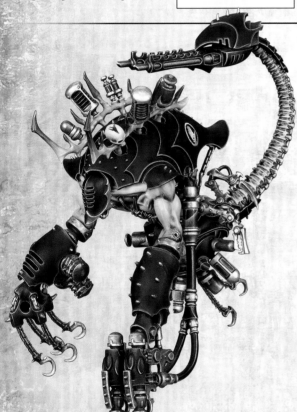

Talos with chain-flails, twin liquifier gun and two splinter cannons

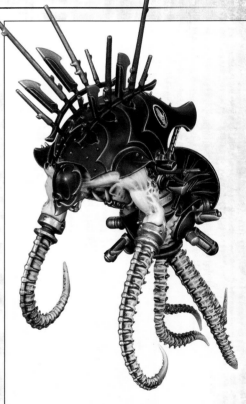

Cronos

Twin liquifier gun

Ichor injector

Stinger pod

Spirit probe

Spirit vortex

INITIATING THE RAID

A Drukhari raiding party is a terrifying presence on the tabletop, and there are many ways to start collecting such an army. Here we present three possible starting forces that are quite different from each other in terms of their composition, look and play style.

The first starting force contains an Archon armed with a splinter pistol and huskblade. Following him is a unit of Kabalite Warriors who, with their splinter cannon and shredder, have a great deal of flexibility on the battlefield. Rounding out this force is a unit of mercenary Scourges with a variety of wargear. With a single HQ, Troops and Fast Attack choice, this force can be taken as a Patrol Detachment.

The second force is led by a Succubus with an archite glaive and agoniser. At her side is a unit of Wyches with various gladiatorial armaments, as well as a Venom to ferry the Succubus swiftly to the fore. Lastly, a squad of Reavers lends the group even more speed and manoeuvrability. This collection also qualifies as a Patrol Detachment, containing a single HQ, Troops, Fast Attack and Dedicated Transport choice.

The last force contains a Haemonculus who is accompanied by a hulking Talos. Marching before their master is a unit of Wracks. Their Acothyst leader bears a hexrifle and scissorhand, and a Venom stands ready to transport them towards their next victims. With one HQ, Troops, Heavy Support and Dedicated Transport choice each, this collection also comprises a Patrol Detachment.

Mordakon Bestruvia, lesser Archon of the Kabal of the Black Heart, leads this raiding part. His Kabalite Warriors hail from the Splinter of the Dying Dream, and are eager to sate their thirst for pain in realspace. The Scourges accompanying them on their raid are a flock from the Murder of Blades, and have been coaxed down from the spires of High Commorragh by the promise of wealth.

These Wyches are from the Circle of Despair Unfolding within the Cult of Strife, and have honed their skills both within and outside of the arena against all manner of alien warriors. Their Succubus, Reethia Bleek, has a keen eye for enemy combatants who could provide a worthy challenge, and with her personal Venom and Reaver attendants, she has little trouble hunting them down.

Graegon Pupaque, a particularly ancient Prophet of Flesh, leads a raid to personally select subjects for his ongoing tortures. His latest creation, the Talos known as Nervemonger, hovers alongside its master – ready to dissect the choicest enemy morsels – while Wracks from the Cell of Endless Sorrow await Pupaque's sadistic instructions.

Splinter cannon

Twin splinter rifle

Venom

GATHERED FOR AGONY

There are countless ways to add to the core of your raiding party. The army shown here combines the three starting forces outlined on the previous page and adds a couple of new units to further bolster its strengths. The resultant alliance of agony is truly imposing on the tabletop, and utilises warriors drawn from every stratum of the Dark City.

This massive raiding party, known as the Nightmare Choir, has Archon Bestruvia from the Kabal of the Black Heart at its head. His Kabalite Warriors still fight by his side, along with his Scourge mercenaries. These Drukhari are armed with a variety of long-range armaments, including splinter weapons to tear through ranks of infantry and haywire blasters to annihilate armoured vehicles, and can provide withering fire support for the rest of the army.

Reethia Bleek and her Wyches join Bestruvia's forces. To work alongside the squad of Reavers, Bleek has included a wing of

hellglaive-wielding Hellions in her coterie. While the Wyches run screaming towards the enemy lines, the jetbikers and skyboard riders – along with Reethia herself, transported within her Venom – can zoom through the air to launch lightning-fast offensives or outflank their foes.

Finally, Graegon Pupaque and his abominable creations bolster the Nightmare Choir with their durability and tools of torture. His Wracks have their Venom ready to transport them where their inherent cruelty can be put to brutal use, whilst Nervemonger the Talos readies its surgically sharp blade. Pupaque has also brought

another of his Engines of Pain to battle – the Cronos Hopestealer – to provide sustaining soul-energy for his own servants, as well as those of the other Drukhari with whom he is in league.

Each of the three forces that comprise the Nightmare Choir can be taken as a separate Patrol Detachment. As such, each Detachment receives the benefits of their own Drukhari Obsession (pg 114), as well as Stratagems, Relics and Warlord Traits specific to the Kabal of the Black Heart, Cult of Strife and Prophets of Flesh respectively. This gives each Detachment a unique set of strengths and allows them to fulfil different sadistic roles on the battlefield. Normally, you would not receive any Command Points for taking Patrol Detachments, but the Raiding Force rule (pg 114) means that you generate 3 Command Points for having a least three Patrol Detachments in the same army. For being Battle-forged, the Nightmare Choir generates a further 3 Command Points for a total of 6 – an ample amount for using various Stratagems to shape the course of battle.

1. **Archon Mordakon Bestruvia**

2. **Kabalite Warriors of the Kabal of the Black Heart**

3. **Scourges of the Murder of Blades**

4. **Succubus Reethia Bleek**

5. **Venom of the Cult of Strife**

6. **Wyches of the Cult of Strife**

7. **Reavers of the Cult of Strife**

8. **Hellions of the Cult of Strife**

9. **Haemonculus Graegon Pupaque**

10. **Wracks of the Prophets of Flesh**

11. **Venom of the Prophets of Flesh**

12. **Talos Nervemonger**

13. **Cronos Hopestealer**

THE DARK AELDARI

This section contains all of the datasheets that you will need to fight battles with your Drukhari miniatures, and the rules for all of the weapons they can wield in battle. Each datasheet includes the characteristics profiles of the unit it describes, as well as any wargear and special abilities it may have. Any abilities that are common to several units are described below and referenced on the datasheets themselves.

KEYWORDS

Throughout this section you will come across keywords that are within angular brackets, specifically <Kabal>, <Wych Cult> and <Haemonculus Coven>. These are shorthand for keywords of your own choosing, as described below.

<Kabal>, <Wych Cult> and <Haemonculus Coven>

Most Drukhari on the battlefield belong to either a Kabal, Wych Cult or Haemonculus Coven. Some datasheets specify what Kabal, Wych Cult or Haemonculus Coven the unit is drawn from (e.g. Lelith Hesperax has the **Cult of Strife** keyword, so belongs to the Cult of Strife). Other Drukhari datasheets may have either the <Kabal>, <Wych Cult> or <Haemonculus Coven> keyword. When

you include such a unit in your army, you must nominate which Kabal, Wych Cult or Haemonculus Coven the unit is from. You then simply replace the <Kabal>, <Wych Cult> or <Haemonculus Coven> keyword in every instance on that unit's datasheet with the name you chose. You can use any of the Kabals, Wych Cults or Haemonculus Covens you have read about, or make up your own.

For example, if you were to include an Archon in your army, and you decided the Archon was from the Kabal of the Black Heart, then their <Kabal> Faction keyword would be changed to **Kabal of the Black Heart** and their Overlord ability would then say 'Re-roll hit rolls of 1 for friendly **Kabal of the Black Heart** units that are within 6" of this model.'

'Some of you thought me dead. Some of you even willed it, and you gathered here in the Nhexus to offer feigned respect. But now you see plainly that my will cannot be undone, my favour cannot be regained and my wrath cannot be tempered. Whether you are loyal or a traitor, you will be slaughtered, for it is only right that my ascension be celebrated with sacrifice. And if I deign to have you resurrected, know that you will serve me by your deeds or by your suffering.'

- Asdrubael Vect, Supreme Overlord of Commorragh

ABILITIES

The following abilities are common to several **Drukhari** units:

Poisoned Weapon

The Drukhari frequently use virulent poisons to slay their prey in excruciating ways.

This weapon wounds on a 4+, unless it is targeting a **Vehicle** or **Titanic** unit, in which case it wounds on a 6+.

Power From Pain

As the Drukhari feed on the souls of the slain, they become imbued with supernatural might, eventually turning into killing machines.

Units with this ability gain a bonus depending upon which battle round it is, as shown in the table below. Note that all bonuses are cumulative; for example, in the second battle round, wounds are ignored on a roll of 6, and you can re-roll the dice when determining how far a unit Advances or charges.

POWER FROM PAIN

BATTLE ROUND	BONUS
1	**Inured to Suffering:** Roll a D6 each time a model with this bonus loses a wound. On a 6 the model does not lose that wound.
2	**Eager to Flay:** You can re-roll the dice when determining how far a unit with this bonus moves when it Advances or charges.
3	**Flensing Fury:** Add 1 to hit rolls made for units with this bonus in the Fight phase.
4	**Emboldened by Bloodshed:** Units with this bonus automatically pass Morale tests (do not roll the dice).
5+	**Mantle of Agony:** Subtract 1 from the Leadership characteristic of enemy units that are within 6" of any units with this bonus in the Morale phase.

Combat Drugs

Chemical stimulants are widely used to heighten combat performance, despite the risk of a deadly and spectacular overdose.

Units with this ability gain a bonus during the battle depending on the drugs injected into their veins. Before the battle, roll on the table below to see which combat drug the unit is using. Alternatively, you can pick the bonus the unit receives, but if you do this you cannot choose a bonus that has already been taken by another unit until all six combat drugs have been taken once each.

COMBAT DRUGS

D6	BONUS
1	**Adrenalight:** +1 to Attacks characteristic
2	**Grave Lotus:** +1 to Strength characteristic
3	**Hypex:** +2 to Move characteristic
4	**Painbringer:** +1 to Toughness characteristic
5	**Serpentin:** +1 to Weapon Skill characteristic (e.g. WS 3+ becomes WS 2+)
6	**Splintermind:** +2 to Leadership characteristic

DRUKHARI WARGEAR LISTS

Many of the units you will find on the following pages reference one or more of the wargear lists below. When this is the case, the unit may take any item from the appropriate list. The profiles for the weapons in these lists can be found in the Armoury of Commorragh section (pg 108-111).

WYCH CULT WEAPONS

- Hydra gauntlets
- Razorflails
- Shardnet and impaler

TOOLS OF TORMENT

- Hexrifle
- Liquifier gun
- Stinger pistol

WEAPONS OF TORTURE

- Agoniser
- Electrocorrosive whip
- Flesh gauntlet
- Mindphase gauntlet
- Scissorhand
- Venom blade

VEHICLE EQUIPMENT

- Chain-snares
- Grisly trophies
- Phantasm grenade launcher *
- Shock prow *

* Cannot be equipped on a Venom.

ARCHON

NAME	M	WS	BS	S	T	W	A	Ld	Sv
Archon	8"	2+	2+	3	3	5	5	9	5+

An Archon is a single model armed with a splinter pistol and a huskblade.

WEAPON	RANGE	TYPE	S	AP	D	ABILITIES
Blast pistol	6"	Pistol 1	8	-4	D6	-
Splinter pistol	12"	Pistol 1	*	0	1	Poisoned Weapon (pg 87)
Agoniser	Melee	Melee	*	-2	1	Poisoned Weapon (pg 87)
Huskblade	Melee	Melee	+1	-2	D3	-
Power sword	Melee	Melee	User	-3	1	-
Venom blade	Melee	Melee	*	0	1	Poisoned Weapon (pg 87). Add 2 to wound rolls made for this weapon, unless it is targeting a **Vehicle**.

WARGEAR OPTIONS	• This model may replace its huskblade with an agoniser, power sword or venom blade. • This model may replace its splinter pistol with a blast pistol.

ABILITIES	**Power From Pain** (pg 87)	**Overlord:** Re-roll hit rolls of 1 for friendly <**Kabal**> units that are within 6" of this model.
	Shadowfield: This model has a 2+ invulnerable save, which cannot be re-rolled for any reason. The first time this invulnerable save is failed the shadowfield ceases to function for the remainder of the battle.	

FACTION KEYWORDS	**Aeldari, Drukhari, <Kabal>**
KEYWORDS	**Character, Infantry, Archon**

DRAZHAR

NAME	M	WS	BS	S	T	W	A	Ld	Sv
Drazhar	7"	2+	2+	4	4	5	4	9	2+

Drazhar is a single model armed with demiklaives. Only one of this model may be included in your army.

WEAPON	RANGE	TYPE	S	AP	D	ABILITIES
Demiklaives	Each time the bearer fights, choose one of the profiles below.					
- Single blade	Melee	Melee	+1	-3	1	-
- Dual blades	Melee	Melee	User	-2	1	A model attacking with dual blades can make 2 additional attacks with them each time it fights.

ABILITIES	**Power From Pain** (pg 87)	**Tormentors:** Each time your opponent takes a Morale test for a unit that is within 6" of any enemy **Incubi** units and the result of the Morale test equals the highest Leadership characteristic in the unit, the test is failed and one model flees the unit.
	Eternal Warrior: Drazhar has a 5+ invulnerable save.	
	Murderous Assault: If Drazhar charges in the Charge phase, he can fight an additional time in the next Fight phase.	**Master of Blades:** Add 1 to hit rolls for friendly **Incubi** units whilst they are within 6" of Drazhar.

FACTION KEYWORDS	**Aeldari, Drukhari, Incubi**
KEYWORDS	**Character, Infantry, Drazhar**

LELITH HESPERAX

NAME	M	WS	BS	S	T	W	A	Ld	Sv
Lelith Hesperax	8"	2+	2+	3	3	5	4	8	6+

Lelith Hesperax is a single model armed with two penetrating blades and a mane of barbs and hooks. Only one of this model may be included in your army.

WEAPON	RANGE	TYPE	S	AP	D	ABILITIES
Impaler	Melee	Melee	User	-1	2	-
Mane of barbs and hooks	Melee	Melee	User	0	1	Each time Lelith Hesperax fights, she can make 2 additional attacks with this weapon.
Penetrating blade	Melee	Melee	User	-4	1	If Lelith Hesperax is armed with two penetrating blades, each time she fights she can make 1 additional attack with them.

WARGEAR OPTIONS	• Lelith Hesperax may replace one penetrating blade with an impaler.

ABILITIES	**Power From Pain** (pg 87)	**Natural Perfection:** At the start of each battle round, choose one of the following of Lelith Hesperax's characteristics: Move, Strength, Toughness, Attacks or Leadership. The characteristic you choose is increased by 1 until the end of this battle round (if you chose Move or Leadership, it is instead increased by 2 until the end of the battle round).
	A League Apart: Re-roll failed hit and wound rolls for attacks made by Lelith Hesperax that target enemy **CHARACTERS**.	
	Brides of Death: In the Fight phase, re-roll hit rolls of 1 for friendly **CULT OF STRIFE** units whilst they are within 6" of Lelith Hesperax.	**No Escape:** Roll off if an **INFANTRY** unit within 1" of any enemy models with this ability wishes to Fall Back. The unit can only Fall Back if the player controlling it wins the roll-off.
	Quicksilver Dodge: Lelith Hesperax has a 3+ invulnerable save.	

FACTION KEYWORDS	**AELDARI, DRUKHARI, CULT OF STRIFE**
KEYWORDS	**CHARACTER, INFANTRY, SUCCUBUS, LELITH HESPERAX**

With lethal grace, Lelith Hesperax bounds ahead of her Cult's warriors in her eagreness to get to grips with the enemy.

SUCCUBUS

NAME	M	WS	BS	S	T	W	A	Ld	Sv
Succubus	8"	2+	2+	3	3	5	4	8	6+

A Succubus is a single model armed with an agoniser and archite glaive.

WEAPON	RANGE	TYPE	S	AP	D	ABILITIES
Blast pistol	6"	Pistol 1	8	-4	D6	-
Splinter pistol	12"	Pistol 1	*	0	1	Poisoned Weapon (pg 87).
Agoniser	Melee	Melee	*	-2	1	Poisoned Weapon (pg 87).
Archite glaive	Melee	Melee	+2	-3	1	When attacking with this weapon, you must subtract 1 from the hit roll.
Impaler	Melee	Melee	User	-1	2	-

WARGEAR OPTIONS	• This model may replace its agoniser and archite glaive with one item from the *Wych Cult Weapons* list. • This model may replace its agoniser with a splinter pistol, blast pistol or impaler.

ABILITIES	**Power From Pain, Combat Drugs** (pg 87)	**Lightning Dodge:** This model has a 4+ invulnerable save.
	Brides of Death: In the Fight phase, re-roll hit rolls of 1 for friendly <**Wych Cult**> units whilst they are within 6" of this model.	**No Escape:** Roll off if an **Infantry** unit within 1" of any enemy models with this ability wishes to Fall Back. The unit can only Fall Back if the player controlling it wins the roll-off.

FACTION KEYWORDS	**Aeldari, Drukhari, <Wych Cult>**
KEYWORDS	**Character, Infantry, Succubus**

A Cult of Strife Succubus breaks away from the body of her raiding party, readying herself for solo slaughter.

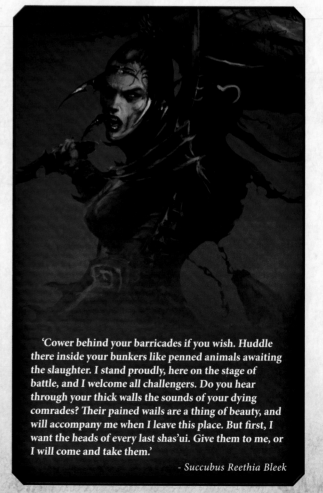

'Cower behind your barricades if you wish. Huddle there inside your bunkers like penned animals awaiting the slaughter. I stand proudly, here on the stage of battle, and I welcome all challengers. Do you hear through your thick walls the sounds of your dying comrades? Their pained wails are a thing of beauty, and will accompany me when I leave this place. But first, I want the heads of every last shas'ui. Give them to me, or I will come and take them.'

- Succubus Reethia Bleek

URIEN RAKARTH

NAME	M	WS	BS	S	T	W	A	Ld	Sv
Urien Rakarth	7"	2+	2+	3	5	5	4	8	6+

Urien Rakarth is a single model armed with the Casket of Flensing, Haemonculus tools and an ichor injector. Only one of this model may be included in your army.

WEAPON	RANGE	TYPE	S	AP	D	ABILITIES
Casket of Flensing	12"	Assault 2D6	3	-2	1	This weapon can only be fired once per battle.
Haemonculus tools	Melee	Melee	*	0	1	Poisoned Weapon (pg 87).
Ichor injector	Melee	Melee	User	-1	1	The bearer can only make a single attack with this weapon each time it fights. You can re-roll failed wound rolls for this weapon. Each time you roll a wound roll of 6+ for this weapon, the target suffers D3 mortal wounds in addition to any other damage.

ABILITIES	Power From Pain (pg 87)	Clone Field: Urien Rakarth has a 4+ invulnerable save.
	Haemovores: Roll a D6 for each enemy unit within 3" of Urien Rakarth at the start of the Fight phase. On a 6 that unit suffers a mortal wound.	**Contempt for Death:** All damage suffered by Urien Rakarth is halved (rounding up).
	Sculptor of Torments: Add 1 to the Strength and Leadership characteristics of **PROPHETS OF FLESH** units whilst they are within 6" of Urien Rakarth.	**Master of Pain:** Add 1 to the Toughness characteristic of **PROPHETS OF FLESH** units whilst they are within 6" of any friendly **PROPHETS OF FLESH** models with this ability.

FACTION KEYWORDS	**AELDARI, DRUKHARI, PROPHETS OF FLESH**
KEYWORDS	**CHARACTER, INFANTRY, HAEMONCULUS, URIEN RAKARTH**

HAEMONCULUS

NAME	M	WS	BS	S	T	W	A	Ld	Sv
Haemonculus	7"	2+	2+	3	4	5	5	8	6+

A Haemonculus is a single model armed with a stinger pistol and Haemonculus tools.

WEAPON	RANGE	TYPE	S	AP	D	ABILITIES
Hexrifle	36"	Heavy 1	4	-1	1	This weapon may target a **CHARACTER** even if it is not the closest enemy unit. Each time you roll a wound roll of 6+ for this weapon, the target suffers a mortal wound in addition to any other damage.
Liquifier gun	8"	Assault D6	3	-D3	1	Each time this weapon is fired, roll a D3 to determine its AP for those attacks. For example, if you rolled a 1, this weapon would have an AP of -1. This weapon automatically hits its target.
Stinger pistol	12"	Pistol 1	*	0	1	Poisoned Weapon (pg 87). Add 2 to wound rolls made for this weapon, unless it is targeting a **VEHICLE**.
Haemonculus tools	Melee	Melee	*	0	1	Poisoned Weapon (pg 87).
Ichor injector	Melee	Melee	User	-1	1	The bearer can only make a single attack with this weapon each time it fights. You can re-roll failed wound rolls for this weapon. Each time you roll a wound roll of 6+ for this weapon, the target suffers D3 mortal wounds in addition to any other damage.

WARGEAR OPTIONS	• This model may take an ichor injector. • This model may replace its stinger pistol with a hexrifle or liquifier gun. • This model may replace its Haemonculus tools with one item from the *Weapons of Torture* list.

ABILITIES	Power From Pain (pg 87)	Master of Pain: Add 1 to the Toughness characteristic of **<HAEMONCULUS COVEN>** units whilst they are within 6" of any friendly **<HAEMONCULUS COVEN>** models with this ability.
	Insensible To Pain: This model has a 5+ invulnerable save.	

FACTION KEYWORDS	**AELDARI, DRUKHARI, <HAEMONCULUS COVEN>**
KEYWORDS	**CHARACTER, INFANTRY, HAEMONCULUS**

Emboldened by the bloodshed of their enemies and allies alike, these Kabalite Warriors stride heedlessly forward to open fire.

KABALITE WARRIORS

NAME	M	WS	BS	S	T	W	A	Ld	Sv
Kabalite Warrior	7"	3+	3+	3	3	1	1	7	5+
Sybarite	7"	3+	3+	3	3	1	2	8	5+

This unit contains 1 Sybarite and 4 Kabalite Warriors. It can include up to 5 additional Kabalite Warriors (**Power Rating +2**), up to 10 additional Kabalite Warriors (**Power Rating +4**) or up to 15 additional Kabalite Warriors (**Power Rating +6**). Each model is armed with a splinter rifle.

WEAPON	RANGE	TYPE	S	AP	D	ABILITIES
Blast pistol	6"	Pistol 1	8	-4	D6	-
Blaster	18"	Assault 1	8	-4	D6	-
Dark lance	36"	Heavy 1	8	-4	D6	-
Phantasm grenade launcher	18"	Assault D3	1	0	1	If a unit is hit by one or more phantasm grenade launchers, subtract 1 from its Leadership characteristic until the end of the turn.
Shredder	12"	Assault D6	6	-1	1	When attacking an **INFANTRY** unit, re-roll failed wound rolls for this weapon.
Splinter cannon	36"	Rapid Fire 3	*	0	1	Poisoned Weapon (pg 87)
Splinter pistol	12"	Pistol 1	*	0	1	Poisoned Weapon (pg 87)
Splinter rifle	24"	Rapid Fire 1	*	0	1	Poisoned Weapon (pg 87)
Agoniser	Melee	Melee	*	-2	1	Poisoned Weapon (pg 87)
Power sword	Melee	Melee	User	-3	1	-

WARGEAR OPTIONS	• The Sybarite may take a power sword or an agoniser. • The Sybarite may take a phantasm grenade launcher. • The Sybarite may replace their splinter rifle with a splinter pistol or a blast pistol. • For every ten models in the unit, one Kabalite Warrior may replace their splinter rifle with a splinter cannon or dark lance. • For every five models in the unit, one Kabalite Warrior may replace its splinter rifle with a shredder or a blaster.
ABILITIES	Power From Pain (pg 87)
FACTION KEYWORDS	AELDARI, DRUKHARI, <KABAL>
KEYWORDS	INFANTRY, KABALITE WARRIORS

WYCHES

NAME	M	WS	BS	S	T	W	A	Ld	Sv
Wych	8"	3+	3+	3	3	1	2	7	6+
Hekatrix	8"	3+	3+	3	3	1	3	8	6+

This unit contains 1 Hekatrix and 4 Wyches. It can include up to 5 additional Wyches (**Power Rating +2**), up to 10 additional Wyches (**Power Rating +4**) or up to 15 additional Wyches (**Power Rating +6**). Each model is armed with a splinter pistol, Hekatarii blade and plasma grenades.

WEAPON	RANGE	TYPE	S	AP	D	ABILITIES
Blast pistol	6"	Pistol 1	8	-4	D6	-
Phantasm grenade launcher	18"	Assault D3	1	0	1	If a unit is hit by one or more phantasm grenade launchers, subtract 1 from its Leadership characteristic until the end of the turn.
Splinter pistol	12"	Pistol 1	*	0	1	Poisoned Weapon (pg 87)
Agoniser	Melee	Melee	*	-2	1	Poisoned Weapon (pg 87)
Hekatarii blade	Melee	Melee	User	0	1	Each time the bearer fights, it can make 1 additional attack with this weapon.
Power sword	Melee	Melee	User	-3	1	-
Plasma grenade	6"	Grenade D6	4	-1	1	-

WARGEAR OPTIONS	
	• The Hekatrix may take a phantasm grenade launcher. • The Hekatrix may replace their splinter pistol with a blast pistol. • The Hekatrix may replace their Hekatarii blade with a power sword or an agoniser. • One Wych may replace their splinter pistol and Hekatarii blade with one item from the *Wych Cult Weapons* list. If the unit numbers 10 or more models, up to two further Wyches can also do this.

ABILITIES	**Power From Pain, Combat Drugs** (pg 87) **Dodge:** Models in this unit have a 6+ invulnerable save, which is increased to a 4+ invulnerable save in the Fight phase.	**No Escape:** Roll off if an **Infantry** unit within 1" of any enemy models with this ability wishes to Fall Back. The unit can only Fall Back if the player controlling it wins the roll-off.

FACTION KEYWORDS	Aeldari, Drukhari, <Wych Cult>
KEYWORDS	Infantry, Wyches

A seasoned Hekatrix calls out well-rehearsed battle manoeuvres as she and her Wyches dash towards the enemy lines.

WRACKS

3 POWER

NAME	M	WS	BS	S	T	W	A	Ld	Sv
Wrack	7"	3+	3+	3	4	1	2	7	6+
Acothyst	7"	3+	3+	3	4	1	3	8	6+

This unit contains 1 Acothyst and 4 Wracks. It can include up to 5 additional Wracks (**Power Rating +2**). Each model is armed with Haemonculus tools.

WEAPON	RANGE	TYPE	S	AP	D	ABILITIES
Liquifier gun	8"	Assault D6	3	-D3	1	Each time this weapon is fired, roll a D3 to determine its AP for those attacks. For example, if you rolled a 1, this weapon would have an AP of -1. This weapon automatically hits its target.
Ossefactor	24"	Assault 1	*	-3	1	Poisoned Weapon (pg 87). Add 2 to wound rolls made for this weapon, unless it is targeting a **VEHICLE**. If a model is slain by this weapon, the model's unit immediately suffers a mortal wound on a D6 roll of 4+.
Haemonculus tools	Melee	Melee	*	0	1	Poisoned Weapon (pg 87).

WARGEAR OPTIONS	
	• For every five models in the unit, one Wrack may take either a liquifier gun or ossefactor.
	• The Acothyst may replace his Haemonculus tools with one item from the *Weapons of Torture* list.
	• The Acothyst may take one item from the *Tools of Torment* list.

ABILITIES	
	Power From Pain (pg 87)
	Insensible To Pain: Models in this unit have a 5+ invulnerable save.

FACTION KEYWORDS	AELDARI, DRUKHARI, <HAEMONCULUS COVEN>
KEYWORDS	INFANTRY, WRACKS

Imbued with their master's patience, these Wracks fire from afar before closing in to collect the writhing survivors.

LHAMAEAN

NAME	M	WS	BS	S	T	W	A	Ld	Sv
Lhamaean	8"	3+	3+	3	3	3	2	8	5+

A Lhamaean is a single model armed with a shaimeshi blade.

WEAPON	RANGE	TYPE	S	AP	D	ABILITIES
Shaimeshi blade	Melee	Melee	*	0	1	Poisoned Weapon (pg 87). Add 2 to wound rolls made for this weapon, unless it is targeting a **VEHICLE**. Each time you roll a wound roll of 6+ for this weapon, other than against a **VEHICLE**, the target suffers a mortal wound in addition to any other damage.

ABILITIES	**Power From Pain** (pg 87)
	Court of the Archon: You can re-roll failed hit rolls for this model whilst it is within 3" of any friendly <**KABAL**> Archons. In addition, if your army is Battle-forged, this model does not take up slots in a Detachment that includes any <**KABAL**> Archons.
FACTION KEYWORDS	**AELDARI, DRUKHARI, <KABAL>**
KEYWORDS	**INFANTRY, COURT OF THE ARCHON, LHAMAEAN**

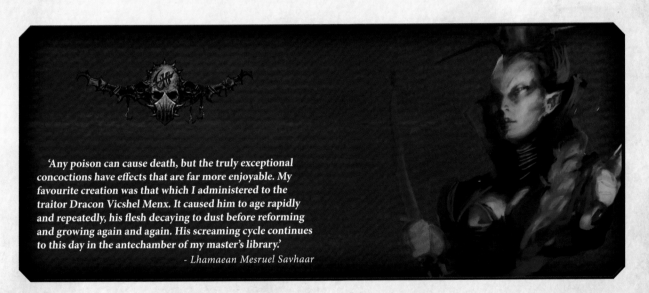

'Any poison can cause death, but the truly exceptional concoctions have effects that are far more enjoyable. My favourite creation was that which I administered to the traitor Dracon Vicshel Menx. It caused him to age rapidly and repeatedly, his flesh decaying to dust before reforming and growing again and again. His screaming cycle continues to this day in the antechamber of my master's library.'

- Lhamaean Mesruel Savhaar

MEDUSAE

NAME	M	WS	BS	S	T	W	A	Ld	Sv
Medusae	8"	3+	3+	3	3	3	1	8	5+

A Medusae is a single model which attacks with an eyeburst.

WEAPON	RANGE	TYPE	S	AP	D	ABILITIES
Eyeburst	9"	Assault 4	4	-2	1	-

ABILITIES	**Power From Pain** (pg 87)
	Court of the Archon: You can re-roll failed hit rolls for this model whilst it is within 3" of any friendly <**KABAL**> Archons. In addition, if your army is Battle-forged, this model does not take up slots in a Detachment that includes any <**KABAL**> Archons.
FACTION KEYWORDS	**AELDARI, DRUKHARI, <KABAL>**
KEYWORDS	**INFANTRY, COURT OF THE ARCHON, MEDUSAE**

SSLYTH

NAME	M	WS	BS	S	T	W	A	Ld	Sv
Sslyth	8"	3+	3+	5	5	3	3	6	5+

A Sslyth is a single model armed with a shardcarbine, splinter pistol and Sslyth battle-blade.

WEAPON	RANGE	TYPE	S	AP	D	ABILITIES
Shardcarbine	18"	Assault 3	*	0	1	Poisoned Weapon (pg 87).
Splinter pistol	12"	Pistol 1	*	0	1	Poisoned Weapon (pg 87).
Sslyth battle-blade	Melee	Melee	User	-1	1	-

ABILITIES	
Court of the Archon: You can re-roll failed hit rolls for this model whilst it is within 3" of any friendly <Kabal> Archons. In addition, if your army is Battle-forged, this model does not take up slots in a Detachment that includes any <Kabal> Archons.	**Insensible To Pain:** This model has a 5+ invulnerable save. **Cold-blooded Bodyguard:** Roll a D6 each time a friendly <Kabal> Archon loses a wound whilst they are within 3" of this model; on a 2+ this model intercepts that hit – the Archon does not lose a wound but this model suffers a mortal wound.

FACTION KEYWORDS	AELDARI, DRUKHARI, <KABAL>
KEYWORDS	INFANTRY, COURT OF THE ARCHON, SSLYTH

Flanked by the deadly members of his court, Archon Vraesque Malindrach strides forth to battle.

UR-GHUL

NAME	M	WS	BS	S	T	W	A	Ld	Sv
Ur-Ghul	8"	3+	-	4	3	3	4	4	7+

An Ur-Ghul is a single model which attacks with claws and talons.

WEAPON	RANGE	TYPE	S	AP	D	ABILITIES
Claws and talons	Melee	Melee	User	0	1	-

ABILITIES	
Insensible To Pain: This model has a 5+ invulnerable save. **Ferocious Charge:** Add 2 to this model's Attacks characteristic if it charged in the same turn.	**Court of the Archon:** You can re-roll failed hit rolls for this model whilst it is within 3" of any friendly <Kabal> Archons. In addition, if your army is Battle-forged, this model does not take up slots in a Detachment that includes any <Kabal> Archons.

FACTION KEYWORDS	AELDARI, DRUKHARI, <KABAL>
KEYWORDS	INFANTRY, COURT OF THE ARCHON, UR-GHUL

INCUBI

NAME	M	WS	BS	S	T	W	A	Ld	Sv
Incubi	7"	3+	3+	3	3	1	3	8	3+
Klaivex	7"	2+	3+	3	3	2	4	9	3+

This unit contains 1 Klaivex and 4 Incubi. It can include up to 5 additional Incubi (**Power Rating +4**). Each model is armed with a klaive.

WEAPON	RANGE	TYPE	S	AP	D	ABILITIES
Klaive	Melee	Melee	+1	-3	1	-

ABILITIES	**Power From Pain** (pg 87)	**Tormentors:** Each time your opponent takes a Morale test for a unit that is within 6" of any enemy **Incubi** units and the result of the Morale test equals the highest Leadership characteristic in the unit, the test is failed and one model flees the unit.
	Lethal Precision: Add 2 to the Damage characteristic of a close combat attack made by a Klaivex if the wound roll for the attack is 6+.	

FACTION KEYWORDS	AELDARI, DRUKHARI, INCUBI
KEYWORDS	INFANTRY

MANDRAKES

NAME	M	WS	BS	S	T	W	A	Ld	Sv
Mandrake	8"	3+	3+	4	3	1	3	7	7+
Nightfiend	8"	3+	3+	4	3	1	4	8	7+

This unit contains 1 Nightfiend and 4 Mandrakes. It can include up to 5 additional Mandrakes (**Power Rating +4**). Each model is armed with a glimmersteel blade, and attacks with a baleblast.

WEAPON	RANGE	TYPE	S	AP	D	ABILITIES
Baleblast	18"	Assault 2	4	-1	1	Each time you roll a wound roll of 6+ for this weapon, the target suffers a mortal wound in addition to any other damage.
Glimmersteel blade	Melee	Melee	User	-1	1	-

ABILITIES	**Power From Pain** (pg 87)	**Shrouded From Sight:** Subtract 1 from the hit rolls of attacks that target this unit. In addition, models in this unit have a 5+ invulnerable save.
	From Out of the Shadows: During deployment, you can set up this unit in the realm of Aelindrach instead of placing it on the battlefield. At the end of any of your Movement phases the Mandrakes can pull themselves into reality – set them up anywhere on the battlefield that is more than 9" away from any enemy models.	

FACTION KEYWORDS	AELDARI, DRUKHARI
KEYWORDS	INFANTRY, MANDRAKES

'The Archon with whom I am in covenant pays me to kill her enemies. Before her, there were others who paid me to kill their enemies. After, there will be others still, and I will kill their enemies also, for as long as I am paid I do not betray those who pay me – but when a covenant is concluded, I go wherever Khaine wills.'

- Veryusess, Incubus of the Shrine of Cursed Night

BEASTMASTER

NAME	M	WS	BS	S	T	W	A	Ld	Sv
Beastmaster	12"	3+	3+	3	3	3	3	7	5+

A Beastmaster is a single model armed with an agoniser. It rides a skyboard equipped with splinter pods.

WEAPON	RANGE	TYPE	S	AP	D	ABILITIES
Splinter pods	18"	Assault 2	*	0	1	Poisoned Weapon (pg 87)
Agoniser	Melee	Melee	*	-2	1	Poisoned Weapon (pg 87)

ABILITIES	**Power From Pain, Combat Drugs** (pg 87)
	Beastmaster: Re-roll hit rolls of 1 for friendly **DRUKHARI BEAST** units whilst they are within 6" of this model. Friendly **DRUKHARI BEAST** units can use this model's Leadership characteristic instead of their own whilst they are within 6" of it. In addition, if your army is Battle-forged, you must include at least one **DRUKHARI BEAST** unit in a Detachment for each Beastmaster in that Detachment. **DRUKHARI BEAST** units do not take up slots in a Detachment that includes any Beastmasters. This model can never have a Warlord Trait.
FACTION KEYWORDS	**AELDARI, DRUKHARI, <WYCH CULT>**
KEYWORDS	**CHARACTER, INFANTRY, SKYBOARD, FLY, BEASTMASTER**

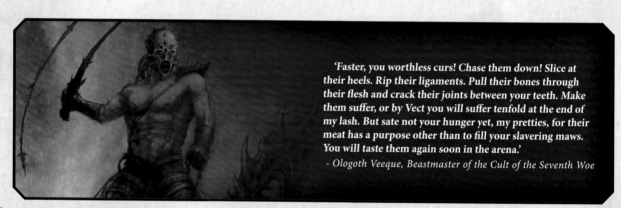

'Faster, you worthless curs! Chase them down! Slice at their heels. Rip their ligaments. Pull their bones through their flesh and crack their joints between your teeth. Make them suffer, or by Vect you will suffer tenfold at the end of my lash. But sate not your hunger yet, my pretties, for their meat has a purpose other than to fill your slavering maws. You will taste them again soon in the arena.'

- Ologoth Veeque, Beastmaster of the Cult of the Seventh Woe

GROTESQUES

NAME	M	WS	BS	S	T	W	A	Ld	Sv
Grotesque	7"	3+	6+	5	5	4	4	8	6+

This unit contains 3 Grotesques. It can include up to 7 additional Grotesques (**Power Rating +2 per model**). Each model is armed with a monstrous cleaver and a flesh gauntlet.

WEAPON	RANGE	TYPE	S	AP	D	ABILITIES
Liquifier gun	8"	Assault D6	3	-D3	1	Each time this weapon is fired, roll a D3 to determine its AP for those attacks. For example, if you rolled a 1, this weapon would have an AP of -1. This weapon automatically hits its target.
Flesh gauntlet	Melee	Melee	User	0	1	Each time you roll a wound roll of 6+ for this weapon, other than against **VEHICLES**, the target suffers a mortal wound in addition to any other damage.
Monstrous cleaver	Melee	Melee	User	-2	1	Each time the bearer fights, it can make 1 additional attack with this weapon.

WARGEAR OPTIONS	• Any model may replace its monstrous cleaver with a liquifier gun.
ABILITIES	**Power From Pain** (pg 87) **Insensible To Pain:** Models in this unit have a 5+ invulnerable save.
FACTION KEYWORDS	**AELDARI, DRUKHARI, <HAEMONCULUS COVEN>**
KEYWORDS	**INFANTRY, GROTESQUES**

CLAWED FIENDS

2 POWER

NAME	M	WS	BS	S	T	W	A	Ld	Sv
Clawed Fiend	10"	4+	-	5	5	4	5	4	5+

This unit contains 1 Clawed Fiend. It may include up to 2 additional Clawed Fiends (**Power Rating +3**) or up to 5 additional Clawed Fiends (**Power Rating +8**). Each model attacks with clawed fists.

WEAPON	RANGE	TYPE	S	AP	D	ABILITIES
Clawed fists	Melee	Melee	User	-1	2	-

ABILITIES	**Berserk Rage:** Increase a Clawed Fiend's Attacks characteristic by 1 whilst it has 3 or fewer wounds remaining.
FACTION KEYWORDS	AELDARI, DRUKHARI
KEYWORDS	BEAST, CLAWED FIENDS

KHYMERAE

1 POWER

NAME	M	WS	BS	S	T	W	A	Ld	Sv
Khymera	10"	3+	-	4	4	1	3	4	6+

This unit contains 2 Khymerae. It may include up to 5 additional pairs of Khymerae (**Power Rating +1 per pair**). Each model attacks with claws and talons.

WEAPON	RANGE	TYPE	S	AP	D	ABILITIES
Claws and talons	Melee	Melee	User	0	1	-

ABILITIES	**Otherworldly:** Models in this unit have a 5+ invulnerable save.
FACTION KEYWORDS	AELDARI, DRUKHARI
KEYWORDS	BEAST, DAEMON, KHYMERAE

RAZORWING FLOCKS

2 POWER

NAME	M	WS	BS	S	T	W	A	Ld	Sv
Razorwing Flock	12"	4+	-	2	2	4	4	4	7+

This unit contains up to 3 Razorwing Flocks. It may include up to 3 additional Razorwing Flocks (**Power Rating +2**) or up to 9 additional Razorwing Flocks (**Power Rating +5**). Each model attacks with its razor feathers.

WEAPON	RANGE	TYPE	S	AP	D	ABILITIES
Razor feathers	Melee	Melee	User	-1	1	-

FACTION KEYWORDS	AELDARI, DRUKHARI
KEYWORDS	BEAST, SWARM, FLY, RAZORWING FLOCKS

REAVERS

NAME	M	WS	BS	S	T	W	A	Ld	Sv
Reaver	18"	3+	3+	3	4	2	2	7	4+
Arena Champion	18"	3+	3+	3	4	2	3	8	4+

This unit contains 1 Arena Champion and 2 Reavers. It can include up to 3 additional Reavers (**Power Rating +3**), up to 6 additional Reavers (**Power Rating +7**) or up to 9 additional Reavers (**Power Rating +10**). Each model is armed with a splinter pistol and rides a Reaver jetbike equipped with a splinter rifle and bladevanes.

WEAPON	RANGE	TYPE	S	AP	D	ABILITIES
Blaster	18"	Assault 1	8	-4	D6	-
Heat lance	18"	Assault 1	6	-5	D6	If the target is within half range of this weapon, roll two dice when inflicting damage with it and discard the lowest result.
Splinter pistol	12"	Pistol 1	*	0	1	Poisoned Weapon (pg 87)
Splinter rifle	24"	Rapid Fire 1	*	0	1	Poisoned Weapon (pg 87)
Agoniser	Melee	Melee	*	-2	1	Poisoned Weapon (pg 87)
Bladevanes	Melee	Melee	4	-1	1	-
Power sword	Melee	Melee	User	-3	1	-

WARGEAR OPTIONS	• The Arena Champion may take either a power sword or an agoniser. • For every three models in the unit, one model may replace its splinter rifle with a heat lance or blaster. • For every three models in the unit, one model may take a grav-talon or cluster caltrops.

ABILITIES	**Power From Pain, Combat Drugs** (pg 87) **Grav-talon:** After this unit has completed a charge move, roll a D6 for each of its models with a grav-talon that is within 1" of an enemy unit – on a 4+ that unit suffers a mortal wound.	**Cluster Caltrops:** Roll a D6 for each enemy unit within 1" of any models with cluster caltrops in a unit that Falls Back – on a 4+ that unit suffers a mortal wound. **Matchless Swiftness:** When this unit Advances, add 8" to its Move characteristic for that Movement phase instead of rolling a dice.

FACTION KEYWORDS	**AELDARI, DRUKHARI, <WYCH CULT>**
KEYWORDS	**BIKER, FLY, REAVERS**

The skills learnt by Reavers in Commorragh's high-speed arenas are swiftly put to use on the battlefields of realspace.

HELLIONS

NAME	M	WS	BS	S	T	W	A	Ld	Sv
Hellion	14"	3+	3+	3	3	1	2	7	5+
Helliarch	14"	3+	3+	3	3	1	3	8	5+

This unit contains 1 Helliarch and 4 Hellions. It can include up to 5 additional Hellions (**Power Rating +4**), up to 10 additional Hellions (**Power Rating +7**) or up to 15 additional Hellions (**Power Rating +11**). Each model is armed with a hellglaive and rides a skyboard equipped with splinter pods.

WEAPON	RANGE	TYPE	S	AP	D	ABILITIES
Phantasm grenade launcher	18"	Assault D3	1	0	1	If a unit is hit by one or more phantasm grenade launchers, subtract 1 from its Leadership characteristic until the end of the turn.
Splinter pistol	12"	Pistol 1	*	0	1	Poisoned Weapon (pg 87)
Splinter pods	18"	Assault 2	*	0	1	Poisoned Weapon (pg 87)
Agoniser	Melee	Melee	*	-2	1	Poisoned Weapon (pg 87)
Hellglaive	Melee	Melee	+1	0	2	-
Power sword	Melee	Melee	User	-3	1	-
Stunclaw	Melee	Melee	+1	0	1	Each time you roll a wound roll of 6+ for this weapon, the target suffers a mortal wound in addition to any other damage.

WARGEAR OPTIONS	• The Helliarch may take a phantasm grenade launcher.
	• The Helliarch may replace their hellglaive with one of the following options:
	  - Splinter pistol and stunclaw
	  - Splinter pistol and power sword
	  - Splinter pistol and agoniser

ABILITIES	**Power From Pain, Combat Drugs** (pg 87) **Hit and Run:** This unit can both Fall Back and charge in the same turn.
FACTION KEYWORDS	**Aeldari, Drukhari, <Wych Cult>**
KEYWORDS	**Infantry, Skyboard, Fly, Hellions**

During a raid, the members of a Hellion gang often compete to see who can make the most spectacular kill.

SCOURGES

NAME	M	WS	BS	S	T	W	A	Ld	Sv
Scourge	14"	3+	3+	3	3	1	1	7	4+
Solarite	14"	3+	3+	3	3	1	2	8	4+

This unit contains 1 Solarite and 4 Scourges. It can include up to 5 additional Scourges (**Power Rating +3**). Each model is armed with a shardcarbine and plasma grenades.

WEAPON	RANGE	TYPE	S	AP	D	ABILITIES
Blast pistol	6"	Pistol 1	8	-4	D6	-
Blaster	18"	Assault 1	8	-4	D6	-
Dark lance	36"	Heavy 1	8	-4	D6	-
Haywire blaster	24"	Assault D3	4	-1	1	If the target is a **Vehicle** and you roll a wound roll of 4+ for this weapon, the target suffers a mortal wound in addition to any other damage. If the wound roll is 6+, inflict D3 mortal wounds instead of 1.
Heat lance	18"	Assault 1	6	-5	D6	If the target is within half range of this weapon, roll two dice when inflicting damage with it and discard the lowest result.
Shardcarbine	18"	Assault 3	*	0	1	Poisoned Weapon (pg 87)
Shredder	12"	Assault D6	6	-1	1	When attacking an **Infantry** unit, re-roll failed wound rolls for this weapon.
Splinter cannon	36"	Rapid Fire 3	*	0	1	Poisoned Weapon (pg 87)
Splinter pistol	12"	Pistol 1	*	0	1	Poisoned Weapon (pg 87)
Agoniser	Melee	Melee	*	-2	1	Poisoned Weapon (pg 87)
Power lance	Melee	Melee	+2	-1	1	-
Venom blade	Melee	Melee	*	0	1	Poisoned Weapon (pg 87). Add 2 to wound rolls made for this weapon, unless it is targeting a **Vehicle**.
Plasma grenade	6"	Grenade D6	4	-1	1	-

WARGEAR OPTIONS	
	• Up to four Scourges may replace their shardcarbine with either a splinter cannon, dark lance, heat lance, shredder, haywire blaster or blaster.
	• The Solarite may replace their shardcarbine with either a splinter pistol or blast pistol.
	• The Solarite may take a venom blade, power lance or agoniser.

ABILITIES	Power From Pain (pg 87)	**Winged Strike:** During deployment, you can set up this unit flying high in the skies instead of placing it on the battlefield. At the end of any of your Movement phases the Scourges can use a winged strike to arrive – set them up anywhere on the battlefield that is more than 9" away from any enemy models.
	Ghostplate Armour: Models in this unit have a 6+ invulnerable save.	

FACTION KEYWORDS	**Aeldari, Drukhari**
KEYWORDS	**Infantry, Fly, Scourges**

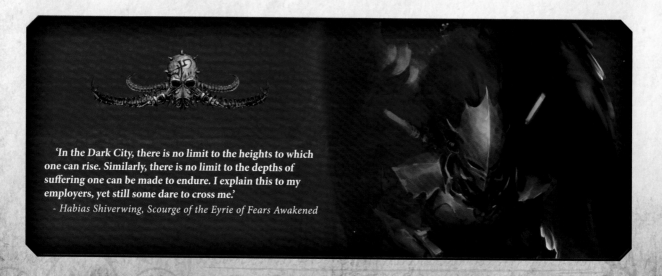

'In the Dark City, there is no limit to the heights to which one can rise. Similarly, there is no limit to the depths of suffering one can be made to endure. I explain this to my employers, yet still some dare to cross me.'

– *Habias Shiverwing, Scourge of the Eyrie of Fears Awakened*

As the battle rages on, Talos are unleashed by their Haemonculi masters to gather choice samples from the most intriguing opponents.

TALOS

NAME	M	WS	BS	S	T	W	A	Ld	Sv
Talos	8"	3+	4+	6	6	7	5	8	3+

This unit contains 1 Talos. It may contain an additional Talos (**Power Rating +6**) or 2 additional Talos (**Power Rating +12**). Each model is equipped with two splinter cannons and two macro-scalpels.

WEAPON	RANGE	TYPE	S	AP	D	ABILITIES
Haywire blaster	24"	Assault D3	4	-1	1	If the target is a **Vehicle** and you roll a wound roll of 4+ for this weapon, the target suffers 1 mortal wound in addition to any other damage. If the wound roll is 6+, inflict D3 mortal wounds instead of 1.
Heat lance	18"	Assault 1	6	-5	D6	If the target is within half range of this weapon, roll two dice when inflicting damage with it and discard the lowest result.
Splinter cannon	36"	Rapid Fire 3	*	0	1	Poisoned Weapon (pg 87)
Stinger pod	24"	Assault 2D6	5	0	1	-
Twin liquifier gun	8"	Assault 2D6	3	-D3	1	Each time this weapon is fired, roll a D3 to determine its AP for those attacks. For example, if you rolled a 1, this weapon would have an AP of -1. This weapon automatically hits its target.
Chain-flails	Melee	Melee	User	0	1	Make 2 hit rolls for each attack with this weapon. You can re-roll failed wound rolls for this weapon.
Ichor injector	Melee	Melee	User	-1	1	The bearer can only make a single attack with this weapon each time it fights. You can re-roll failed wound rolls for this weapon. Each time you roll a wound roll of 6+ for this weapon, the target suffers D3 mortal wounds in addition to any other damage.
Macro-scalpel	Melee	Melee	+1	-2	2	If a model is equipped with two macro-scalpels, each time it fights it can make 1 additional attack with them.
Talos gauntlet	Melee	Melee	+2	-3	D3	When attacking with this weapon, you must subtract 1 from the hit roll.

WARGEAR OPTIONS	• Any Talos may replace one of its macro-scalpels with an ichor injector or a twin liquifier gun.
	• Any Talos may replace one of its macro-scalpels with chain-flails or a Talos gauntlet.
	• Any Talos may replace its two splinter cannons with a stinger pod, two heat lances or two haywire blasters.

ABILITIES	Power From Pain (pg 87)	**Explodes:** If a model in this unit is reduced to 0 wounds, roll a D6 before removing the model from the battlefield. On a 6 it explodes, and each unit within 6" suffers a mortal wound.
	Insensible To Pain: Models in this unit have a 5+ invulnerable save.	

FACTION KEYWORDS	**Aeldari, Drukhari, <Haemonculus Coven>**
KEYWORDS	**Monster, Talos**

CRONOS

NAME	M	WS	BS	S	T	W	A	Ld	Sv
Cronos	8"	4+	3+	5	6	7	3	9	3+

This unit contains 1 Cronos. It may contain an additional Cronos (**Power Rating +4**) or 2 additional Cronos (**Power Rating +8**). Each model is equipped with a spirit syphon and spirit-leech tentacles.

WEAPON	RANGE	TYPE	S	AP	D	ABILITIES
Spirit syphon	8"	Assault D6	3	-2	1	This weapon automatically hits its target. Each time you make a wound roll of 6+ for this weapon, that hit is resolved with a Damage characteristic of D3.
Spirit vortex	18"	Assault D6	3	-2	1	Each time you make a wound roll of 6+ for this weapon, that hit is resolved with a Damage characteristic of D3.
Spirit-leech tentacles	Melee	Melee	User	-1	1	Each time you make a wound roll of 6+ for this weapon, that hit is resolved with a Damage characteristic of D3.

WARGEAR OPTIONS	• Any model may take a spirit vortex. • Any model may take a spirit probe.	
ABILITIES	**Power From Pain** (pg 87) **Insensible To Pain:** Models in this unit have a 5+ invulnerable save. **Explodes:** If a model in this unit is reduced to 0 wounds, roll a D6 before removing the model from the battlefield. On a 6 it explodes, and each unit within 6" suffers a mortal wound.	**Spirit Probe:** Re-roll wound rolls of 1 for **DRUKHARI** units in the Fight phase whilst they are within 6" of any friendly Cronos with a spirit probe. In addition, if a Cronos with a spirit probe inflicts one or more unsaved wounds in the Fight phase, you can pick a friendly **DRUKHARI** unit within 6" of it that is not a **VEHICLE**. The unit you pick regains 1 lost wound.
FACTION KEYWORDS	**AELDARI, DRUKHARI, <HAEMONCULUS COVEN>**	
KEYWORDS	**MONSTER, CRONOS**	

RAVAGER

DAMAGE
Some of this model's characteristics change as it suffers damage, as shown below:

REMAINING W	M	BS	A
6-10+	14"	3+	3
3-5	10"	4+	D3
1-2	6"	5+	1

NAME	M	WS	BS	S	T	W	A	Ld	Sv
Ravager	*	4+	*	6	6	10	*	7	4+

A Ravager is a single model equipped with bladevanes and three dark lances.

WEAPON	RANGE	TYPE	S	AP	D	ABILITIES
Dark lance	36"	Heavy 1	8	-4	D6	Change this weapon's Type from Heavy to Assault if it is equipped on a **VEHICLE**.
Disintegrator cannon	36"	Assault 3	5	-3	2	-
Bladevanes	Melee	Melee	4	-1	1	-

WARGEAR OPTIONS	• This model may replace one dark lance with one disintegrator cannon, two dark lances with two disintegrator cannons, or three dark lances with three disintegrator cannons. • This model may take items from the *Vehicle Equipment* list.	
ABILITIES	**Night Shield:** This model has a 5+ invulnerable save against ranged weapons. **Hovering:** Instead of measuring distance and ranges to and from this model's base, measure to and from this model's hull or base (whichever is closer).	**Explodes:** If this model is reduced to 0 wounds, roll a D6 before removing it from the battlefield. On a 6 it explodes, and each unit within 6" suffers D3 mortal wounds.
FACTION KEYWORDS	**AELDARI, DRUKHARI, <KABAL>**	
KEYWORDS	**VEHICLE, FLY, RAVAGER**	

RAIDER

NAME	M	WS	BS	S	T	W	A	Ld	Sv
Raider	*	4+	*	6	5	10	*	7	4+

DAMAGE

Some of this model's characteristics change as it suffers damage, as shown below:

REMAINING W	M	BS	A
6-10+	14"	3+	3
3-5	10"	4+	D3
1-2	6"	5+	1

A Raider is a single model equipped with a dark lance and bladevanes.

WEAPON	RANGE	TYPE	S	AP	D	ABILITIES
Dark lance	36"	Heavy 1	8	-4	D6	Change this weapon's Type from Heavy to Assault if it is equipped on a **VEHICLE**.
Disintegrator cannon	36"	Assault 3	5	-3	2	-
Bladevanes	Melee	Melee	4	-1	1	-

WARGEAR OPTIONS	• This model may replace its dark lance with a disintegrator cannon. • This model may take splinter racks. • This model may take items from the *Vehicle Equipment* list.

ABILITIES	**Open-topped:** Models embarked on this model can attack in their Shooting phase. Measure the range and draw line of sight from any point on this model. When they do so, any restrictions or modifiers that apply to this model also apply to its passengers; for example, the passengers cannot shoot if this model has Fallen Back in the same turn, cannot shoot (except with Pistols) if this model is within 1" of an enemy unit, and so on. Note that the passengers cannot shoot if this model Falls Back, even though the Raider itself can. **Hovering:** Instead of measuring distance and ranges to and from this model's base, measure to and from this model's hull or base (whichever is closer).	**Night Shield:** This model has a 5+ invulnerable save against ranged weapons. **Explodes:** If this model is reduced to 0 wounds, roll a D6 before removing it from the battlefield and before any embarked models disembark. On a 6 it explodes, and each unit within 6" suffers D3 mortal wounds. **Splinter Racks:** If this model has splinter racks, then each time a model that is embarked upon it shoots a splinter pistol or splinter rifle and you roll a 6+ to hit with that weapon, it scores 2 hits instead of 1. This does not apply to Artefacts of Cruelty.

TRANSPORT	This model can transport 10 **DRUKHARI INFANTRY** models. Each Grotesque takes the space of two models. This model cannot transport Scourges or **SKYBOARD** models.

FACTION KEYWORDS	**AELDARI, DRUKHARI, <HAEMONCULUS COVEN>** or **<KABAL>** or **<WYCH CULT>**

KEYWORDS	**VEHICLE, TRANSPORT, FLY, RAIDER**

VENOM

NAME	M	WS	BS	S	T	W	A	Ld	Sv
Venom	16"	4+	3+	5	5	6	2	7	4+

A Venom is a single model equipped with a twin splinter rifle, a splinter cannon and bladevanes.

WEAPON	RANGE	TYPE	S	AP	D	ABILITIES
Splinter cannon	36"	Rapid Fire 3	*	0	1	Poisoned Weapon (pg 87)
Twin splinter rifle	24"	Rapid Fire 2	*	0	1	Poisoned Weapon (pg 87)
Bladevanes	Melee	Melee	4	-1	1	-

WARGEAR OPTIONS	• This model may replace its twin splinter rifle with an additional splinter cannon. • This model may take items from the *Vehicle Equipment* list.

ABILITIES	**Open-topped:** Models embarked on this model can attack in their Shooting phase. Measure the range and draw line of sight from any point on this model. When they do so, any restrictions or modifiers that apply to this model also apply to its passengers; for example, the passengers cannot shoot if this model has Fallen Back in the same turn, cannot shoot (except with Pistols) if this model is within 1" of an enemy unit, and so on. Note that the passengers cannot shoot if this model Falls Back, even though the Venom itself can.	**Flickerfield:** Subtract 1 from hit rolls for attacks that target this model in the Shooting phase. **Explodes:** If this model is reduced to 0 wounds, roll a D6 before removing it from the battlefield and before any embarked models disembark. On a 6 it explodes, and each unit within 6" suffers 1 mortal wound. **Night Shield:** This model has a 5+ invulnerable save against ranged weapons.

TRANSPORT	This model can transport 5 **DRUKHARI INFANTRY** models other than Grotesques, Scourges and **SKYBOARD** models.

FACTION KEYWORDS	**AELDARI, DRUKHARI, <HAEMONCULUS COVEN>** or **<KABAL>** or **<WYCH CULT>**

KEYWORDS	**VEHICLE, TRANSPORT, FLY, VENOM**

RAZORWING JETFIGHTER

8 POWER

DAMAGE
Some of this model's characteristics change as it suffers damage, as shown below:

REMAINING W	M	BS	A
6-10+	20-72"	3+	3
3-5	20-48"	4+	D3
1-2	20-32"	5+	1

NAME	M	WS	BS	S	T	W	A	Ld	Sv
Razorwing Jetfighter	*	6+	*	6	6	10	*	7	4+

A Razorwing Jetfighter is a single model equipped with two disintegrator cannons, a twin splinter rifle and Razorwing missiles.

WEAPON	RANGE	TYPE	S	AP	D	ABILITIES
Dark lance	36"	Heavy 1	8	-4	D6	Change this weapon's Type from Heavy to Assault if it is equipped on a **Vehicle**.
Disintegrator cannon	36"	Assault 3	5	-3	2	-
Razorwing missiles	When attacking with this weapon, choose one of the profiles below.					
- Monoscythe missile	48"	Assault D6	6	0	2	-
- Necrotoxin missile	48"	Assault 3D3	*	0	1	Poisoned Weapon (pg 87). Add 2 to wound rolls made for this weapon, unless it is targeting a **Vehicle**.
- Shatterfield missile	48"	Assault D6	7	-1	1	Re-roll failed wound rolls for this weapon.
Splinter cannon	36"	Rapid Fire 3	*	0	1	Poisoned Weapon (pg 87)
Twin splinter rifle	24"	Rapid Fire 2	*	0	1	Poisoned Weapon (pg 87)

WARGEAR OPTIONS	• This model may replace its two disintegrator cannons with two dark lances. • This model may replace its twin splinter rifle with a splinter cannon.

ABILITIES	**Supersonic:** Each time this model moves, first pivot it on the spot up to 90° (this does not contribute to how far the model moves), and then move the model straight forwards. Note that it cannot pivot again after the initial pivot. When this model Advances, increase its Move characteristic by 20" until the end of the phase – do not roll a dice. **Night Shield:** This model has a 5+ invulnerable save against ranged weapons.	**Hard to Hit:** Your opponent must subtract 1 from hit rolls for attacks that target this model in the Shooting phase. **Airborne:** This model cannot charge, can only be charged by units that can **Fly**, and can only attack or be attacked in the Fight phase by units that can **Fly**. **Crash and Burn:** If this model is reduced to 0 wounds, roll a D6 before removing it from the battlefield. On a 6 it crashes in a fiery explosion and each unit within 6" suffers D3 mortal wounds.

FACTION KEYWORDS	**Aeldari, Drukhari, <Kabal>** or **<Wych Cult>**
KEYWORDS	**Vehicle, Fly, Razorwing Jetfighter**

With terrifying swiftness, the Razorwing Jetfighter swats the Ork flyers from the sky, reducing them to burning comets of scrap.

From the smog-choked clouds, a wing of Voidraven Bombers rain destruction down upon the T'au gun-line.

9 POWER

VOIDRAVEN BOMBER

NAME	M	WS	BS	S	T	W	A	Ld	Sv
Voidraven Bomber	*	6+	*	6	6	12	*	7	4+

DAMAGE
Some of this model's characteristics change as it suffers damage, as shown below:

REMAINING W	M	BS	A
7-12+	20-60"	3+	3
4-6	20-40"	4+	D3
1-3	20-25"	5+	1

A Voidraven Bomber is a single model equipped with two void lances.

WEAPON	RANGE	TYPE	S	AP	D	ABILITIES
Dark scythe	24"	Assault D3	8	-4	D3	-
Void lance	36"	Assault 1	9	-4	D6	-
Voidraven missiles	When attacking with this weapon, choose one of the profiles below.					
- Implosion missile	48"	Assault D3	6	-3	1	-
- Shatterfield missile	48"	Assault D6	7	-1	1	Re-roll failed wound rolls for this weapon.

WARGEAR OPTIONS	• This model may replace its two void lances with two dark scythes. • This model may take Voidraven missiles.

ABILITIES	**Crash and Burn:** If this model is reduced to 0 wounds, roll a D6 before removing it from the battlefield. On a 6 it crashes in a fiery explosion and each unit within 6" suffers D3 mortal wounds. **Hard to Hit:** Your opponent must subtract 1 from hit rolls for attacks that target this model in the Shooting phase. **Airborne:** This model cannot charge, can only be charged by units that can **FLY**, and can only attack or be attacked in the Fight phase by units that can **FLY**. **Night Shield:** This model has a 5+ invulnerable save against ranged weapons.	**Supersonic:** Each time this model moves, first pivot it on the spot up to 90° (this does not contribute to how far the model moves), and then move the model straight forwards. Note that it cannot pivot again after the initial pivot. When this model Advances, increase its Move characteristic by 20" until the end of the phase – do not roll a dice. **Void Mine:** Once per battle, a Voidraven Bomber can drop a void mine on an enemy unit it moves over in one of its Movement phases. After the Voidraven Bomber has moved, pick one enemy unit that it flew over. Then, roll three D6 for each **VEHICLE** or **MONSTER** in the unit, or one D6 for every other model in the unit, up to a maximum of 10 D6. For each roll of 3+, the unit being bombed suffers a mortal wound.

FACTION KEYWORDS	**AELDARI, DRUKHARI, <KABAL>** or **<WYCH CULT>**
KEYWORDS	**VEHICLE, FLY, VOIDRAVEN BOMBER**

ARMOURY OF COMMORRAGH

The Drukhari utilise all manner of weaponry, from simple yet effective blades to arcane devices that unleash the power of captive stars. Yet all of these weapons have a shared purpose – to swiftly obliterate the enemy's defences so that the suffering of those who survive can be savoured. The profiles for each item of Drukhari wargear is listed below.

RANGED WEAPONS

WEAPON	RANGE	TYPE	S	AP	D	ABILITIES
Baleblast	18"	Assault 2	4	-1	1	Each time you roll a wound roll of 6+ for this weapon, the target suffers a mortal wound in addition to any other damage.
Blast pistol	6"	Pistol 1	8	-4	D6	-
Blaster	18"	Assault 1	8	-4	D6	-
Casket of Flensing	12"	Assault 2D6	3	-2	1	This weapon can only be fired once per battle.
Dark lance	36"	Heavy 1	8	-4	D6	Change this weapon's Type from Heavy to Assault if it is equipped on a VEHICLE.
Dark scythe	24"	Assault D3	8	-4	D3	-
Disintegrator cannon	36"	Assault 3	5	-3	2	-
Eyeburst	9"	Assault 4	4	-2	1	-
Haywire blaster	24"	Assault D3	4	-1	1	If the target is a VEHICLE and you roll a wound roll of 4+ for this weapon, the target suffers a mortal wound in addition to any other damage. If the wound roll is 6+, inflict D3 mortal wounds instead of 1.
Heat lance	18"	Assault 1	6	-5	D6	If the target is within half range of this weapon, roll two dice when inflicting damage with it and discard the lowest result.
Hexrifle	36"	Heavy 1	4	-1	1	This weapon may target a CHARACTER even if it is not the closest enemy unit. Each time you roll a wound roll of 6+ for this weapon, the target suffers a mortal wound in addition to any other damage.
Liquifier gun	8"	Assault D6	3	-D3	1	Each time this weapon is fired, roll a D3 to determine its AP for those attacks. For example, if you rolled a 1, this weapon would have an AP of -1. This weapon automatically hits its target.
Ossefactor	24"	Assault 1	*	-3	1	Poisoned Weapon (pg 87). Add 2 to wound rolls made for this weapon, unless it is targeting a VEHICLE. If a model is slain by this weapon, the model's unit immediately suffers a mortal wound on a D6 roll of 4+.
Phantasm grenade launcher	18"	Assault D3	1	0	1	If a unit is hit by one or more phantasm grenade launchers, subtract 1 from its Leadership characteristic until the end of the turn.
Plasma grenade	6"	Grenade D6	4	-1	1	-
Razorwing missiles	When attacking with this weapon, choose one of the profiles below.					
- Monoscythe missile	48"	Assault D6	6	0	2	-
- Necrotoxin missile	48"	Assault 3D3	*	0	1	Poisoned Weapon (pg 87). Add 2 to wound rolls made for this weapon, unless it is targeting a VEHICLE.
- Shatterfield missile	48"	Assault D6	7	-1	1	Re-roll failed wound rolls for this weapon.
Shardcarbine	18"	Assault 3	*	0	1	Poisoned Weapon (pg 87)
Shredder	12"	Assault D6	6	-1	1	When attacking an INFANTRY unit, re-roll failed wound rolls for this weapon.
Spirit syphon	8"	Assault D6	3	-2	1	This weapon automatically hits its target. Each time you make a wound roll of 6+ for this weapon, that hit is resolved with a Damage characteristic of D3.
Spirit vortex	18"	Assault D6	3	-2	1	Each time you make a wound roll of 6+ for this weapon, that hit is resolved with a Damage characteristic of D3.
Splinter cannon	36"	Rapid Fire 3	*	0	1	Poisoned Weapon (pg 87)
Splinter pistol	12"	Pistol 1	*	0	1	Poisoned Weapon (pg 87)
Splinter pods	18"	Assault 2	*	0	1	Poisoned Weapon (pg 87)
Splinter rifle	24"	Rapid Fire 1	*	0	1	Poisoned Weapon (pg 87)
Stinger pistol	12"	Pistol 1	*	0	1	Poisoned Weapon (pg 87). Add 2 to wound rolls made for this weapon, unless it is targeting a VEHICLE.
Stinger pod	24"	Assault 2D6	5	0	1	-

RANGED WEAPONS						
WEAPON	**RANGE**	**TYPE**	**S**	**AP**	**D**	**ABILITIES**
Twin liquifier gun	8"	Assault 2D6	3	-D3	1	Each time this weapon is fired, roll a D3 to determine its AP for those attacks. For example, if you rolled a 1, this weapon would have an AP of -1. This weapon automatically hits its target.
Twin splinter rifle	24"	Rapid Fire 2	*	0	1	Poisoned Weapon (pg 87)
Void lance	36"	Assault 1	9	-4	D6	-
Voidraven missiles	When attacking with this weapon, choose one of the profiles below.					
- Implosion missile	48"	Assault D3	6	-3	1	-
- Shatterfield missile	48"	Assault D6	7	-1	1	Re-roll failed wound rolls for this weapon.

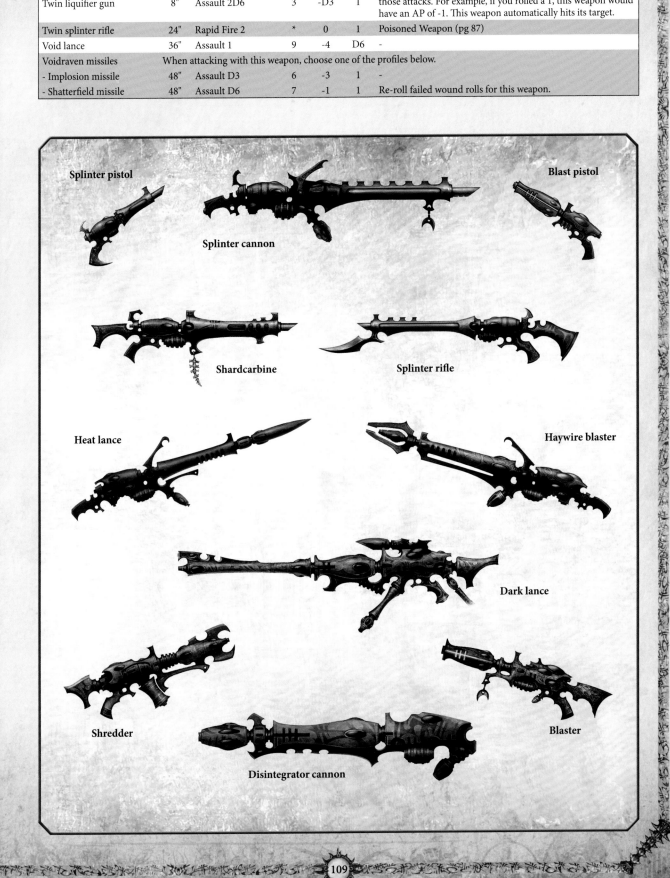

Splinter pistol

Splinter cannon

Blast pistol

Shardcarbine

Splinter rifle

Heat lance

Haywire blaster

Dark lance

Shredder

Blaster

Disintegrator cannon

MELEE WEAPONS

WEAPON	RANGE	TYPE	S	AP	D	ABILITIES
Agoniser	Melee	Melee	*	-2	1	Poisoned Weapon (pg 87)
Archite glaive	Melee	Melee	+2	-3	1	When attacking with this weapon, you must subtract 1 from the hit roll.
Bladevanes	Melee	Melee	4	-1	1	-
Chain-flails	Melee	Melee	User	0	1	Make 2 hit rolls for each attack with this weapon, instead of 1. You can re-roll failed wound rolls for this weapon.
Clawed fists	Melee	Melee	User	-1	2	-
Claws and talons	Melee	Melee	User	0	1	-
Demiklaives	Each time the bearer fights, choose one of the profiles below.					
- Single blade	Melee	Melee	+1	-3	1	-
- Dual blades	Melee	Melee	User	-2	1	A model attacking with dual blades can make 2 additional attacks with them each time it fights.
Electrocorrosive whip	Melee	Melee	*	-2	2	Poisoned Weapon (pg 87)
Flesh gauntlet	Melee	Melee	User	0	1	Each time you roll a wound roll of 6+ for this weapon, other than against **Vehicles**, the target suffers a mortal wound in addition to any other damage.
Glimmersteel blade	Melee	Melee	User	-1	1	-
Haemonculus tools	Melee	Melee	*	0	1	Poisoned Weapon (pg 87)
Hekatarii blade	Melee	Melee	User	0	1	Each time the bearer fights, it can make 1 additional attack with this weapon.
Hellglaive	Melee	Melee	+1	0	2	-
Huskblade	Melee	Melee	+1	-2	D3	-
Hydra gauntlets	Melee	Melee	User	-1	1	Each time the bearer fights, it can make 1 additional attack with this weapon. You can re-roll failed wound rolls for this weapon.
Ichor injector	Melee	Melee	User	-1	1	The bearer can only make a single attack with this weapon each time it fights. You can re-roll failed wound rolls for this weapon. Each time you roll a wound roll of 6+ for this weapon, the target suffers D3 mortal wounds in addition to any other damage.
Impaler	Melee	Melee	User	-1	2	-
Klaive	Melee	Melee	+1	-3	1	-
Macro-scalpel	Melee	Melee	+1	-2	2	If a model is equipped with two macro-scalpels, each time it fights it can make 1 additional attack with them.
Mane of barbs and hooks	Melee	Melee	User	0	1	Each time Lelith Hesperax fights, she can make 2 additional attacks with this weapon.
Mindphase gauntlet	Melee	Melee	User	0	2	-

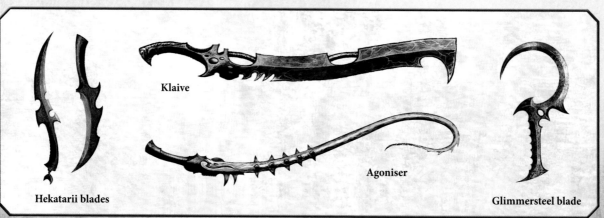

Klaive

Agoniser

Hekatarii blades

Glimmersteel blade

MELEE WEAPONS

WEAPON	RANGE	TYPE	S	AP	D	ABILITIES
Monstrous cleaver	Melee	Melee	User	-2	1	Each time the bearer fights, it can make 1 additional attack with this weapon.
Penetrating blade	Melee	Melee	User	-4	1	If Lelith Hesperax is armed with two penetrating blades, each time she fights she can make 1 additional attack with them.
Power lance	Melee	Melee	+2	-1	1	-
Power sword	Melee	Melee	User	-3	1	-
Razor feathers	Melee	Melee	User	-1	1	-
Razorflails	Melee	Melee	User	-1	1	Each time the bearer fights, it can make D3 additional attacks with this weapon. You can re-roll failed hit rolls for this weapon.
Scissorhand	Melee	Melee	*	-1	1	Poisoned Weapon (pg 87). Each time the bearer fights, it can make 1 additional attack with this weapon.
Shaimeshi blade	Melee	Melee	*	0	1	Poisoned Weapon (pg 87). Add 2 to wound rolls made for this weapon, unless it is targeting a **VEHICLE**. Each time you roll a wound roll of 6+ for this weapon, other than against a **VEHICLE**, the target suffers a mortal wound in addition to any other damage.
Shardnet and impaler	Melee	Melee	User	-1	2	Each time the bearer fights, it can make 1 additional attack with this weapon. If an **INFANTRY** unit is affected by the No Escape ability whilst it is within 3" of an enemy model armed with this weapon, the unit's controlling player rolls a D3 instead of a D6 when making the roll-off.
Shock prow	Melee	Melee	User	-1	1	The bearer can only make a single attack with this weapon each time it fights. If the bearer charged this turn, this weapon has a Damage characteristic of D3 instead of 1.
Spirit-leech tentacles	Melee	Melee	User	-1	1	Each time you make a wound roll of 6+ for this weapon, that hit is resolved with a Damage characteristic of D3 instead of 1.
Sslyth battle-blade	Melee	Melee	User	-1	1	-
Stunclaw	Melee	Melee	+1	0	1	Each time you roll a wound roll of 6+ for this weapon, the target suffers a mortal wound in addition to any other damage.
Talos gauntlet	Melee	Melee	+2	-3	D3	When attacking with this weapon, you must subtract 1 from the hit roll.
Venom blade	Melee	Melee	*	0	1	Poisoned Weapon (pg 87). Add 2 to wound rolls made for this weapon, unless it is targeting a **VEHICLE**.

VEHICLE EQUIPMENT

Chain-snares	Re-roll hit rolls of 1 for a model with chain-snares whenever it attacks with its bladevanes.
Grisly trophies	Roll a D6 each time a model flees from a unit that is within 6" of any enemy models with grisly trophies. For each roll of 6, one additional model flees that unit (these cannot cause additional models to flee).

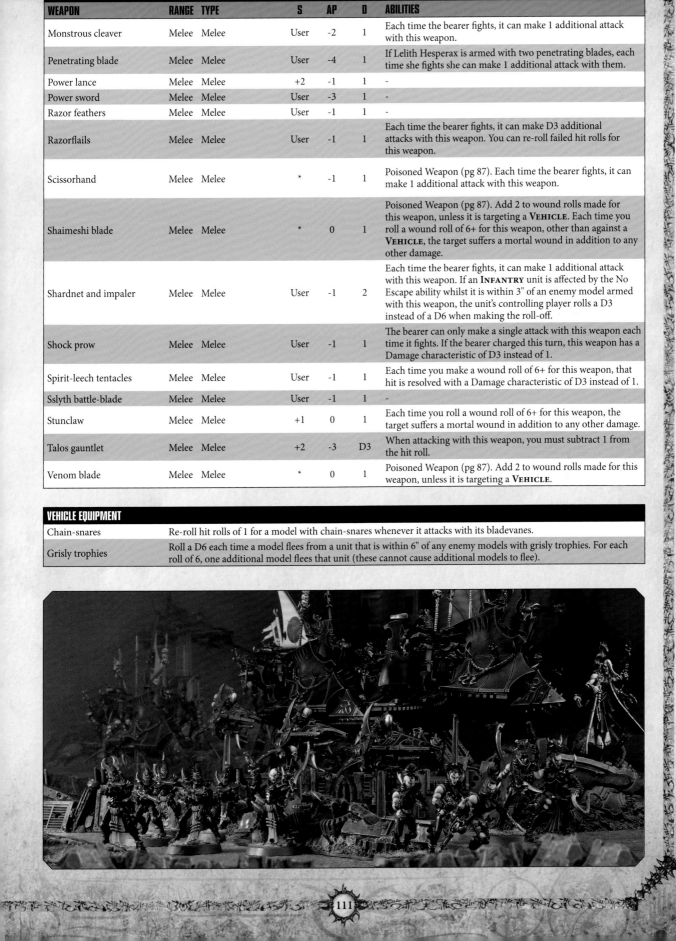

A vast raiding party tears across the blasted cityscape towards their enemy, eager to capture greenskins for the Dark City's arenas and to test the Orks' infamous insensibility to pain.

COMMORRITE RAIDERS

In this section you'll find rules for Battle-forged armies that include DRUKHARI Detachments – that is, any Detachment which includes only DRUKHARI units (as defined below). These rules include the abilities below and a series of Stratagems that can only be used by the Drukhari. This section also includes the Drukhari's unique Warlord Traits, Relics and Tactical Objectives. Together, these rules reflect the character and fighting style of the Drukhari in your games of Warhammer 40,000.

DRUKHARI UNITS

In the rules described in this section we often refer to 'DRUKHARI units' and 'DRUKHARI Warlords'. This is shorthand for a unit or Warlord that has the DRUKHARI keyword. Note that other Aeldari, such as the Harlequins and Craftworlds, deviate significantly in terms of organisation and fighting styles. These Aeldari cannot make use of any of the rules or abilities listed in this section, and instead have their own rules.

YNNARI is a keyword that some units in this book can gain when taken as part of a Reborn army, as detailed in other publications. If a Detachment includes any YNNARI units, it is no longer a DRUKHARI Detachment and will not gain any of the abilities listed below.

ABILITIES

All DRUKHARI Detachments (excluding Super-heavy Auxiliary Detachments) gain the following abilities:

VANGUARD OF THE DARK CITY

When the Drukhari visit their horrors on the denizens of realspace, they do so filled with arrogant assurance of their own superiority, seeing the galaxy's other inhabitants not as threats but as fodder to fuel the hungering soul of Commorragh.

If your army is Battle-forged, all Troops units in DRUKHARI Detachments gain this ability. Such a unit that is within range of an objective marker (as specified in the mission) controls that objective marker even if there are more enemy models within range of it. If an enemy unit within range of the same objective marker has a similar ability, then the objective marker is controlled by the player who has the most models within range of it as normal.

RAIDING FORCE

The fractious animosities that pervade the Dark City are set aside when orchestrating raids upon the worlds of lesser races.

If your Battle-forged army includes at least 3 DRUKHARI Patrol Detachments, you receive +4 Command Points. If your army includes 6 or more DRUKHARI Patrol Detachments, you receive +8 Command Points instead.

DRUKHARI OBSESSIONS

Over their millennia-long lives, the Drukhari have cultivated highly specific tastes for different types of suffering, and have refined to an art form the methods required to create their preferred flavours of pain.

If your army is Battle-forged, all <KABAL>, <WYCH CULT> and <HAEMONCULUS COVEN> units in a DRUKHARI Detachment gain a Drukhari Obsession, so long as every other unit in their Detachment is from the same Kabal, Wych Cult or Haemonculus Coven (if you include a mix of <KABAL>, <WYCH CULT> and/or <HAEMONCULUS COVEN> units in the same Detachment, none of those units gain an obsession). Note that for this purpose, Lelith Hesperax is a <WYCH CULT> unit and Urien Rakarth is a <HAEMONCULUS COVEN> unit.

The obsession gained depends on <KABAL>, <WYCH CULT> or <HAEMONCULUS COVEN> that unit is from, as shown over the next few pages. For example, a KABAL OF THE BLACK HEART unit with the Drukhari Obsessions ability gains the Thirst for Power obsession.

If you have chosen a Kabal, Wych Cult or Haemonculus Coven that does not feature on these lists, you can choose the Kabal, Wych Cult or Haemonculus Coven Obsession (respectively) that best suits the fighting style and battlefield strategies of the warriors that hail from it.

Blades for Hire

DRUKHARI BEASTS, INCUBI, Mandrakes and Scourges units can be included in a Drukhari Detachment without preventing other units in that Detachment from gaining a Drukhari Obsession. Note, however, that these units listed can never themselves benefit from a Drukhari Obsession.

MATCHED PLAY RULES

If you are using a Battle-forged army in a matched play game, the following rules apply:

COURT OF THE ARCHON

You can only include <KABAL> COURT OF THE ARCHON models in a Detachment that also includes one or more <KABAL> Archons, and you can only include a maximum of 4 COURT OF THE ARCHON models in the same Detachment.

DRUKHARI BEASTS

You can only include DRUKHARI BEAST units in a Detachment that also includes one or more Beastmasters, and you can only include a maximum of 3 DRUKHARI BEAST units in the same Detachment.

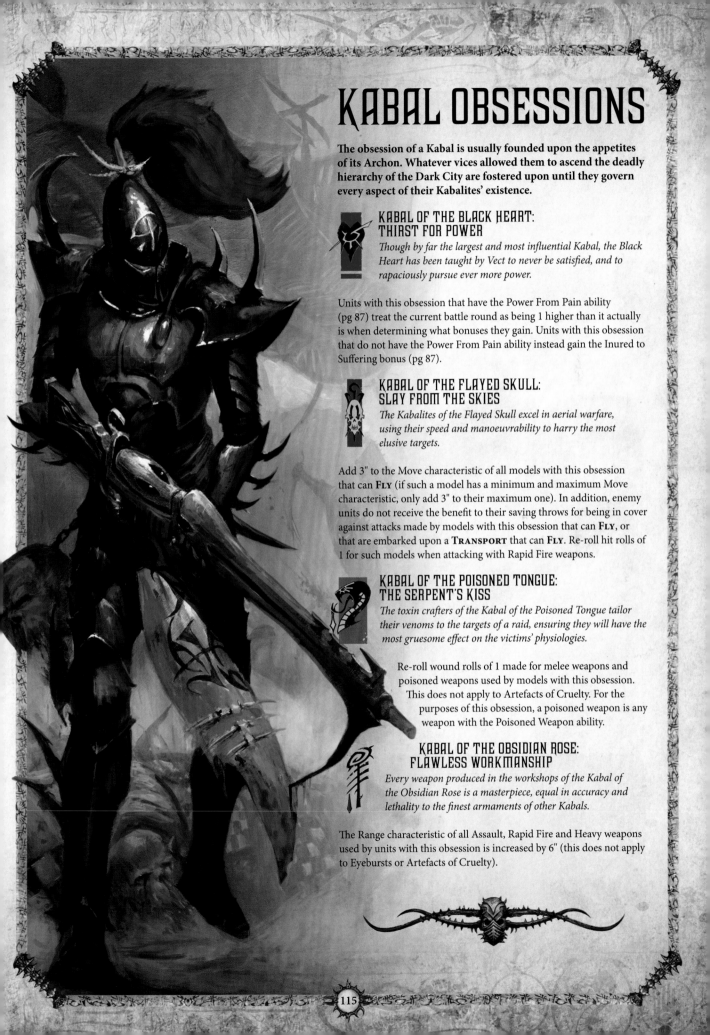

KABAL OBSESSIONS

The obsession of a Kabal is usually founded upon the appetites of its Archon. Whatever vices allowed them to ascend the deadly hierarchy of the Dark City are fostered upon until they govern every aspect of their Kabalites' existence.

KABAL OF THE BLACK HEART: THIRST FOR POWER

Though by far the largest and most influential Kabal, the Black Heart has been taught by Vect to never be satisfied, and to rapaciously pursue ever more power.

Units with this obsession that have the Power From Pain ability (pg 87) treat the current battle round as being 1 higher than it actually is when determining what bonuses they gain. Units with this obsession that do not have the Power From Pain ability instead gain the Inured to Suffering bonus (pg 87).

KABAL OF THE FLAYED SKULL: SLAY FROM THE SKIES

The Kabalites of the Flayed Skull excel in aerial warfare, using their speed and manoeuvrability to harry the most elusive targets.

Add 3" to the Move characteristic of all models with this obsession that can **FLY** (if such a model has a minimum and maximum Move characteristic, only add 3" to their maximum one). In addition, enemy units do not receive the benefit to their saving throws for being in cover against attacks made by models with this obsession that can **FLY**, or that are embarked upon a **TRANSPORT** that can **FLY**. Re-roll hit rolls of 1 for such models when attacking with Rapid Fire weapons.

KABAL OF THE POISONED TONGUE: THE SERPENT'S KISS

The toxin crafters of the Kabal of the Poisoned Tongue tailor their venoms to the targets of a raid, ensuring they will have the most gruesome effect on the victims' physiologies.

Re-roll wound rolls of 1 made for melee weapons and poisoned weapons used by models with this obsession. This does not apply to Artefacts of Cruelty. For the purposes of this obsession, a poisoned weapon is any weapon with the Poisoned Weapon ability.

KABAL OF THE OBSIDIAN ROSE: FLAWLESS WORKMANSHIP

Every weapon produced in the workshops of the Kabal of the Obsidian Rose is a masterpiece, equal in accuracy and lethality to the finest armaments of other Kabals.

The Range characteristic of all Assault, Rapid Fire and Heavy weapons used by units with this obsession is increased by 6" (this does not apply to Eyebursts or Artefacts of Cruelty).

WYCH CULT OBSESSIONS

Wych Cult obsessions arise from the performed slaughters in Commorragh's arenas. Each Cult has developed its signature style, a practised method of barbarity that continues to enthral the baying crowds.

CULT OF STRIFE: THE SPECTACLE OF MURDER
Whether enthralling spectators in the arena or slaughtering their way through an enemy army, the Cult of Strife have developed a penchant for bombastically violent opening manoeuvres.

Increase the Attacks characteristic of models with this obsession by 1 during any turn in which they charged, were charged or made a Heroic Intervention.

CULT OF THE CURSED BLADE: ONLY THE STRONG WILL THRIVE
There is no place for frailties amongst the Cult of the Cursed Blade, for they teach that weakness exists only to be exploited by the strong. Those Wyches who survive in the Cult's arena are the physical embodiment of this philosophy.

Increase the Strength characteristic of models with this obsession by 1. In addition, when a unit with this obsession fails a Morale test, only one model from that unit must flee.

CULT OF THE RED GRIEF: THE SPEED OF THE KILL
Wyches of the Cult of the Red Grief revel in high-speed murder, and there is fierce competition amongst their ranks as to who can butcher their victims the quickest.

Units with this obsession can charge in the same turn in which they Advanced. In addition, you can re-roll failed charge rolls for units with this obsession.

'The galaxy's battlefields provide almost as great a thrill as the arenas, but some adaptations are necessary. Without a proper audience, I must slice the eyelids off my victims so that I know they are witnessing the true extent of my skill. And when I am finished, I must make do with the wet applause that comes from the flapping of their rent flesh.'

- Resputia the Razor, Wych of the Red Grief

HAEMONCULUS COVEN OBSESSIONS

The obsession of each Haemonculus Coven was developed in the oubliettes and laboratories of the undercity, where over millennia these twisted immortals have indulged themselves in their favoured form of fleshcraft.

THE PROPHETS OF FLESH: CONNOISSEURS OF PAIN

The Prophets of Flesh have modified their own bodies and those of their servants to an extraordinary extent – so much so that few weapons their enemies bring to bear against them can inflict damage greater than that they have already endured.

If a model has this obsession, the invulnerable save conferred by its Insensible to Pain ability is increased to 4+.

THE DARK CREED: DISTILLERS OF FEAR

The Coven of the Dark Creed has perfected every method of inducing terror, to the extent that their mere presence fills the minds of their enemies with nightmarish dread.

Models in enemy units must subtract 1 from their Leadership characteristic for each unit with this obsession that is within 6" of theirs (to a maximum of -3).

COVEN OF TWELVE: BUTCHERS OF FLESH

The practice of internecine assassinations that exists amongst the Coven of Twelve ensures that weapons and wits are kept razor-sharp at all times, and only those members who are master flesh-carvers survive long.

Improve the Armour Penetration characteristic of all melee weapons used by a model with this obsession by 1. For example, an Armour Penetration characteristic of 0 becomes -1, an Armour Penetration characteristic of -1 becomes -2, and so on. This does not apply to any Artefacts of Cruelty.

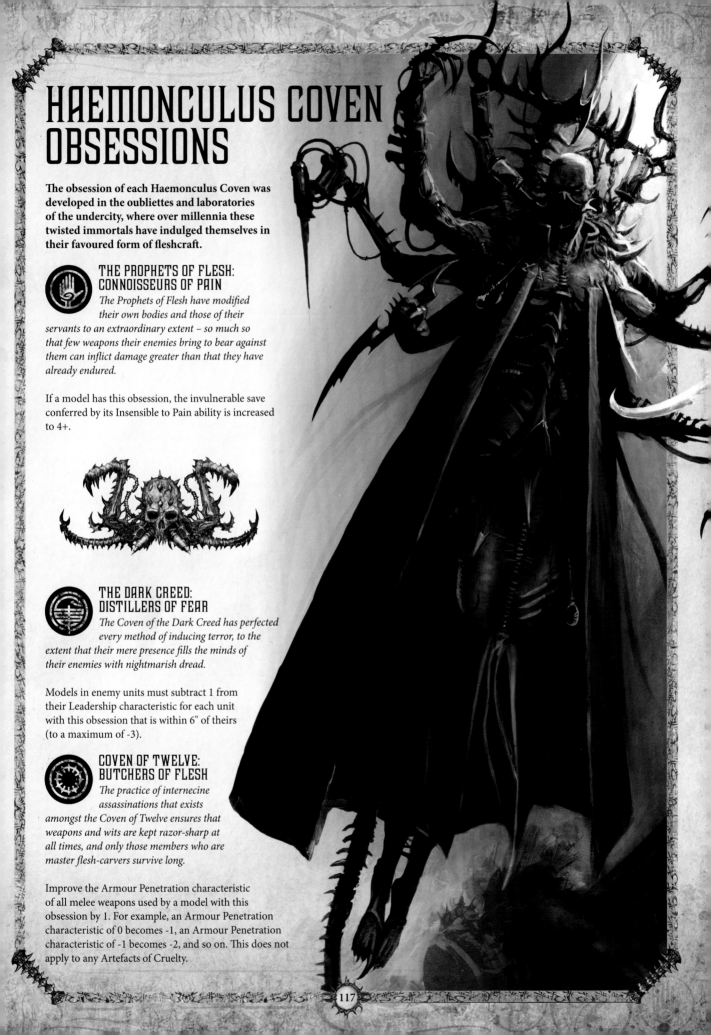

STRATAGEMS

If your army is Battle-forged and includes any DRUKHARI Detachments (excluding Auxiliary Support Detachments), you have access to the Stratagems shown here, meaning you can spend Command Points to activate them. These help to reflect the unique strategies used by the Drukhari on the battlefield.

WEBWAY PORTAL
1CP/3CP
Drukhari Stratagem

By hurling jagged rune-graven orbs into the air, the Drukhari can tear a rent in the skein of reality, flaying a route into the webway through which more of their kin can pour.

Use this Stratagem during deployment if you have not used the Screaming Jets Stratagem this battle. If you spend 1 CP, you can set up one DRUKHARI INFANTRY, BIKER or BEAST unit from your army in the webway instead of placing it on the battlefield. If you spend 3 CPs, you can place two such units in the webway instead. Any units in the webway can emerge at the end of any of your Movement phases – set them up anywhere on the battlefield that is more than 9" from any enemy units. You can only use this Stratagem once.

ALLIANCE OF AGONY
1CP
Drukhari Stratagem

In preparing a raid upon a shared enemy, even the most bloodthirsty Drukhari will veil their enmity and temporarily halt any assassination attempts, allowing these disparately twisted individuals to work together towards the same gruesome purpose.

Use this Stratagem before the battle if your Warlord is an Archon. Choose up to one HAEMONCULUS and up to one SUCCUBUS from your army. Generate a Warlord Trait for each character you chose (note that these characters are only regarded as your Warlord for the purposes of these Warlord Traits).

ARCHITECTS OF PAIN
1CP
Drukhari Stratagem

The Drukhari learnt long ago to orchestrate the agonies of those on the battlefield, preserving and enhancing the suffering of their victims so that they may drink of it at their leisure.

Use this Stratagem at the start of the battle round. Choose a unit from your army that has the Power From Pain ability. Until the end of the battle round, that unit treats the current battle round as being 1 higher than it actually is when determining what bonuses it gains from the Power From Pain table. This is cumulative with other, similar effects (such as the Kabal of the Black Heart's 'Thirst for Power' obsession).

HAYWIRE GRENADE
1CP
Drukhari Stratagem

Haywire grenades send out a powerful electromagnetic pulse to debilitate and damage enemy vehicles.

Use this Stratagem before a DRUKHARI model from your army throws a plasma grenade at a VEHICLE unit. Only make a single hit roll for that grenade; if it hits, the enemy unit suffers D3 mortal wounds.

LIGHTNING-FAST REACTIONS
2CP
Drukhari Stratagem

The hyper-fast reflexes of the Drukhari allow them to duck and weave to avoid all but the swiftest enemy strikes.

Use this Stratagem when a DRUKHARI INFANTRY, VEHICLE or BIKER unit from your army (excluding Urien Rakarth or a <HAEMONCULUS COVEN> unit) is targeted by a ranged or melee weapon. Subtract 1 from hit rolls made against that unit for the rest of the phase.

PRIZES FROM THE DARK CITY
1CP/3CP
Drukhari Stratagem

A warlord who wants their high status to be known will equip their raiding parties with the most extravagant weaponry.

Use this Stratagem before the battle. Your army can have one extra Artefact of Cruelty for 1 CP, or two extra Artefacts of Cruelty for 3 CPs. All of the Artefacts of Cruelty that you include must be different and be given to different DRUKHARI CHARACTERS. You can only use this Stratagem once per battle.

EVISCERATING FLY-BY
1CP
Drukhari Stratagem

The airborne combatants of a Wych Cult have no need to slow down in order to carry out their slaughter.

Use this Stratagem when a <WYCH CULT> unit from your army that can FLY Advances. If that unit moves over any enemy units this phase, choose one of those enemy units and roll a D6 for each model in your unit, adding 1 to the result if the enemy unit you picked is INFANTRY. For each roll of 6+ the enemy unit you chose suffers a mortal wound.

FLESHCRAFT
Drukhari Stratagem
With practised efficiency, a Haemonculus can re-mould the damaged flesh of his creations.

Use this Stratagem at the end of your Movement phase. Select a <Haemonculus Coven> Monster or Grotesque model from your army that is within 3" of any <Haemonculus Coven> Haemonculus from your army. The model you selected regains D3 lost wounds.

1CP

HYPERSTIMM BACKLASH
Drukhari Stratagem
Heedless of the brutal effects of overdosing, members of a Wych Cult may take a massive dose of combat drugs to further enhance their combat prowess.

Use this Stratagem at the start of the battle round. Choose a unit from your army that has the Combat Drugs ability. Until the end of the battle round, the bonus that unit receives from its Combat Drugs is doubled. At the end of the battle round, roll a D6 for each model in that unit. For each roll of 1, that unit suffers a mortal wound. If you use this Stratagem on a model that has the Stimm Addict Warlord Trait and/or the Phial Bouquet Artefact of Cruelty, all its bonuses are doubled but it automatically suffers D3 mortal wounds at the end of the battle round.

2CP

FIRE AND FADE
Drukhari Stratagem
The Drukhari are masters at using hit-and-run tactics, engaging a target with a flurry of shots before quickly manoeuvring into cover or out of sight.

Use this Stratagem after a Drukhari unit from your army shoots in your Shooting phase. The unit can immediately move up to 7" as if it were the Movement phase (it cannot Advance as part of this move). However, it cannot charge in the same turn that it does so.

1CP

SCREAMING JETS
Drukhari Stratagem
Just as terrifying as a sudden emergence from the webway is the meteoric descent of a Drukhari raiding craft behind enemy lines.

Use this Stratagem during deployment if you have not used the Webway Portal Stratagem this battle. You can set up a Drukhari Vehicle from your army that can Fly in the sky instead of placing it on the battlefield. It can descend at the end of any of your Movement phases – set it up anywhere on the battlefield more than 9" from any enemy models. If you use this Stratagem on a Transport, all units embarked inside it remain so when it is set up in the sky.

1CP

CRUEL DECEPTION
Drukhari Stratagem
Commorrite society is founded upon deception, and the Drukhari are quick to use a perceived weakness to annihilate their enemies.

Use this Stratagem if a Drukhari unit from your army Falls Back. That unit can still shoot and charge this turn.

2CP

THE GREAT ENEMY
Drukhari Stratagem
The Chaos God Slaanesh is reviled by the Aeldari, who hate and despise his followers with a ferocious loathing.

Use this Stratagem when a Drukhari unit from your army is chosen to fight. Until the end of the phase, re-roll failed wound rolls for attacks made by this unit that target Slaanesh units.

1CP

FREAKISH SPECTACLE
Drukhari Stratagem
The very sight of the mutilated Haemonculi and their creations is enough to break the spirits of even the most stalwart warriors.

Use this Stratagem when an enemy unit fails a Morale test within 6" of Urien Rakarth or a <Haemonculus Coven> unit from your army. One additional model flees from the enemy unit.

1CP

RELEASE THE BEASTS
Drukhari Stratagem
A skilled Beastmaster will foster the bloodlust of his creatures right up to the point that it can no longer be contained.

Use this Stratagem at the start of your Charge phase. Choose a Beastmaster from your army. Until the end of the phase you can re-roll failed charge rolls for units of Drukhari Beasts from your army if they are within 6" of that Beastmaster when the roll is made.

1CP

THE TORTURER'S CRAFT
Drukhari Stratagem
Over long millennia in Commorragh's undercity, the Haemonculus Covens have perfected the craft of carving flesh.

Use this Stratagem before Urien Rakarth or a <Haemonculus Coven> unit from your army fights in the Fight phase. Until the end of the phase, you can re-roll failed wound rolls for that unit.

2CP

HUNT FROM THE SHADOWS
1CP

Drukhari Stratagem

The denizens of Commorragh live and die in murky twilight, and are expert at using the shadows to their advantage.

Use this Stratagem when a **DRUKHARI INFANTRY** unit from your army that is receiving the benefit of cover is targeted in the Shooting phase. Until the end of that phase, add 2 to that unit's saving throws instead of only adding 1 (this does not affect invulnerable saving throws).

PRAY THEY DON'T TAKE YOU ALIVE
1CP

Drukhari Stratagem

Few armies are able to maintain their mettle when the sounds of their leader's tortured screams fill the air.

Use this Stratagem if a **DRUKHARI** unit from your army slays the enemy Warlord in the Fight phase. For the remainder of the battle, every model in the enemy army subtracts 1 from its Leadership characteristic.

SOUL-TRAP
1CP

Drukhari Stratagem

Soul-traps vary in size and appearance, from pyramidal prisms to jewelled skulls engraved with vampiric runes, but all serve to capture the spirit essence of powerful enemies and empower the bearer with stolen energies.

Use this Stratagem when an Archon from your army kills an enemy **CHARACTER** in the Fight phase. Increase the Attacks, Strength and Leadership characteristics of that Archon by 1 for the remainder of the battle.

ENHANCED AETHERSAILS
1CP

Drukhari Stratagem

Drukhari raiding craft bear many enhancements that allow for lightning-fast attacks and swift withdrawals.

Use this Stratagem when a Raider or a Ravager from your army Advances. Add 8" to that model's Move characteristic for that phase instead of rolling a dice.

ONSLAUGHT
1CP

Drukhari Stratagem

When loosed upon masses of enemies, Incubi will eagerly demonstrate the speed with which they can kill.

Use this Stratagem before an **INCUBI** unit from your army fights in the Fight phase. Until the end of the phase, each time you roll an unmodified hit roll of 6 for a model in this unit, that attack scores 2 hits instead of 1.

CRUCIBLE OF MALEDICTION
2CP

Drukhari Stratagem

When released, the souls of psykers tortured unto death that are held within a crucible of malediction spew outward, driving insane any nearby whose minds are attuned to the warp.

Use this Stratagem in your Psychic phase. Select a **HAEMONCULUS** from your army and roll a D6 for each **PSYKER** unit within 12" of it; on a 4+ the unit being rolled for suffers D3 mortal wounds. You can only use this Stratagem once per battle.

TORMENT GRENADE
1CP

Drukhari Stratagem

Upon impact this grenade releases an ochre cloud of phantasmal gas that eats away at the enemy's psyche.

Use this Stratagem before a model from your army fires a phantasm grenade launcher. If an enemy unit is hit by an attack made with this weapon this phase, then, in addition to the usual effects, roll 3D6. If the result is higher than the highest Leadership characteristic in the enemy unit, it suffers D3 mortal wounds.

AGENTS OF VECT
3CP

Kabal of the Black Heart Stratagem

The Supreme Overlord of Commorragh develops counter-measures for every conceivable course of events, and he teaches his Kabalites to bring the enemy's best-laid plans to ruin.

Use this Stratagem just after your opponent has spent CPs to use a Stratagem, but before the effects of that Stratagem are resolved. Roll a D6; on a 1 your opponent's Stratagem is resolved as normal. On a 2-5 your opponent's CPs are refunded, but the Stratagem they were using is not resolved and cannot be attempted again this phase. On a 6 the Stratagem they were attempting to use is not resolved, cannot be attempted again this phase and the CPs spent are lost. This Stratagem cannot be used to affect Stratagems used 'before the battle' or 'during deployment'.

INSIDIOUS MISDIRECTION
2CP

Kabal of the Poisoned Tongue Stratagem

The Kabalites of the Poisoned Tongue excel at wrong-footing their enemies before an attack is launched.

Use this Stratagem at the start of the first battle round, but before the first turn has begun. Pick up to 3 **KABAL OF THE POISONED TONGUE** units from your army that are on the battlefield; immediately remove these units from the battlefield and then set them up again as described in the Deployment section of your mission (if you redeploy a **TRANSPORT**, all units embarked inside it remain so when it is set up again). You can only use this Stratagem once per battle.

FAILURE IS NOT AN OPTION
1CP
Kabal of the Obsidian Rose Stratagem
Even when faced with insurmountable odds, the Kabalites of the Obsidian Rose know that anything less than the perfect execution of their deadly art is utterly unacceptable.

Use this Stratagem when a **KABAL OF THE OBSIDIAN ROSE** unit from your army fails a Morale test. Select which models will flee, but before removing them, each can either shoot as if it were the Shooting phase or make a single close combat attack as if it were the Fight phase. If any enemy models are slain by these attacks, none of the models flee from your unit. If no enemy models were slain, the fleeing models are removed as normal.

MASTERS OF THE SHADOWED SKY
1CP
Kabal of the Flayed Skull Stratagem
The Kabalites of the Flayed Skull view the skies above the battlefield as their rightful territory, and will scour from existence those enemies who dare trespass.

Use this Stratagem when you select a **KABAL OF THE FLAYED SKULL** unit to shoot with in the Shooting phase. Until the end of the phase, add 1 to hit rolls made for this unit's attacks that target units that can **FLY**.

NO METHOD OF DEATH BEYOND OUR GRASP
3CP
Cult of Strife Stratagem
The Cult of Strife are well versed in every conceivable method of murder, and after completing one act of slaughter they will often showcase another from their repertoire.

Use this Stratagem just after a **CULT OF STRIFE** unit from your army has destroyed an enemy unit in either the Shooting or Fight phase (if used in the Fight phase, use this Stratagem after the attacking unit has consolidated). If the enemy unit was destroyed in the Shooting phase, your unit can immediately shoot an additional time this phase. If the enemy unit was destroyed in the Fight phase, your unit can immediately fight an additional time this phase.

CONCEALED BOOBY TRAPS
1CP
Cult of the Cursed Blade Stratagem
After luring their enemies towards them, the Cult of the Cursed Blade detonate hidden charges that riddle the attackers with barbed shards of shrapnel.

Use this Stratagem when an enemy unit finishes a charge move within 1" of a **CULT OF THE CURSED BLADE** unit from your army that is wholly on or within a terrain feature. Roll a dice; on a 4+ that enemy unit suffers D3 mortal wounds.

ATHLETIC AERIALISTS
2CP
Cult of the Red Grief Stratagem
Wyches of the Red Grief set foot on solid ground only for as long as it takes to butcher the enemy.

Use this Stratagem just before a **CULT OF THE RED GRIEF INFANTRY** unit consolidates. Instead of moving towards the nearest enemy, the unit consolidates up to 6" towards the nearest **CULT OF THE RED GRIEF TRANSPORT** from your army. If all models in the unit end this move within 3" of the Transport, the unit may immediately embark upon it (if it has sufficient capacity remaining) as if it were the Movement phase, and can do so even if they disembarked from the Transport during the same turn.

BLACK CORNUCOPIANS
2CP
Prophets of Flesh Stratagem
The Prophets of Flesh have innumerable servants, waves of whom are sent screaming forward during their largest raids.

Use this Stratagem at the end of your Movement phase. Pick a unit of **PROPHETS OF FLESH** Wracks from your army and remove it from the battlefield, then set it up again at its full starting strength wholly within 6" of the edge of the battlefield and more than 9" from any enemy models.

AN ESOTERIC KILL, DELIVERED FROM AFAR
2CP
The Dark Creed Stratagem
The Coven of the Dark Creed have a well-earned reputation for novel methods of assassination.

Use this Stratagem when you select a **DARK CREED** unit to shoot with in the Shooting phase. Until the end of the phase, models in that unit can target enemy **CHARACTERS** even if they are not the closest enemy unit.

ADMINISTER PUNISHMENT
1CP
Coven of Twelve Stratagem
Amidst the treacherous Coven of Twelve, any opportunity to inflict suffering upon a fellow member is pounced upon eagerly.

Use this Stratagem when you select a **COVEN OF TWELVE** unit from your army to shoot with in the Shooting phase. Until the end of the phase, models in that unit can target enemy units that are within 1" of friendly **COVEN OF TWELVE** units, but each time you roll a hit roll of 1 for such an attack, it is instead resolved against one of your **COVEN OF TWELVE** units that is within 1" of the target (you decide which). For weapons that hit automatically, roll a D6 for each hit; on a 1-3 that hit is resolved against one of your units, and on a 4+ that hit is resolved against the target. This Stratagem cannot be used if the shooting unit is itself within 1" of an enemy unit.

ARTEFACTS OF CRUELTY

The spires of High Commorragh and the oubliettes of the undercity are replete with tools of esoteric cruelty. Amongst these are artefacts that, through their ability to inflict untold suffering on those who oppose their bearer, exemplify the exquisite craftsmanship and dark science of the Drukhari.

If your army is led by a **DRUKHARI** Warlord, then before the battle you may give one of the following Artefacts of Cruelty to a **DRUKHARI CHARACTER**. Named characters such as Urien Rakarth already have one or more artefacts and cannot be given any of the following artefacts.

Note that some weapons replace one of the character's existing weapons or items of wargear. Where this is the case, if you are playing a matched play game or are otherwise using points values, you must still pay the cost of the weapon or item of wargear that is being replaced. Write down any Artefacts of Cruelty your characters have on your army roster.

PARASITE'S KISS

Thought to be the finest splinter pistol ever crafted, this weapon spits out crystalline darts bound with psycho-vampiric circuitry. Upon biting into flesh, the target's very soul is leeched, and transferred back to the gun's wielder. As the luckless victim withers like rotten fruit, their killer flushes with vigour.

Model with a splinter pistol only. The Parasite's Kiss replaces the bearer's splinter pistol and has the following profile:

WEAPON	RANGE	TYPE	S	AP	D
Parasite's Kiss	12"	Pistol 2	*	-2	2
Abilities: Poisoned Weapon (pg 87). Add 2 to wound rolls made for this weapon, unless it is targeting a **VEHICLE**. Each time this weapon kills an enemy model, the bearer regains 1 lost wound.					

THE DJIN BLADE

Forged from an unknown alloy, the Djin Blade reflects an idealised reflection of whoever looks at it. Though the blade lends its wielder incredible prowess, it will feed off their essence until it turns upon them. On that day the wielder's reflection shifts into something malefic, the true face of the Djin leering out at them before it turns their heart to ash and their soul to drifting cinders.

Archon with a huskblade only. The Djin Blade replaces the bearer's huskblade and has the following profile:

WEAPON	RANGE	TYPE	S	AP	D
The Djin Blade	Melee	Melee	+1	-3	D3
Abilities: Each time the bearer fights, it can make 2 additional attacks with this weapon. Roll a D6 at the end of each Fight phase in which the bearer attacked using this weapon; on a 1 they suffer a mortal wound.					

THE HELM OF SPITE

The Drukhari look down upon those who use psychic witchery. Not only do they tempt the gaze of She Who Thirsts, but they also risk the wrath of Asdrubael Vect. Through necessity, the Drukhari's psychic abilities have atrophied, leaving them vulnerable to the warpcraft of their foes. The Helm of Spite redresses this balance, shielding its wearer from harm and setting up a field of violent psionic feedback.

The bearer can attempt to deny one psychic power in each enemy Psychic phase in the same manner as a **PSYKER**. In addition, each time the bearer makes a successful Deny the Witch test, the psyker that attempted to manifest that power suffers Perils of the Warp.

THE NIGHTMARE DOLL

Should the owner of the Nightmare Doll be harmed in battle, his injuries are absorbed by this creature. If its owner is riddled with bullets, tiny holes appear in the thing's writhing body whilst its master remains whole. Should the Haemonculus be hit by a decapitating strike, the foe's blade will pass through his gnarled neck without leaving so much as a scratch.

Haemonculus only. Whenever you make an Inured to Suffering roll (pg 87) for the bearer, that wound is not lost on a roll of 4+ instead of 6.

THE ANIMUS VITAE

The Animus Vitae appears to be a smooth orb, until it is thrown at the feet of a victim and explodes into a lashing tangle of barbed wires that wrap around its prey. Slowly and spitefully, the Animus Vitae begins to constrict, cutting through armour, flesh and bone until its victim's agonised cries become desperate screams. All the while the foul weapon radiates this agony, saturating the battlefield with pain so that the bearer and his kin can drink it in like a potent draught.

The Animus Vitae has the following profile:

WEAPON	RANGE	TYPE	S	AP	D
The Animus Vitae	6"	Grenade 1	-	-	-
Abilities: You can only use this weapon once per battle. If it hits, the target suffers D3 mortal wounds. If any enemy models are slain by this weapon then, for the remainder of the turn, friendly units with the Power from Pain ability treat the current battle round as being 1 higher than it actually is when determining what bonuses they gain, so long as they remain within 6" of the bearer. This is cumulative with other, similar effects.					

THE TRIPTYCH WHIP

Created in the nascent days of Commorragh's arenas, the Triptych Whip is a fusion of three masterfully balanced agonisers. Since then it has been borne by only a handful of Succubi, passed down to one skilled enough to slay its bearer in gladiatorial combat.

Succubus with agoniser only. The Triptych Whip replaces the bearer's agoniser and has the following profile:

WEAPON	RANGE	TYPE	S	AP	D
The Triptych Whip	Melee	Melee	*	-2	1
Abilities: Poisoned Weapon (pg 87). Each time the bearer fights, it can make 3 additional attacks with this weapon.					

WRIT OF THE LIVING MUSE

When intoned, the words of Vect embossed upon this iron tablet invigorate the members of his Kabal.

KABAL OF THE BLACK HEART Archon only. Re-roll wound rolls of 1 for friendly **KABAL OF THE BLACK HEART** units within 6" of the bearer.

SOUL-SEEKER

The Soul-seeker fires splinters of toxic spirit stones, each of which shatters upon impact to create clouds of empaphagic vapours.

KABAL OF THE POISONED TONGUE Archon with splinter pistol only. Soul-seeker replaces the model's splinter pistol and has the following profile:

WEAPON	RANGE	TYPE	S	AP	D
Soul-seeker	18"	Pistol 2	*	-1	D3

Abilities: Poisoned Weapon (pg 87). Add 2 to wound rolls made for this weapon, unless it is targeting a **VEHICLE**. This weapon can target enemy units that are not visible to the firer and can target enemy **CHARACTERS** even if they are not the closest enemy model. Units attacked by this weapon do not gain any bonus to their saving throws for being in cover.

THE ARMOUR OF MISERY

Crafted using psycho-empathic shards of poisoned wraithbone, this armour emanates crippling waves of dread, causing foes to quail.

KABAL OF THE OBSIDIAN ROSE Archon only. The wearer has a 3+ Save characteristic. In addition, subtract 1 from hit rolls for attacks that target the wearer in the Fight phase.

THE OBSIDIAN VEIL

Utilising the same night-shield technology as Drukhari attack craft, the Obsidian Veil projects a broad-spectrum displacement field around its bearer, surrounding them in a cloud of murky shadow.

KABAL OF THE FLAYED SKULL Archon only. The first time this model fails its invulnerable save and its shadowfield ceases to function, it immediately gains a 4+ invulnerable save for the remainder of the battle.

THE PHIAL BOUQUET

Worn decoratively on the wrist or shoulder, the Phial Bouquet contains a cocktail of artisanal combat drugs that is decanted into the Succubus' spinal column over the course of a battle.

CULT OF STRIFE Succubus only. Roll a D6 at the start of each battle round to randomly determine a Combat Drug from the table on page 87. Until the start of the next battle round, this model gains that bonus in addition to any other Combat Drug bonuses they have (duplicate results are cumulative).

TRAITOR'S EMBRACE

The Traitor's Embrace comprises a pair of metal rods that are sewn into the skin. At the moment of death, these rods cause their bearer's bones to explode outward, rapidly growing into a jagged cage.

CULT OF THE CURSED BLADE Succubus only. Roll a D6 if the bearer is slain in the Fight phase. On a 2+ the unit that killed this model suffers D6 mortal wounds after it has finished making all of its attacks.

THE BLOOD GLAIVE

Forged by Organghast the Haemomancer, the Blood Glaive absorbs the viscera of those victims it slays, sloughing off parts of its blade that have become nicked in battle and using the freshly harvested gore to re-hone the crimson edge.

CULT OF THE RED GRIEF Succubus with archite glaive only. The Blood Glaive replaces the bearer's archite glaive and has the following profile:

WEAPON	RANGE	TYPE	S	AP	D
The Blood Glaive	Melee	Melee	+3	-3	D3

THE VEXATOR MASK

Fashioned from the flayed face of a Shadowseer, this mask plays tricks on the mind. Those who approach it find themselves staring into the face of their most respected leader, a cherished parent, or even their lover. The moment of hesitation this affords is enough for the wearer to plunge a surgical blade into the gawping viewer's heart.

PROPHETS OF FLESH Haemonculus only. Enemy units cannot fire overwatch at the bearer. In addition, at the start of each Fight phase, select an enemy unit within 6" of the bearer. That unit cannot fight until all other units that are able to have done so. If the unit has an ability that allows it to fight first in the Fight phase, it instead fights as if it did not have this ability. If both players have units that cannot fight until all other unit have done so, then alternate choosing which of those units to fight with, starting with the player whose turn is taking place.

SPIRIT-STING

The needles fired by Spirit-sting are loaded with dew collected from a sconce at the bottom of the Chasm of Echoes. When injected, it causes the victims fears to manifest physically, bursting from their brain in an explosion of gore before dissipating into vapour.

DARK CREED Haemonculus with stinger pistol only. Spirit-sting replaces the bearer's stinger pistol and has the following profile:

WEAPON	RANGE	TYPE	S	AP	D
Spirit-sting	12"	Pistol 3	*	-4	1

Abilities: Poisoned Weapon (pg 87). Add 2 to wound rolls made for this weapon, unless it is targeting a **VEHICLE**. Invulnerable saves cannot be taken against this weapon.

THE FLENSING BLADE

The necro-ionised metal of the Flensing Blade draws fleshy tissue towards it whilst simultaneously repelling bone, chitin and inorganic armour. This allows its wielder to expertly carve samples of skin, fat and musculature from his victims for his experiments.

COVEN OF TWELVE Haemonculus only. The Flensing Blade replaces the model's Haemonculus tools and has the following profile:

WEAPON	RANGE	TYPE	S	AP	D
The Flensing Blade	Melee	Melee	*	-2	D3

Abilities: Poisoned Weapon (pg 87). Add 1 to wound rolls made for this weapon, unless it is targeting a **VEHICLE**. Increase this weapon's Damage characteristic to 3 when attacking enemy **CHARACTERS**.

WARLORD TRAITS

If a **DRUKHARI CHARACTER** is your Warlord, they can generate a Warlord Trait from the appropriate table below (depending on whether they have the <KABAL>, <WYCH CULT> or <HAEMONCULUS COVEN> keyword) instead of the one in the *Warhammer 40,000* rulebook. You can either roll on the table to randomly generate a Warlord Trait, or you can select the one that best suits their temperament and preferred style of waging war.

KABAL WARLORD TRAITS

D3 RESULT

1 HATRED ETERNAL

The Warlord is disgusted by the younger races that infest the galaxy, sickened by the unwashed and unrefined multitudes. They will take any opportunity to exterminate such vermin, revelling in every unworthy life they and their followers extinguish.

You can re-roll failed wound rolls for this Warlord.

2 SOUL THIRST

In place of a soul this Warlord plays host to a howling chasm of horror and madness. They must swallow thousands of souls each day to stave off complete degeneration, yet this thirst lends them a lethal ferocity.

Add 1 to this Warlord's Attacks characteristic in any turn in which they charged, were charged or made a Heroic Intervention. In addition, this Warlord regains 1 lost wound each time they slay an enemy model in the Fight phase.

3 ANCIENT EVIL

So long has this Warlord lived, steeped in horror and cruelty, that they are now shrouded in a malefic aura capable of paralysing their foes with fear.

The opposing player must roll an extra dice when taking Morale tests for units within 3" of this Warlord and use the highest result.

WYCH CULT WARLORD TRAITS

D3 RESULT

1 QUICKSILVER FIGHTER

This Warlord strikes with preternatural speed, slaying their foes before they even realise the fight has begun.

This Warlord always fights first in the Fight phase, even if they didn't charge. If the enemy has units that charged, or that have a similar ability, then alternate choosing units to fight with, starting with the player whose turn is taking place.

2 STIMM ADDICT

Though it dramatically reduces their lifespan, this Warlord is addicted to using artificial stimulants to boost their combat effectiveness.

Before the battle, when determining the bonus this Warlord receives from its Combat Drugs ability, roll two dice instead of one and apply both results (duplicate results are cumulative). Alternatively, you can pick two different bonuses to apply to this Warlord.

3 PRECISION BLOWS

This Warlord is adept at slaying their victims in stunning displays of violence, every blow placed perfectly to maim, dismember or decapitate.

Each time you roll a wound roll of 6+ for this Warlord in the Fight phase, the target suffers a mortal wound in addition to the normal damage.

HAEMONCULUS COVEN WARLORD TRAITS

D3 RESULT

1 MASTER REGENESIST

Not content with limiting their work to the flesh of others, this ancient Warlord has experimented on their own body for many centuries. The combination of countless excruciating surgeries and untested elixirs have borne dark fruit, and now their flesh regenerates at a frightening rate.

This Warlord regains D3 lost wounds at the start of each of your turns.

2 MASTER NEMESINE

Out of a twisted scientific curiosity, this Warlord knows a variety of ways to kill every realspace species they have ever discovered. There is no weak point unknown to them, and no nerve cluster they cannot excise with their scalpels.

Add 1 to wound rolls made for this Warlord in the Fight phase.

3 MASTER ARTISAN

This Warlord is not only gifted in the arts of fleshcraft and mettalosculpture, but also in the more metaphysical arts. Irrespective of the medium they work with, all of their creations are works of dark genius.

Re-roll Inured to Suffering rolls (pg 87) of 1 for friendly <HAEMONCULUS COVEN> models within 6" of this Warlord.

'The creatures of realspace are so possessive of their flesh, hiding it from their peers and betters beneath skin and armour. The same is true of their bones, which they are quick to mend when broken. How tedious an existence they must lead, bound to one form forever. That is, of course, until I find them, and introduce them to a life of ever-changing torment.'

- Exen Bal'reyn,
Wrack of the Coven of Twelve

KABAL, WYCH CULT AND HAEMONCULUS COVEN WARLORD TRAITS

If you wish, you can pick a Warlord Trait from the list below instead of using one of the three Drukhari Warlord Traits tables on the previous page, but only if your Warlord is from the relevant Kabal, Wych Cult or Haemonculus Coven.

KABAL OF THE BLACK HEART: LABYRINTHINE CUNNING

The Archons of the Kabal of the Black Heart have minds like steel traps, assimilating every detail of a situation. There is no circumstance they cannot turn to their benefit, nor any vagary of fate that can take them by surprise.

Whilst your Warlord is alive, roll a D6 each time you or your opponent spends a Command Point to use a Stratagem; you gain one Command Point for each roll of a 6.

KABAL OF THE POISONED TONGUE: TOWERING ARROGANCE

The Archons of the Kabal of the Poisoned Tongue are aloof in the extreme and have nothing but scorn for their foes. Such is the power of their conviction that their underlings will stand their ground no matter the odds.

Friendly **KABAL OF THE POISONED TONGUE** units can use this Warlord's Leadership whilst they are within 12" of them.

KABAL OF THE OBSIDIAN ROSE: DEATHLY PERFECTIONIST

The Archons of the Kabal of the Obsidian Rose are all skilled weaponsmiths, and have a reputation for perfectionism in their craftsmanship. Their personal armaments are the finest examples of their Kabal.

Increase the Damage characteristic of weapons (other than Artefacts of Cruelty) used by this Warlord by 1.

KABAL OF THE FLAYED SKULL: FAMED SAVAGERY

The Archons of the Kabal of the Flayed Skull are renowned for their savagery, slaying their foes and removing the skin from their skulls before their corpse has even hit the floor.

Increase this Warlord's Strength and Attacks characteristics by 1 during any turn in which they charged, were charged or made a Heroic Intervention.

CULT OF STRIFE: BLOOD DANCER

The Succubi of the Cult of Strife are renowned for their expertise at close-quarters combat within the arenas of Commorragh. The skill they display before the baying crowds on the blood-soaked sands is equally as deadly on the battlefield.

Each time you roll a hit roll of 6+ for this Warlord in the Fight phase, that hit scores 3 hits instead of 1.

CULT OF RED GRIEF: HYPER-SWIFT REFLEXES

The Succubi of the Cult of the Red Grief believe the best defence is simply not to be there when the opponent's blade falls. Such are their reflexes that they dodge blows with supernatural speed.

Add 1 to invulnerable saving throws made for this Warlord.

CULT OF THE CURSED BLADE: TREACHEROUS DECEIVER

The Succubi of the Cult of the Cursed Blade are cunning and treacherous, exploiting any opportunity to wrong-foot and deceive their foes before striking them with concealed weapons.

Each time you roll an unmodified saving throw of 6 for this Warlord in the Fight phase, the enemy unit that made that attack suffers a mortal wound after it has resolved all of it attacks.

PROPHETS OF FLESH: DIABOLICAL SOOTHSAYER

Many Haemonculi of the Prophets of Flesh dabble in soothsaying, despite the prohibition on psychic activity that pervades Commorragh. The insights they gain by doing so give them a great advantage before launching a realspace raid.

Once per battle, you can re-roll a single hit roll, wound roll, saving throw or damage roll for your Warlord. In addition, if your army is Battle-forged, roll a D3 before the battle begins; you gain a number of additional Command Points equal to the result.

THE DARK CREED: FEAR INCARNATE

The twisted Haemonculi of the Dark Creed have orchestrated the terror of others for so long that they exude an insanity-inducing aura so powerful that their mere presence is enough to drive their foes into such depths of despair that their hearts stop beating.

Roll 2D6 for each enemy unit that is within 3" of your Warlord at the start of the Fight phase. If the result exceeds the highest Leadership characteristic in that unit, it suffers a mortal wound.

COVEN OF TWELVE: SCARLET EPICUREAN

The Haemonculi of the Coven of Twelve have been slain and resurrected so many times that there are few methods of death they are not intimately familiar with. Unless they wish to experience a new fatality, they are notoriously difficult to kill.

Reduce all damage inflicted on your Warlord by 1 (to a minimum of 1). For example, if your Warlord fails a saving throw against a weapon that inflicts 3 damage, he will only lose 2 wounds.

NAMED CHARACTERS AND WARLORD TRAITS

If one of the following named characters is your Warlord, they must be given the associated Warlord Trait shown below.

NAMED CHARACTER	WARLORD TRAIT
Drazhar	Hatred Eternal
Lelith Hesperax	Blood Dancer
Urien Rakarth	Diabolical Soothsayer

POINTS VALUES

If you are playing a matched play game, or a game that uses a points limit, you can use the following lists to determine the total points cost of your army. Simply add together the points costs of all your models and the wargear they are equipped with to determine your army's total points value.

HQ

UNIT	MODELS PER UNIT	POINTS PER MODEL (Does not include wargear)
Archon	1	70
Haemonculus	1	70
Succubus	1	50

TROOPS

UNIT	MODELS PER UNIT	POINTS PER MODEL (Does not include wargear)
Kabalite Warriors	5-20	6
Wracks	5-10	9
Wyches	5-20	8

ELITES

UNIT	MODELS PER UNIT	POINTS PER MODEL (Does not include wargear)
Beastmaster	1	36
Grotesques	3-10	32
Incubi	5-10	16
Lhamaean	1	15
Mandrakes	5-10	16
Medusae	1	21
Sslyth	1	27
Ur-Ghul	1	15

FAST ATTACK

UNIT	MODELS PER UNIT	POINTS PER MODEL (Does not include wargear)
Clawed Fiends	1-6	32
Hellions	5-20	14
Khymerae	2-12	10
Razorwing Flocks	1-12	12
Reavers	3-12	19
Scourges	5-10	12

HEAVY SUPPORT

UNIT	MODELS PER UNIT	POINTS PER MODEL (Does not include wargear)
Cronos	1-3	65
Ravager	1	80
Talos	1-3	75

DEDICATED TRANSPORTS

UNIT	MODELS PER UNIT	POINTS PER MODEL (Does not include wargear)
Raider	1	65
Venom	1	55

FLYERS

UNIT	MODELS PER UNIT	POINTS PER MODEL (Does not include wargear)
Razorwing Jetfighter	1	105
Voidraven Bomber	1	155

NAMED CHARACTERS

UNIT	MODELS PER UNIT	POINTS PER MODEL (Includes wargear)
Drazhar	1	120
Lelith Hesperax	1	80
Urien Rakarth	1	90

'PAIN IS POWER, AND POWER IS EVERYTHING. WE THEREFORE SEEK EVERY OPPORTUNITY TO INFLICT PAIN, AND WE DO NOT ALLOW LIMITS TO BE IMPOSED UPON OUR IMAGINATION. THE FLESH, THE MIND, THE SOUL – ALL CAN BE MADE TO FEEL TORMENTS ETERNAL. AND WHEN ALL THREE SCREAM IN AGONY WITHIN A SINGLE BEING, THE PATH TO IMMORTALITY LIES OPEN BEFORE US. SO IT HAS BEEN SINCE THE BEGINNING, AND SO IT WILL CONTINUE UNTIL WE EXTINGUISH THE STARS AND THE GALAXY LIES DARK AND FALLOW.'

- *Mantra of the Kabal of the Dying Sun*

RANGED WEAPONS

WEAPON	POINTS PER WEAPON
Baleblast	0
Blast pistol	10
Blaster	17
Dark lance	20
Dark scythe	0
Disintegrator cannon	15
Eyeburst	0
Haywire blaster	8
Heat lance	12
Hexrifle	5
Liquifier gun	11
Ossefactor	7
Phantasm grenade launcher	3
Razorwing missiles	0
Shardcarbine	0
Shredder	8
Spirit syphon	0
Spirit vortex	10
Splinter cannon	10
Splinter pistol	0
Splinter pods	0
Splinter rifle	0
Stinger pistol	5
Stinger pod	15
Twin liquifier gun	22
Twin splinter rifle	0
Void lance	0
Voidraven missiles	10

OTHER WARGEAR

WARGEAR	POINTS PER ITEM
Chain-snares	2
Cluster caltrops	3
Grav-talon	3
Grisly trophies	2
Spirit probe	5
Splinter racks	10

MELEE WEAPONS

WEAPON	POINTS PER WEAPON
Agoniser	4
Archite glaive	0
Bladevanes	0
Chain-flails	3
Clawed fists	0
Claws and talons	0
Electrocorrosive whip	6
Flesh gauntlet	3
Glimmersteel blade	0
Haemonculus tools	0
Hekatarii blade	0
Hellglaive	0
Huskblade	6
Hydra gauntlets	4
Ichor injector	5
Impaler	5
Klaive	0
Macro-scalpel	4
Mindphase gauntlet	4
Monstrous cleaver	0
Power lance	4
Power sword	4
Razor feathers	0
Razorflails	4
Scissorhand	8
Shaimeshi blade	0
Shardnet and impaler	5
Shock prow	1
Spirit-leech tentacles	0
Sslyth battle-blade	0
Stunclaw	4
Talos gauntlet	15
Venom blade	2

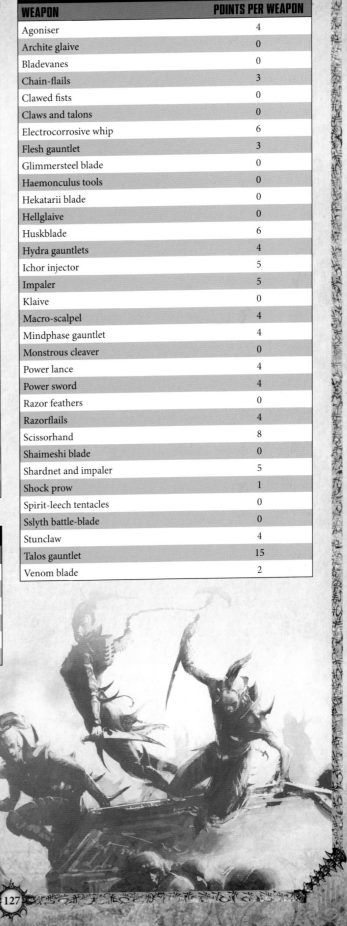

TACTICAL OBJECTIVES

The Drukhari view the lesser races with hateful contempt, and they launch raids to sow the greatest amount of fear, torment and suffering throughout the worlds of realspace.

If your army is led by a **DRUKHARI** Warlord, these Tactical Objectives replace the Capture and Control Tactical Objectives (numbers 11-16) in the *Warhammer 40,000* rulebook. If a mission uses Tactical Objectives, players use the normal rules for using Tactical Objectives with the following exception: when a Drukhari player generates a Capture and Control objective (numbers 11-16), they instead generate the corresponding Drukhari Tactical Objective, as shown below. Other Tactical Objectives (numbers 21-66) are generated normally.

D66	TACTICAL OBJECTIVE
11	Take Them Alive!
12	Fear and Terror
13	Death by a Thousand Cuts
14	Trophy Hunter
15	There Is No Escape
16	Pain, In All Its Forms

11 TAKE THEM ALIVE! — *Drukhari*

Commorragh is always in need of fresh slaves. Close with the prey and capture them alive.

Score 1 victory point if at least one enemy **INFANTRY** unit was destroyed during the Fight phase this turn. If an enemy **INFANTRY CHARACTER** was slain during the Fight phase this turn, score D3 victory points instead.

12 FEAR AND TERROR — *Drukhari*

Sow terror and panic in the ranks of your foes. Drink in their fear like a fine wine.

Score 1 victory point if at least one enemy unit failed a Morale test during this turn.

13 DEATH BY A THOUSAND CUTS — *Drukhari*

Strike and fade! Watch the enemy's army weaken and die as you bleed it one warrior at a time.

Score 1 victory point if at least one model was destroyed from at least three different enemy units during this turn. If at least one model was destroyed from 6 or more different enemy units during this turn, score D3 victory points instead.

14 TROPHY HUNTER — *Drukhari*

The lords of Commorragh demand a trophy, either a bauble from the field of battle or the head of an enemy champion.

When this Tactical Objective is generated, your opponent must nominate one objective marker and one **CHARACTER** from their army. Score 1 victory point if you control this objective marker and/or the nominated character has been slain.

15 THERE IS NO ESCAPE — *Drukhari*

No enemy can hide from our sight. Murder any who would seek to escape the kiss of our blades.

Score 1 victory point if at least one enemy unit that was completely on or within terrain at the start of the turn was destroyed this turn.

16 PAIN, IN ALL ITS FORMS — *Drukhari*

Revel in the suffering of others, unleash pain in all its forms.

Score 1 victory point if at least one enemy unit was destroyed in both the Shooting and Fight phases of this turn. If at least two enemy units were destroyed in each of these phases, score D3 victory points instead. If at least one of these units was destroyed by a <KABAL> unit, one by a <WYCH CULT> unit and one by a <HAEMONCULUS COVEN> unit, score D3+3 victory points instead.

'TO THOSE LEFT IN THE DARK CITY WHO REFUSE MY RULE, HEAR ME NOW. WHEN I FIND YOU – AND I WILL FIND YOU – YOUR SUFFERING WILL BE ENDLESS. AND TO THOSE WHO HAVE REMAINED LOYAL, GO NOW INTO REALSPACE. LET THE VERMINOUS RACES KNOW THAT I COME FOR THEM, AND THAT I AM COMMORRAGH.'

- *Declaration of Asdrubael Vect, Supreme Overlord of Commorragh*